Gentle Rebel
Letters of
Eugene V. Debs

Edited by
J. Robert Constantine

University of Illinois Press

Urbana and Chicago

Publication of this book was supported by a grant from the
National Historical Publications and Records Commission.

This book is printed on acid-free paper.

Library of Congress Cataloging-in-Publication Data

Debs, Eugene V. (Eugene Victor), 1855–1926.
    Gentle rebel : letters of Eugene V. Debs / edited by J. Robert
Constantine.
        p.   cm.
    Includes index.
    ISBN 0-252-02018-9 (cloth : alk. paper). — ISBN 0-252-06324-4
(pbk. : alk. paper)
    1. Debs, Eugene V. (Eugene Victor), 1855–1926—Correspondence.
2. Socialists—United States—Correspondence. 3. Socialism—United
States—History—Sources. 4. United States—Politics and
government—1865–1933—Sources. I. Constantine, J. Robert (James
Robert), 1924–   . II. Title
HX84.D3A4   1995
335'.3.'092—dc20   93-48601
                                                                        CIP

Gentle Rebel

Contents

Illustrations

Preface

IN THE YEARS following Eugene V. Debs's death in 1926, his brother Theodore received numerous inquiries concerning the disposition of EVD's correspondence. Often such inquiries came from men and women who were interested in writing a biography of Debs or in editing his correspondence for publication, or who were doing research in areas in which Debs's correspondence was seen to be of significance. Theodore Debs's responses to such inquiries made it clear that much of EVD's correspondence had been systematically and periodically destroyed. In a letter dated August 30, 1934, Theodore wrote, "Periodically our files were cleaned as we had not the office room to care for the volume of letters that came to my brother, especially during the three years he was in prison. However, not all correspondence was destroyed. Letters, fine and beautiful, were transferred to our private files." Theodore Debs preserved the private files until his death in 1945, at which time they became the property of his daughter, Marguerite Debs Cooper, who donated them to Indiana State University in 1967.

The letters donated by Mrs. Cooper became the nucleus of the large Debs Collection in the Cunningham Memorial Library at Indiana State University. The selection of letters for inclusion in this edition of Debs's correspondence was made chiefly from the Cunningham Library holdings, but important and essential letters came from other public and university libraries and archives and from private holdings. The private collections consulted include those of Mrs. Theresa Branstetter Taft, Needham, Mass.; Mr. Harry T. Fleischman, New York City; Ms. Merrily Cummings Ford, Glendora, Calif.; Mr. Leo Miller, New York City; Ms. Annelle Creel Rouse, Concord, Calif.; and Mrs. Gertrude Warren, Schenectady, N.Y. The provenance for each letter is given at the end of the letter. Many letters mentioned in Debs's correspondence have not been found, in part, no doubt, the result of the disposal practice described by his brother. Readers who would dig deeper into Debs's letters are referred to *The Papers of Eugene V. Debs, 1834–1945* (microfilm edition with *Guide*, Microfilming Corporation of America, 1983), which includes nearly ten thousand Debs letters, and to *The Letters of Eugene V. Debs* (3 volumes, University of Illinois Press, 1990), an annotated edition of some fifteen hundred of Debs's letters.

The letters included in this edition are intended to illuminate EVD's public career and his private life, the variety of interests, issues, and movements in which he was engaged, and his relationship with the many prominent and obscure men and women (and children) of his time. The headnotes to the letters are designed merely to identify the correspondent and to place the letters in context. Throughout the correspondence there are references to Debs's speeches, editorials, essays, articles, pamphlets, and letters to the editors of various publications; these are reproduced in the microfilm edition of *The Papers of Eugene V. Debs,* and much greater background material on both the correspondents and the issues raised in the letters is provided in the annotated, three-volume edition of *The Letters of Eugene V. Debs.*

As a general principle I have tried to reproduce the original text of each letter as accurately as possible. All the letters are transcribed in full, and idiosyncratic spelling, punctuation, and usage have been preserved. The heading of each letter is not transcribed from the text but is entered in standardized form: name of correspondent, date, and place of origin. Information supplied by the editor is included in square brackets, with or without a question mark. Places are identified by city name and state or foreign country, written out in full (e.g., Chicago, Illinois; Colmar, France); the only exceptions are New York City and Washington, D.C. Letterhead information has not been transcribed but is often cited for identification purposes in the headnote. Miscellaneous headings that are part of the original text of the letter but are not included in the standardized heading have been transcribed (e.g., Personal; Treasurer's Report; 10 P.M. Thanksgiving Eve).

Underlinings and marginal notations have been included only if they are judged to have been written by the author of the letter rather than by the recipient, by Debs's relatives, or by archivists, librarians, or others. Marginal notes are placed at the end of the letter, treated as postscripts. When there are several marginal notes (as there often are in EVD's letters), they are listed at the end, in order, beginning at the top of the letter. If a marginal note relates to a specific paragraph of a letter, it has been inserted into the text at that point, as a new paragraph introduced by "[in margin]." Frequently, especially during Debs's imprisonment from 1919 to 1921, EVD wrote notes on letters he had received and sent them to his brother Theodore in Terre Haute, to be answered or otherwise disposed of. Debs's notes on such letters are preceded by "[Debs's note to Theodore]" or "[Debs's reply to Theodore]."

Errors in spelling, punctuation, and so on, have been left in the text except in cases where it was judged that they were the result of a typographical error or a slip of the pen. In cases where a word was obviously left out, the word has been supplied in brackets, with a question mark if the judgment is uncertain. Illegible words are indicated by "[illegible]" or "[two words illegible]," and so on. Where a version of the text was crossed out and rewritten but is still legible, the crossed-out version has been included, followed by the correct version. Illegible crossouts, or errors crossed out and rewritten, have been omitted. Words inserted above the line are indicated by curly braces.

Where a writer used a symbol for "and" (or a plus sign), as EVD often did, an ampersand has been substituted. When the writer used a dash in place of a period, as EVD often did, a period has been substituted. Hyphens and dashes have been standardized in the transcription: - indicates a hyphen, and — indicates a dash, regardless of the usage of the letter writer.

In the preparation of this edition of Debs's letters (as in the preparation of the microfilm and annotated editions of his work), I have received the encouragement and cooperation of literally scores of academic colleagues, librarians, and archivists from this country and abroad, who provided me with biographical and bibliographical information and with photocopies of letters found in their holdings. To all of them I repeat the expression of gratitude that I have made to them individually and in the preface of *The Letters of Eugene V. Debs*. No less important has been the support given by the National Endowment for the Humanities and the National Historical Publications and Records Commission, whose grants greatly accelerated the completion of my work. I am particularly indebted to Roger Bruns, director of publications at the NHPRC, for his advice and counsel and for his steady encouragement of the project. Finally, I want to acknowledge the encouragement and help I have received over the years from Richard L. Wentworth, the director and editor in chief of the University of Illinois Press, and his staff.

I also wish to acknowledge the generosity of the following individuals who donated manuscript material to the Debs Papers Project: Mr. W. B. Kilpatrick, Jr., Warren, Ohio; Ms. Naomi S. Lang, Beverly Hills, Calif.; Mrs. Eleanor Lowenthal, Kensington, Md.; Mrs. Wrisley B. Oleson, Sarasota, Fla.; Miss Gertrude Traubel, Philadelphia, Pa.

Symbols and Abbreviations

TxU	University of Texas, Austin, Barker Texas History Center
WHi	Wisconsin State Historical Society, Madison

Document Symbols

A	Autograph
AL	Autograph letter, not signed or signature missing
ALc	Autograph letter, copy
ALS	Autograph letter, signed
AN	Autograph note, not signed
ANS	Autograph note, signed
AS	Autograph, signed
EVD	Eugene Victor Debs
MS(S)	Manuscript(s)
PLS	Printed form letter, signed
T	Typed
Tc	Transcript copy
TDc	Typed document, copy
TDS	Typed document, signed
TL	Typed letter
TLc	Typed letter, copy
TLS	Typed letter, signed
TLSc	Typed letter, signed copy
TS	Typed, signed
(Y)	Initial of Bart Young, Debs's secretary

Biographical Sketch:
Eugene Victor Debs, 1855–1926

EUGENE VICTOR DEBS was born in Terre Haute, Indiana, on November 5, 1855. His parents, Jean Daniel Debs and Marguerite Marie Bettrich, had migrated from their native Colmar in Alsace in 1849, were married that same year in New York City, and, after brief stops in Cincinnati and Brooklyn, settled in Terre Haute. Called "Dandy" and "Daisy" by their six surviving children (Debs was the third surviving child, and the first son), Debs's parents raised an unusually close-knit family. For more than fifty years they operated a small retail grocery store, first in a front downstairs room of their home and later on the city's main street. According to Debs's brother Theodore, the enterprise provided the family with a "comfortable" living, although Gene recalled that in his early years the grocery business struggled to survive.

Of the three institutions that are said to have shaped the lives of nineteenth-century Americans—the family, the church, and the school—it seems clear that Debs's family was the most important influence on his career. His father, whose family had been a leading one in Colmar for generations, was a man of considerable education with a strong respect for the life of the mind. He was fluent in French and German, and the reading of the classics in those languages was a family ritual (Gene was named after Victor Hugo and Eugene Sue). Debs wrote repeatedly and lovingly of his mother, to whom he attributed saintly qualities of character and personality that bound and held the family together. Some of his earliest letters, written as a teenager in East St. Louis and as a young man in Terre Haute, also reflect his regard and concern for his sisters—Marie Marguerite, Louise, Eugenie, and Emily—with whom he shared his interests and plans for the future and whose support he sought throughout his career. It was for his brother, Theodore, however, that Debs developed the deepest, most intimate, and most lasting bond of affection. Their letters, spanning nearly half a century, describe a rare relationship that evolved from one in which Gene was an admonishing big brother (he was almost nine years older) to a full partnership in which Theodore became his secretary, agent, manager, adviser, and, most important, devoted friend.

Except perhaps in a negative sense, the church played only a small part in Debs's early development. His father was baffled, if not appalled, by the quality of Terre Haute's Protestant clergy. His mother, a Catholic, had her first four children baptized as Catholics, but she did not have Gene baptized and in fact dropped out of the church shortly after his birth in 1855. In later life Debs recalled having attended the Catholic church in Terre Haute on one occasion and being so offended by the priest's descriptions of hell and the punishment of sinners that he vowed he would "never go inside a church again." As an adult he adopted a broad tolerance toward religion based on a pragmatic test: "I wouldn't if I could disturb anyone's religion. If he sincerely believes it, it is the right creed." As a number of his letters reveal, Debs used some of his most blistering invective on Protestant and Catholic clergymen when he encountered them in the political arena. Still, many of his most devoted supporters were found among the clergy.

Debs's formal education ended well before he completed high school, but there was significant compensation in the fact that his home life was one in which ideas and reading were cherished and encouraged. As a teenager he began to assemble a personal library, and one of his first acquisitions, Voltaire's *Philosophical Dictionary*, was a gift from his father, whose own impressive collection of books was eventually given to the Terre Haute Public Library. Another early acquisition was Hugo's *Les Misérables*, which Debs said had impressed him more than any other book he had ever read. Although he quit school in 1870 at the age of fourteen, he was active as a teenager and as a young adult in Terre Haute's Occidental Literary Club, whose meetings were given over to the discussion of books and current issues. As president of the group in the late 1870s, Debs was responsible for the Terre Haute appearance of a number of noted Americans, including Wendell Phillips, who was championing the cause of labor, Robert Ingersoll, who became Debs's friend and model as a public speaker, the controversial Susan B. Anthony, whose devotion to woman's rights strongly impressed him, and James Whitcomb Riley, who became his life-long friend. Debs's writings, speeches, and correspondence were liberally sprinkled with allusions to the writers—particularly Hugo, Robert Burns, and Walt Whitman—he first knew as a teenager. In later years, one of his greatest sources of pride, which he could not conceal, was his wide range of acquaintances, friends, and loyal supporters among his generation's leading poets, novelists, artists, and other intellectuals.

Debs's first job in 1870 paid him fifty cents a day for scraping paint and grease off locomotives in the Terre Haute yards of the Terre Haute and Indianapolis Railroad. His advancement to fireman in the switching yards in December 1871 doubled his wages, and he was soon working as a fireman on the trains running between Terre Haute and Indianapolis. He lost his job during the depression that followed the Panic of 1873, and his first surviving letters were written from East St. Louis where he went in search of work. Thus, by the time he was eighteen Debs had learned the nature of employment in one of the nation's most dangerous occupations and had felt the impact of a downturn in the business cycle. The experiences made a powerful impression on the high school dropout.

At the end of 1874 Debs returned to Terre Haute, where one of his father's friends, Herman Hulman, gave him a job at his wholesale grocery firm. For the next five years Debs combined his interest in his job with an active participation in the affairs of the Occidental Literary Club and a growing involvement in the infancy of the organized labor movement and in the local Democratic party.

In February 1875 Debs joined the newly founded Vigo Lodge of the Brotherhood of Locomotive Firemen (BLF) and was soon serving as an organizer and recording secretary of the local, the minutes of whose meetings reflected the group's interests in providing assistance to injured members and to the widows of those killed on the job, in job safety issues, and, often, in monitoring the morality of its members and disciplining those found guilty of excessive drinking, sexual promiscuity, or making "slanderous remarks" about their brothers. Debs was not an on-the-job railroader during these years, but his service as recording secretary of the BLF local put him in close touch with conditions in an industry whose great strike in 1877 altered the thinking of many Americans concerning the nature of labor-management relations in general and the role of labor unions in particular. In 1876 Debs attended for the first time the national convention of the BLF and began to write short articles for the *BLF Magazine*. In 1878 he was elected associate editor of the magazine and in 1880 became its editor and national secretary-treasurer of the union.

During the years of his employment at Hulman's Wholesale Grocery, Debs became increasingly active in local Democratic party affairs. The members of the BLF local provided him with a nucleus of support in the party, and in 1879, at the age of twenty-four, he was elected as Terre Haute's city clerk; two years later he led the party's ticket in his re-election campaign. Debs declined a nomination for a third term in 1883, but the following year he was elected to the lower house of the Indiana General Assembly. During his one term in that body Debs supported a number of pro-labor laws and a woman suffrage bill (which was defeated), but he was frustrated and disappointed in his experience as a state legislator and, much later (1923), recalled that he was "as ashamed of that [permitting himself as a Democrat to be elected to a state legislature] as I am proud of having gone to jail."

A few months after the adjournment of the Indiana General Assembly in 1885, Debs married Katherine "Kate" Metzel, the stepdaughter of a prominent Terre Haute druggist, John Jacob Baur. For a time after their marriage Gene and Kate lived in rented rooms, but in 1890 they built a large house in Terre Haute's most fashionable neighborhood. Their home (now a state and national historical landmark) was from time to time the subject of controversy: it was cited as evidence of Kate Debs's upper-class taste and proof of the shallowness of Debs's working-class roots; it was said to have been built and maintained by scab labor; and an often-repeated charge (especially during Debs's presidential campaigns) was that Kate Debs refused to permit working men or women to enter the home. Some of the correspondence between Gene and Kate suggests a lifetime of mutual loyalty and devotion; still other letters make it clear that, late in life, Debs developed a strong bond of affection for Mabel Dunlap Curry, the wife of an Indiana State Normal School English professor, who worked as a volunteer in Debs's Terre Haute office during his imprisonment in 1919–21. Gene and Kate had no children of their own, but Gene became renowned for his affection for and interest in children, hundreds of whom—male and female—were named after him. Many of the most poignant letters in his correspondence came from scores of children while he was imprisoned in Atlanta.

During the course of the 1880s, Debs's roles as secretary-treasurer of the BLF and editor of the *BLF Magazine* brought him growing recognition as a skilled union organizer and a talented labor journalist. In addition to organizing numerous BLF locals, Debs organized locals for the Brotherhood of Railroad Brakemen, the Switchmen's Mutual Aid Association, the Brotherhood of Railway Carmen, and the Order of Railway Telegraphers. Meanwhile, the *BLF Magazine* was recognized as one of the leading labor journals of the day, and in 1890 the editor of the *Labor Engineer* described Debs as "by far the ablest labor speaker and writer in America."

As editor of the *BLF Magazine,* Debs stressed the common interests of capital and labor and the mutual advantages to be gained by cooperation between labor and management. Strikes and boycotts were, he wrote in 1883, "the knives with which laborers cut their throats," and he regularly praised the achievements of the leading businessmen of the day as models his readers might well emulate. But he began to alter his conservative stance in the latter years of the decade and to find, as he wrote in 1887, that strikes were "the weapons of the oppressed" and that "the nation had as its cornerstone a strike." At the same time his editorials were given over increasingly to the idea of a federation of railroad unions along the lines formulated in 1886 by the newly founded American Federation of Labor (AFL). The idea was given a brief trial in the formation in 1889 of the Supreme Council of the United Orders of Railway Employees, the rather grand name given to an alliance of firemen, trainmen, and switchmen. But in a series of strikes during the next few years, the various unions broke ranks, management effectively capitalized on the resulting disunity, and, in June 1892, the Supreme Council dissolved itself.

Increasingly frustrated by the weakness of the existing railroad unions and the attitudes of the "aristocracy" of the unions, as he called the engineers and conductors, Debs resigned as secretary-treasurer of the BLF in 1892 (though he continued to edit the *BLF Magazine* until 1894) and began to think through a plan for an industrial union for *all* railroad workers, regardless of craft or skill, an idea that was abhorrent to both the existing brotherhoods and to the rapidly growing AFL. In a June 1893 meeting in Chicago, Debs and some fifty other dissident railroad workers organized the American Railway Union (ARU), of which Debs served as the first (and only) president. Throughout its brief and dramatic career the ARU was "Debs's union," attracting tens of thousands of members in its first months of recruitment and winning a notable victory for its members in an eighteen-day strike against James J. Hill's Great Northern Railroad in April 1894. A few months later, in June 1894, the new union (against Debs's advice), in sympathy with striking Pullman Palace Car workers, voted to launch a boycott of Pullman cars on all the roads served by the ARU membership. The resulting Pullman strike of 1894, possibly the most famous strike in American labor history, paralyzed much of the commerce in the western half of the nation before it was broken by an alliance of management and the full legal and military power of the federal government.

The ARU never recovered from the failure of the Pullman strike, and in its aftermath Debs was imprisoned for six months at the Woodstock, Illinois, jail for violation of a blanket injunction handed down by the federal court in Chicago against the ARU leadership during the course of the strike. It was during this imprisonment, Debs later said, that he became convinced that no union, no matter how it was structured, could protect the interests of workers in the prevailing economic and political system. In January 1897, Debs announced in the ARU paper *Railway Times* his conversion to socialism. In explaining his decision, he mentioned as contributing factors the role of the federal government in breaking the Pullman strike, his reading of socialist literature and meetings with socialist leaders during his imprisonment, and the crushing defeat of William Jennings Bryan by William McKinley in the November 1896 presidential election.

During the course of the next thirty years, Debs carried a message of industrial unionism and democratic socialism to millions of Americans, arguing passionately that unbridled capitalism was destroying democracy at home and leading inevitably to war abroad. Only through industrial unionism in the economic realm and socialism in the political realm, he insisted, could workers' interests be protected. At the same time, there was scarcely a single social reform movement of the Progressive Era (with the exception of Prohibition, if that be included among Progressive Era reforms) in which he did not take an active, often leading part. The range of causes for which his support was sought or in which he volunteered his time and energy included the early attacks on child labor, on racial and sexual discrimination, on militarism, on prison brutality, on capital punishment, and a host of other social legacies, some of them ancient and some of recent origin.

Debs's influence in shaping his generation's attitudes and opinions on economic, political, and social issues resulted chiefly from his presidential campaigns, his extensive writings, and his seemingly endless speaking and lecture tours, the latter of which brought him an impressive income while contributing, no doubt, to his frequent and prolonged bouts of illness. After joining in the creation of the Socialist Party of America, Debs was that party's presidential candidate in 1900, 1904, 1908, 1912, and 1920 (he declined the nomination in 1916, instead running [unsuccessfully] for Congress in Indiana's Fifth Congressional District). With only the faintest hope of victory, Debs nonetheless waged energetic and dramatic campaigns that criss-crossed the country, attracted enormous crowds, and, most important from his point of view, familiarized millions of Americans with ideas that were considered radical in the early years of the century but were gradually adopted by the major parties and have become orthodox public policy. (A cartoon from the 1912 presidential election portrays Debs in a swimming hole, his clothes, labeled "Socialism," being carried away by Theodore Roosevelt.) Among those ideas were the abolition of child labor, the right of women to vote, a graduated income tax, the direct election of United States senators, unemployment compensation for workers, employer liability laws, national departments of education and health, pensions for retired men and women, and others embodied in the Socialist party platform's "immediate demands." Debs was, of course, not alone in his advocacy of many of these proposals, but his presidential campaigns contributed to the public's knowledge and acceptance of them and to their gradual adoption by the Democratic and Republican parties.

Debs's most dramatic and colorful presidential campaign was the 1908 campaign, in which the Socialist party chartered a train, the Red

Special, which carried Debs on a whistle-stop tour of the nation—a fifteen thousand–mile trip that drew huge crowds and was widely reported in both the socialist and nonsocialist press. The public's interest in the Red Special caused a number of papers to predict that Debs would do well in November—the *Chicago Tribune* thought he would get a million votes—but on election day he received only 420,793 votes, an increase of just 20,000 over his 1904 total. Many socialists were deeply disappointed in the 1908 election (won by William Howard Taft), but Debs thought the Red Special had been a wonderful "educational enterprise" and he urged his supporters to begin immediately to prepare for the 1912 campaign.

During the years between the campaign of 1908 and the election of 1912 the history of the Socialist Party of America was characterized by a significant growth in membership and by a series of astonishing victories in local and state elections, including the 1910 elections of Victor Berger to the United States Congress and of Emil Seidel as mayor of Milwaukee. But the period also witnessed a hardening of the rivalry between the dominant conservative wing of the party and its more radical, largely western factions. Debs was given a large share of the credit for the growth of the party, but he played only a small part in the intraparty struggles (which he deplored). At the 1912 Socialist party convention he easily overcame a challenge by Emil Seidel to win his fourth presidential nomination (Seidel was chosen his vice-presidential running mate). Debs's 1912 presidential campaign against William Howard Taft (the incumbent), Theodore Roosevelt (the popular Bull Moose candidate), and Woodrow Wilson (the Democratic governor of New Jersey), rivaled his 1908 effort in miles traveled and crowds attracted. (During one stretch, he spoke five or six times a day for sixty-eight consecutive days.) Contemporaries noted during the campaign that both Wilson (who won the election) and Roosevelt had "stolen Debs's thunder," that is, had taken over a number of the ideas of the Socialist party and made them their own. Debs got nearly a million votes, or roughly 6 percent of the total number cast, which was his best performance in a presidential race and which he interpreted as a moral victory for ideas he had long espoused.

Most historians consider Debs's 1912 presidential campaign to have been the high point of the socialist movement in America. In the years that followed, part of the movement's strength was sapped by the New Freedom reforms of the Wilson administration, whose policies and programs drew members and potential converts from the Socialist Party of America. More important, however, in bringing on the winter of American socialism was the party's chronic addiction to savage and destructive factionalism, centering on issues such as the use of violence in in-

dustrial disputes, the efficacy of political action, and, after 1914, the
nature of the party's stance on World War I. In 1916, before America's
entry into the war, Debs declined the Socialist party's presidential nomination and, as noted, ran third in a race for Congress in Indiana's fifth
district. Though not a presidential candidate, Debs nonetheless influ-
enced the campaign. His criticisms of war in general, as well as his specific attack on the role of the United States in the war in a June 1918
speech in Canton, Ohio, set the stage for one of the strangest presidential election campaigns in American history.

In 1920 Debs, once again (for the fifth time) nominated as the Socialist Party of America's presidential candidate, was obliged to campaign from the Atlanta federal penitentiary, where he was serving a
ten-year sentence for violation of the wartime Espionage Act. During
the campaign (one of its slogans was "From the Jail House to the White
House"), Debs was formally notified of his nomination by a delegation
of socialists whom he received in the warden's office and with whom
he had his picture taken on the steps leading up to the prison's entrance. He was permitted to issue one campaign statement each week,
and he used the opportunity to attack his opponents, Warren Harding and James Cox, and the "Too Old Parties" for their fence-strad-
dling positions on issues such as the League of Nations. He also criticized the government's role in the Red Scare of 1919–20, in which
hundreds of anarchists, communists, socialists, Wobblies, and others
who were considered un-American were the victims of a hysterical and
tragic abuse, ranging from physical violence to warrantless arrests and
deportation (Debs himself being perhaps the most famous victim of
the atmosphere created by the Red Scare). Warren Harding won the
1920 election in a landslide victory, but once again Debs received nearly a million votes, despite the fact that the Socialist party had by that
time suffered mortal wounds from massive wartime defections and the
secession of thousands of members attracted to the new Communist
party splinter groups. In his five presidential campaigns Debs had slowly won over thousands, then hundreds of thousands, of men and wom-
en to his vision of a democratic society that would provide labor, dig-
nity, and security to all citizens. From a handful of "radicals" in 1900
the vision came to be shared by farmers in Oklahoma, miners in Colorado, textile mill workers in New Jersey, Jewish immigrant garment
workers in New York, and, in short, working men and women all over
the country. They were joined by many of the leading writers of the
time—Upton Sinclair, Sinclair Lewis, Carl Sandburg, and Theodore
Dreiser among them—by prominent university professors, clergymen,
social workers, and social reformers, and by a perhaps surprising number of men and women of considerable wealth.

In addition to his five presidential campaigns, Debs spread his ideas on the vital issues of his time through the thousands of editorials, articles, essays, printed interviews, letters to editors, and pamphlets that he wrote over a period of half a century. It was noted earlier that Debs's formal education was limited but that he had the great advantage of a home life in which books and literature were cherished. Early in life he became an avid reader, and throughout his career his writings were sprinkled with allusions to classical and modern literature.

When he was named editor of the *BLF Magazine* in 1880, Debs had little experience as a writer, but during his on-the-job training he developed a skill for turning out hard-hitting and provocative editorials on a wide range of current issues and affairs. In hundreds of editorials in the magazine over a period of fourteen years, Debs focused on worker-related issues—the need for workers to educate themselves on vital issues, to strengthen their unions' political clout at election time, and to maintain constant pressure on politicians to secure the passage and enforcement of pro-labor laws—though he gradually broadened the scope of his writing to deal with wider social issues. For example, he denounced the American Protective Association, a rabidly anti-Catholic organization of the late 1880s and early 1890s, as a tool with which management divided the ranks of labor. In 1884 he added a women's section to the magazine and placed Ida Husted Harper, a Terre Haute friend, in charge of it (Harper later became an ally and biographer of Susan B. Anthony). Debs published a series of editorials in the magazine in 1890 that advocated equality for women in politics, in the workplace, and in marital relations, triggering a chorus of angry letters from a predominantly male readership whose views on the subject were clearly at odds with those of the editor. On other social issues, Debs's editorials reflected the governing prejudices of his time: he opposed unrestricted immigration as a menace to workers' security; he wrote particularly bitter attacks on Italian immigrants who "fatten on garbage" and "underbid the American worker"; and he frequently printed popular black dialect stories, which more often than not contributed to the unflattering stereotypes of blacks that white America accepted. During the 1890s and the early years of the new century, Debs's attitudes on both the immigration question and the racial issue were dramatically changed and he would become immensely popular among immigrant workers and a leading critic of the Jim Crow system. As noted, by 1890 the *BLF Magazine* was recognized as one of the leading labor journals in the country, and Debs was regularly asked by others in the field of labor, including Samuel Gompers and Terence Powderly, to contribute articles to their publications.

After leaving the BLF, Debs became editor of *Railroad Times,* the weekly paper of the ARU, later served on the editorial staffs of the *Appeal to Reason,* a socialist weekly, and the *National Rip-Saw,* a socialist monthly, and in the last year of his life (1926) launched and edited the *New Appeal.* At the same time his articles were sought by and contributed to scores of newspapers and magazines, ranging from the *Birth Control Review* to the *American Legion Monthly* and including all the major socialist and many of the nonsocialist papers and magazines of the time. As in his presidential campaigns, his writings following his conversion to socialism stressed the need for workers to organize in industrial unions (in 1905 he joined with Daniel De Leon and William Haywood in launching the Industrial Workers of the World, known as the Wobblies, but soon left that organization in protest against its policies regarding the use of sabotage and the repudiation of political action in favor of direct action) and to break away from the "Too Old Parties," the Democrats and Republicans, and join the Socialist party. In addition to these basic themes, Debs wrote constantly in defense of the nation's outsiders: striking coal miners, textile workers, railroad, streetcar, and subway workers, and government workers; women seeking the right to vote, the right to earn equal pay for equal work, and the right to choose or not to choose birth control measures; blacks who were living through the worst excesses of the Jim Crow system (Debs was perhaps the most prominent critic of the classic movie *Birth of a Nation,* citing its appeal to racial hatred); immigrants, for many of whom the introduction to American life included the sweatshop, the company town, or the warm embrace of political bosses; and radicals of many kinds, such as Joe Hill, "Big Bill" Haywood, Emma Goldman, Margaret Sanger, Sacco and Vanzetti, and Kate O'Hare. As an editor of radical journals Debs was sensitive to First Amendment rights, particularly freedom of speech and freedom of the press, and his editorials in the *Appeal to Reason* attacking the federal courts and in the *National Rip-Saw* attacking America's entry into World War I pushed First Amendment protections to their limits—and, finally, beyond. His interest in free speech and free press issues preceded by years his joining in the founding of the American Civil Liberties Union following World War I.

In accounting for the impact of Debs's career on the ideas and ideals of his generation (in a 1990 *Life* magazine poll, Debs was chosen as one of the twentieth century's most important men), his role as a gifted public speaker must be added to his roles as a colorful presidential candidate and prolific writer. As in the case of his writing skills, Debs's skills as a public speaker were self-taught and only slowly acquired. Taking as his models men such as Wendell Phillips and Robert Ingersoll, whose speeches he heard in Terre Haute as a young man,

Debs eventually developed a speaking style that was called fiery by his admirers and incendiary by his critics. However they were characterized, his speeches, especially after the national fame that followed upon the Pullman strike, attracted huge crowds (fifteen thousand people paid fifteen cents to a dollar each to hear him in New York's Madison Square Garden), and many people over the years wrote to him to say that their own conversion to socialism or, at least, the alerting of their social consciousness had resulted from one of his speeches. Whenever there was a major strike or other industrial unrest, Debs was likely to be invited (or to volunteer) to be on the scene, urging worker solidarity and helping to raise funds for striking workers and their families. Debs spoke without benefit of electrical amplification or a ghostwriter. He regularly set out on speaking tours that took him to both coasts and most of the regions between, and efforts by local chambers of commerce and (after World War I) American Legion posts to prevent him from speaking only seemed to enlarge the crowds that turned out to hear him.

In the years between presidential campaigns, Debs's speaking and lecture tours were managed by one or the other of the socialist papers for which he wrote, as the tours had as an important secondary goal increasing the number of subscribers to the *Appeal to Reason* or the *National Rip-Saw*. As he grew older, Debs complained of the rigors of the speaking tours that were arranged for him, and his brother Theodore, his wife, and he agreed that the months-long tours contributed to his increasingly frequent medical problems.

As in the case of his printed works, the central theme of Debs's speeches was his vision of a better day to be ushered in by industrial unionism and socialism. Many of his speeches, however, were given in support of one of the countless reform movements of his time—including Margaret Sanger's work on behalf of women and the NAACP's attacks on Jim Crow—or in defense of those he considered to be victims of an unfair legal and judicial system—such as Bill Haywood, Sacco and Vanzetti, Emma Goldman, and dozens more. Occasionally Debs's friends and supporters (including his wife) cautioned him to adopt a more moderate style and language in his speeches, and he seemed to agree with the implied criticism. But usually the crowds' reactions to him and his reaction to the crowds resulted in speeches in which someone's "hide was nailed to the wall," as Debs himself described them.

As it turned out, the most controversial of Debs's many speeches was the one he gave in Canton, Ohio, on June 18, 1918. In his writings and speeches since the outbreak of the war in 1914, Debs had not only denounced the war but opposed the Wilson administration's "preparedness" program and demanded that the United States remain neutral. When America entered the war in April 1917, the Socialist party met in an emergency convention in St. Louis and passed a resolution of opposition. Debs endorsed the resolution but by 1918 was calling for a revision on the grounds that the resolution was causing mass defections from the party and would critically weaken the SPA in the off-year elections of 1918. Debs's Canton speech contained little that was new—the relationship between capitalism and war, the uneven burden of war on capitalists and workers, the injustice of the convictions and imprisonments being carried out under the government's wartime loyalty program—but it was taken by the federal government as a violation of the Espionage Act and became the basis of Debs's indictment and conviction under that law. At his trial in Cleveland in September 1918, Debs acknowledged that he had made the Canton speech as reported, but he insisted that his criticism of the war was protected by the First Amendment. He was found guilty and sentenced to ten years in prison. In March 1919 his conviction and sentence were upheld by the United States Supreme Court.

Debs's imprisonment from April 1919 to December 1921 seemed to elevate him from his role as a nationally known labor and socialist agitator and social critic to a symbolic martyrdom. The "Debs Case" became a rallying point for socialists and nonsocialists who deplored the nature of the wartime loyalty program and the excesses of the Red Scare following the war. (The one million votes Debs received in the 1920 election clearly included the votes of many nonsocialists.) Amnesty and "Free Debs" rallies were held around the country (the American Legion was busy conducting a "Keep Debs in Prison" campaign), and President Wilson and Attorney General A. Mitchell Palmer were flooded with letters and telegrams seeking Debs's release. At Atlanta, Debs insisted that he wanted no release unless other "political prisoners" were released at the same time. He declared that he would not ask for a pardon, since he believed he had committed no crime, and in March 1921 announced that he was "relieved" he had not been given a pardon by Wilson—which in his mind would have been akin to "Benedict Arnold pardoning George Washington."

Debs's ties with his followers in the Socialist party and with the larger public were kept intact by a steady stream of visitors (including Samuel Gompers), by journalists whose interviews with Debs found a ready market in the press, and through correspondence with hundreds of men and women (and children). On his incoming mail (which was temporarily suspended in the spring of 1921 following his published attack on the president) Debs wrote marginal notes and comments, and these were sent in a bundle once a week to his brother Theodore, in Terre Haute, who then put Debs's replies into a formal letter. (The-

odore later explained that the volume of Gene's mail during his imprisonment was so large that much of it was periodically destroyed for
lack of office space.) Debs was also permitted to mail one letter each
week and a letter on special occasions (such as Thanksgiving, Christmas, Confederate Memorial Day, etc.).

Given the standards of the penal systems of the time, Debs's treatment as a prisoner at Atlanta was as humane as the law and the rules
would allow. Befriended by Wardens Frederick Zerbst and James E.
Dyche, Debs was assigned to duty in the prison hospital and, later, to
"healthful" work on the prison farm. On one occasion, at least, he was
permitted to be taken for an automobile ride in and around Atlanta,
and in March 1921 he was permitted to make an unescorted train trip
to Washington, D.C., to confer with the new attorney general, Harry
Daugherty; on his return to Atlanta he was met at the station by the
warden. The socialist paper *New Day* reported that Debs had traveled
"as silently as a ghost," but news of the trip was published immediately and brought down on President Harding and the attorney general
a flood of protests against "discrimination in favor of a criminal duly
convicted by constituted authorities," as the *Atlanta Georgian* put it. The
photographs of Debs taken at the time of his release from the Atlanta
prison made it clear that, despite the decency of the wardens and the
"privileges" he had enjoyed, two and a half years of incarceration had
taken their toll on a man who celebrated his sixty-sixth birthday a few
months before his release.

It was one of the ironies of Debs's career that the calls for his release from prison found a warmer reception in the administration of
the conservative Warren Harding that they had gotten from the liberal Woodrow Wilson. Responding to a growing chorus of groups and
individuals who had joined in an amnesty movement (the SPA, the
American Federation of Labor, the American Civil Liberties Union,
etc.), and risking the wrath of other constituencies (the American Legion, countless chambers of commerce, and powerful segments of the
press), Harding ordered Debs's release at Christmastime in 1921.

Debs's remaining years were divided between losing battles to recover his health and to revive the Socialist Party of America. During
World War I the party suffered tens of thousands of defections (including many of its leading figures) by men and women who deplored its
antiwar stance. The socialist press was decimated not only by the loss
of subscribers but by the loss of its essential fourth-class mailing privileges. The Department of Justice monitored the behavior and activities of socialists all over the country, and in the heated (sometimes
hysterical) atmosphere of the war and the postwar Red Scare, socialists were branded as subversive and un-American and were ostracized

by their fellow citizens. Added to these war-related wounds, the party's chronic internal factionalism and dissension resulted in 1919 in the breaking away of its left-wing members, who organized (or joined) the new Communist Party of America (as it came to be called following several years of bewildering groupings and regroupings). The bitter, long-lasting struggle between the remnants of the Socialist party and the new Communist party dated from the very years Debs was in Atlanta.

In the early months following his release from prison, Debs was under great pressure to declare his allegiance to the new Communist party or to reaffirm his dedication to the Socialist party. His hope that he could reunite the socialists and communists in a new revolutionary movement may have accounted for his apparent temporizing in responding immediately to these pressures, but by the end of 1922 he had publicly declared his intention to remain in the SPA, "the party in whose service I have spent the better part of my life." Debs acknowledged his respect for the "best of motives" that had led to the formation of the Communist party, but he rejected its goal of establishing a proletarian dictatorship along a Russian model and its tactics of violence and "underground" activity. While praising the Russian Revolution and the overthrow of the czar in 1917, and expressing sympathy for the Russian people (some of his first articles following his release from prison were on Russian famine relief), Debs rejected the Soviet system as a model for America and attacked its suppression and execution of political dissidents.

In 1923 Debs agreed to serve as national chairman of the Socialist party, ending his long holdout against being a party official. Once again he made extended speaking tours to rekindle the fires, win back the membership, and replenish party coffers. Despite the organized opposition of the American Legion, local chambers of commerce, and a variety of service clubs, his tours—which took him once again to both coasts—attracted huge and enthusiastic crowds and provided much-needed financial aid to the SPA. His speeches now often had as their theme the need for prison reform in general and the release of Sacco and Vanzetti in particular. His own prison experience had convinced him that blacks and/or the poor received far harsher penalties for their crimes than did affluent whites and that their treatment was correspondingly harsher. The conviction and death sentences of the Italian immigrant anarchists Nicola Sacco and Bartolomeo Vanzetti, were, Debs argued, the result of prejudice against their radical political and economic beliefs and a reflection of the bias built into the capitalist judicial system. Debs's ideas on the subject were summed up in "Sacco and Vanzetti: An Appeal to American Labor," a popular 1926 pamphlet whose proceeds were given over to the Sacco-Vanzetti Defense Committee.

The large crowds and outpouring of affection that marked Debs's speaking tours (he was flooded with gifts and money at a series of seventieth birthday banquets in the fall of 1925) did not, however, reverse the decline of the Socialist party's membership nor add to its appeal to voters. The extent of the decline of the party by 1924 could be measured in part by its failure to nominate a candidate for that year's presidential election. Many people urged Debs to run again, but he made it clear that he would not be a candidate and that he agreed with the party's national convention decision in July 1924 to support Robert M. La Follette, the candidate of the new Progressive party. In the past Debs consistently opposed fusion with reformist parties, but he thought that the party had no practical alternative in 1924 and that support for La Follette would permit socialists to "keep the red flag flying" within the coalition of La Follette supporters. (A contemporary analyst of the 1924 campaign believed that socialists had played an important part in La Follette's receiving five million votes.) As he approached his seventieth birthday, Debs must have found little comfort in the fact that Calvin Coolidge, for whom "the business of government [was] business," won in a landslide victory over the equally conservative Democratic candidate John W. Davis. (The 1924 campaign served to widen the already considerable gap between Debs and the Communist party, whose leadership attacked him and charged that his endorsement of La Follette was proof of his loss of revolutionary principles.) In March 1925 the Socialist party called a special convention in Cleveland to assess its condition, but the convention was so poorly attended and, in Debs's view, so poorly organized that he judged the party to be "as near a corpse as a thing can be." Perhaps in response to Debs's criticism, the party's publicity director confided to a friend that "Debs cannot draw [a crowd] as he once did," and the national secretary concurred, noting that "what Debs does not realize is that his imprisonment is an old story and he is not the drawing card he once was."

Nonetheless, Debs's 1925 national speaking tour (and the seventieth birthday banquets) raised enough money for him to launch the *American Appeal,* a socialist weekly whose first edition appeared on January 1, 1926. As editor in chief and a regular contributor, Debs hoped that the new paper would do for its readers what the *Appeal to Reason* and the *National Rip-Saw* had done before World War I—namely, convert workers and farmers to socialism. For a short time his editorials against the open shop, the Ku Klux Klan, and the treatment of Sacco and Vanzetti showed signs of the vitality that had characterized his earlier writing, but in the spring of 1926 it became clear to his Terre Haute physician and, grudgingly, to Debs himself that the symptoms of his declining health had become ominous. Since his release from prison he had spent extended periods between speaking tours at Lindlahr Sanitarium, a nature-cure facility in the Chicago suburb of Elmhurst. His hospital room became as powerful an attraction as his prison cell had been, and the steady stream of visitors probably retarded his recovery while at the same time making bearable his long stays there. He seemed particularly pleased by visits from Sinclair Lewis, whose novels *Main Street* and *Babbitt* had made him an internationally famed writer, and Carl Sandburg, to whose home in nearby Lombard, Illinois, Debs frequently escaped for parties and picnics. Lewis promised to, but did not, write a novel based on Debs's life, and Sandburg told Debs that he "hoped to get the strong truth of those hands of yours into a poem." Sandburg called his Lincoln biography "the book in which you [Debs] have collaborated."

Debs's stays at Lindlahr in 1922, 1923, and 1924 provided him with a rather fanciful diet of grain and fresh fruit and some exotic exercises, and each time he left the sanitarium feeling, he said, "like a young colt." But by the spring of 1926 neither larger prescriptions of digitalis nor a month-long trip with his wife to Bermuda had their intended effect. In late September he returned to Lindlahr and died there a little more than a month later, on October 20, 1926. A few days after his death, following a memorial service at which Norman Thomas gave the eulogy, Debs's ashes were buried in Terre Haute. According to his brother Theodore, Debs's last will, written in the summer of 1926 but never probated by his widow, had left virtually his entire estate to the Socialist Party of America. If that is true—and Theodore insisted for the remainder of his life that it was—Debs was at the time of his death one of a dwindling number of those men and women who continued to believe that the SPA was a wave of the future.

Eugene Victor Debs's place in American history seems secure but, like his life, subject to controversy. Two facts about his career are certain: he played an important part in popularizing ideas and ideals that were denounced as radical, even un-American, early in the twentieth century but that later became orthodox and are now viewed as traditional; and, taking his successes and failures together, his career was an honorable chapter in the history of American dissent, a history significantly enhanced by Debs's willingness to pay a very high price for holding unpopular views.

Eugene V. Debs (Eugene V. Debs Foundation)

EVD's wife, Katherine Metzel Debs
(Cunningham Memorial Library,
Indiana State University)

EVD (*right*) and Theodore at work in the Red Special, 1908 (Eugene V. Debs Foundation)

EVD (*first row, left*) at fourteen in a group picture of the Terre Haute & Indianapolis Railroad paint crew (Eugene V. Debs Foundation)

EVD's 1908 campaign train, the Red Special. Debs is standing under the "R" in the banner, holding a child; Theodore Debs is on his left, Stephen Marion Reynolds on his right (Eugene V. Debs Foundation)

EVD (*right*) and Fred Warren, managing editor of the *Appeal to Reason* (Eugene V. Debs Foundation)

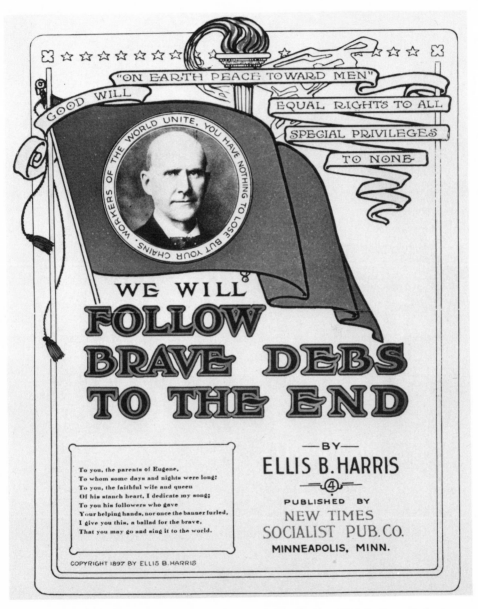

The cover of "Follow Brave Debs to the End," 1897 (Eugene V. Debs Foundation)

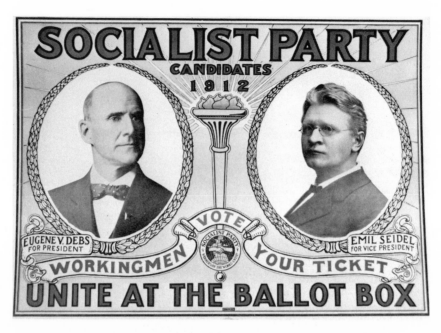

A 1912 Socialist party campaign poster (Eugene V. Debs Foundation)

EVD (*left*) and Victor Berger (Eugene V. Debs Foundation)

EVD on the stump (Eugene V. Debs Foundation)

Mabel Dunlap Curry, EVD's "Juno" (Lilly Library, Indiana University)

Morris Hillquit (Cunningham Memorial Library, Indiana State University)

EUGENE V. DEBS

"I know of no man living whose greatness of heart and mind is so generally conceded as is Mr. Debs."
—FRANK P. WALSH,
Chairman of Industrial Relations.

"Every Man that thinks a child is worthy of more consideration than a dollar, ought to vote for EUGENE V. DEBS for Congress."
—BASIL M. MANLY
Formerly Director United States Commission on Industrial Relations.

Go, search the earth from end to end,
And where's a better all-round friend
Than Eugene Debs?—a man that stands
And jest holds out in his two hands,
As warm a heart as ever beat
Betwixt here and the Mercy Seat!
—JAMES WHITCOMB RILEY.

"Among all the Speakers I have ever heard there has not been one who came nearer my idea of Abraham Lincoln than Eugene V. Debs."
—REV. DEWITT TALMAGE

SOCIALIST CANDIDATE FOR

CONGRESS

Fifth District of Indiana

WILL SPEAK

AT _____

DATE _____

HOUR _____

A 1916 congressional campaign poster (Eugene V. Debs Foundation)

The Atlanta Federal Penitentiary (Eugene V. Debs Foundation)

"Our Gene" at the start of his journey to Prison, from Cleveland, Ohio,
Sunday morning, April 13, 1919.

EVD en route to prison in Moundsville, West Virginia, 1919 (Amalgamated Meat Cut-
ters and Butcher Workmen of North America)

EVD (*center*) and Dr. Madge Patton Stephens, a Terre Haute physician who was a member of the committee that notified Debs of his presidential nomination in 1920 (Cunningham Memorial Library, Indiana State University)

EVD (*left*) and Seymour Stedman, his 1920 running mate (Eugene V. Debs Foundation)

A 1920 presidential campaign poster (Eugene V. Debs Foundation)

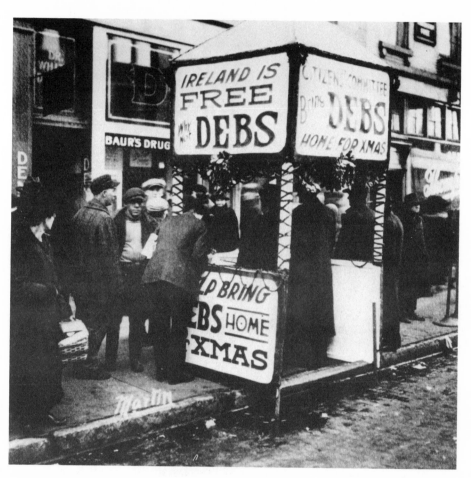

A "Free Debs" petition booth in Terre Haute, 1921 (Eugene V. Debs Foundation)

EVD at the time of his release from prison, December 1921 (Eugene V. Debs Foundation)

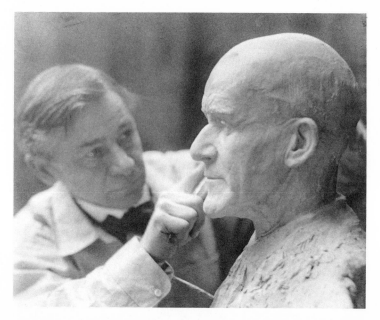

Louis Mayer at work on his bust of EVD, for which Debs sat at the time of his trial in September 1918 (Cunningham Memorial Library, Indiana State University)

EVD in early 1922, shortly after his release from prison (National Archives)

EVD and Carl Sandburg at Lindlahr Sanitarium, 1924 (Eugene V. Debs Foundation)

The last known photograph of Eugene V. Debs, 1926 (Eugene V. Debs Foundation)

A memorial service poster, 1926 (Eugene V. Debs Foundation)

Gentle Rebel

□ *Debs's search for employment as a locomotive fireman during the depression that followed the Panic of 1873 took him to East St. Louis, Illinois. In the following letters to his parents and his sister he describes his experiences there and in St. Louis, where he came face-to-face with the effects of the "dull" economy.*

EVD to Jean Daniel Debs and Marguerite Bettrich Debs

September 29, 1874
East St. Louis, Illinois

Dear Parents:

I take time to write to you a few words in haste to comply with my promise. I arrived here safely and am in good health up to the present time. It seems to me, it has been a year since I left home, at times I have a little company but sometimes I am all alone and I am so homesick, I hardly know what to do, but hope that after I get to work I will get a little accustomed to being away from home. It has rained pretty steadily since my arrival, but has been real fair yesterday and today. Saturday I crossed the bridge and took a stroll through some of the principal streets of Saint Louis. I went to Shaw's Garden, also Lafayette and Missouri Parks which are all very beautiful, and can only be appreciated by being seen. As I was returning I saw one of our old time Snoozers, one that used to cause a great deal of unnecessary talk in our household viz: Samuel Howell. He was just across the street from where I was, but I did not hail him, nor did he recognize me, and I thought we'd better not renew our acquaintance.

Dear Mother I was very sorry not to see you, before I left home, but it was quite unavoidable as I am not acquainted with all the men on the west division of this road, and had I not gone, perhaps I could not have went for over a week. Tell John and Mary also, that I was quite sorry not to see *them*, but I hope to see you all before a great while. I hope that you are all enjoying good health and that you are all happy as I am just at the present time. While I am writing, there is a little girl playing on the piano, and singing also, which sounds very beautifully and which reminds me of home. Dear Parents If I am as successful as I am prospective I will soon get where I can make some money, which prospects are very flattering, as I can tell you that times are indeed dull. It makes a person's heart ache to go along some of the main sts in the city and see men women & children begging for something to eat. Sisters Lou, Jennie and Emma and brother Theodore dont know how happy they ought to be to have a comfortable home, and parents kind, to help them. I did not know it either till I came over here. I could write to you a great while longer, but I suppose that you are tired of reading a letter of so little significance. This morning I went to Carondelet with an Engineer that I was acquainted with and on my return I stopped at the Belleville Machine Shop where I saw Tom McCabe who used to be machinist at Seath and Hager's. I had a little talk with him when he told me that he had acquired the foremanship of the Machine Shop, and consequently he possesses great influence. We together went to the Master Mechanic and Tom spoke to him for me, and I showed him my letter of recommendation upon which he immediately promised me the first chance as fireman on the "St Louis, Belleville, and Southern Ills Rail Road. It may be a while before I get it, but I tell you It will be a good job, and I will have a chance to make some money. A road that runs from St Louis to Belleville, a distance of 78 miles. Dear Sister Lou, tell Alex {mullen} that I aint dead yet, and tell him also that I hope he has got over his spell of sickness. Give all the boys and girls my kind regards, and accept the same from a brother. Tell Charly Hirzel that after I get everything in good shape I will write to him, as I promised. Tell John that I hope he was successful at the Indianapolis fair and that he took a good many premiums. Tell John and Mary that I hope they are well, and little Flaxy Heinl also. and Tell Theodore to take good care of the chickens, and to be a good boy and obey pa and ma. Once more, give my kind regards to Friends inquiring. I need not say answer my letter, for I know you will respond without hesitation, I am very anxious to hear from you. But love to you all, and much, too. I shall tell you of my methods of economy in my next

Your affectionate son
Eugene

Address on the other side

[on reverse: Address. Eugene Debs East St Louis Ills. St Clair County]

ALS, InTI, Debs Collection.

EVD to Eugenie Debs

October 3, 1874
East St. Louis, Illinois

My dear Sister:

Your welcome response to my letter was gladly received this morning at an early hour, and contents eagerly read. Your first words are that you would like to see me home again, to this I must object, the reasons of which I will disclose to you. You see the approaching winter is predicted as one of unusual severity, also pecuniary matters do not seem very prospective, and altogether it is plainly to be seen that this winter will see this Country in the worst pecuniary embarrassment possible. I can see it here, better than I could in Terre Haute, for if you had any idea of the hundreds of starving people that I see daily, without exception, you would not urge me to return to T.H. for awhile at least, as long as I have prospects of an occupation at which I can at least support my self and perhaps save a little money besides. I dont expect to stay away from home for ever, nor for even an unreasonable length of time; I only want to stay long enough to save up a little money and to prove that I can act manly when must be. I dont go anywhere at all, except to a french family by the name of Dûches, that reside in the vicinity of my boarding house. They are very nice people and they think the world and all of me, I feel myself perfectly at home when in their company. The family is not a very large one, it consists only of Father Mother and an only daughter. They would willingly do anything for me, they make it, indeed, their study to surround me with comforts, and are constantly devising some fresh plans, which they think will make me feel myself at home. They volunteered to do my washing free of charge, but I do not want to take advantage of good nature and disposition. The first time I went there I was accompanied by an Engineer who was acquainted with them, in fact neighbor acquaintances, when I became introduced To Mr & Mrs Dûches, and then to Lena, a pretty girl of about 17 years of age. They did not know that I was french, and the first words of Lena to her mother, after the introduction, were, "Ma! He is a railroad boy; spoken in french of course, she little suspecting that I understood it. I immediately made known that I was french myself, and then we had a good laugh over it. We now speak french altogether. Now for a change of subject; In your last, you allude to a young man who was killed close to T.H. By the name of Stewart. I suppose I was aware of that before you, as I was personally acquainted with him, and to tell you the truth of my opinion, I do not sympathize with him a particle, as he was a genuine Dead Beat of the first order. The road that I intend working on is as safe as a bed, never having had any ill luck in any manner, although it is an old road. Now for your Saur Krout; I hope you will Stuff yourselves with it till you cant rest, and enjoy it too. There is something important that I wish to acquaint you with that perhaps will surprise you somewhat. I was down to Dûches house the other evening and they asked me If I knew a young man in Terre Haute, lately arrived, by the name of Johnnie Clay, gave me his full descriptions, and it cannot be any other but the one that was at our dance shortly before I came away. What I was going to tell you was this. He was Clerk in this city, in a bank, and not a long while since purloined One Hundred and Sixty Dollars from the bank, and run away with it. He is not allowed to return here, ~~under~~ as he should be arrested immediately. Dont say anything about it to anybody, I only want you to stay away from him, all of you.

I expect to get my job next week and then you may expect your Gold Watch. Tell ma that I know it is best for me to stay here where I am, until dull times are at an end when I will again return to T.H. I hope that you are all well as I am myself   Health is more valuable than money after all, as long as a person has there health, they should not complain. Give all my Rail Road Friends my regards, and dont sack[?] them promiscuously   Tell Otto that I am still alive and well and that I will write to him when I get myself fixed permanently, give him my best respects, and tell him that I was sorry not to see him before I came away. Give all my friends my regards, and {present} my most special Compliments to the Meyer family, also to all inquirers. I was very much pleased to learn through the important information conveyed by Theodore, that all the game chickens are doing well, and his efforts to write a letter were duly appreciated, and afforded me great pleasure, as I pulled it out of the envellope so grandly, and sat down on the Post Office steps to read it. I showed his writing to Mrs Dûches, and she said that I had a very intelligent young brother indeed. How is everything and everybody in Terre Haute, the only place in this world that I have any love for. Actually it seems a lifetime to me since I left that sacred little spot. I dont know whether I could recognize T.H. or not. Give my love to Father and Mother and tell them that probably I will be at Home on a visit ere long. Give my love to all the family, and lots of it too. Excuse irregularity in writing, also bad penmanship as I am in haste to go to the shop.

Write soon and write much and I remain for ever in affection

Your Brother

Eugene

ALS, InTI, Debs Collection.

□ *James Whitcomb Riley gained national acclaim as the "Hoosier Poet" for the whimsical, friendly verses he published in numerous collections, beginning in 1883 with* The Old Swimming Hole and 'Leven More Poems. *His long friendship with Debs dated from 1880 when Debs arranged three Riley appearances at the Occidental Literary Club. In the following letter Debs inquires about a mutual friend's health and mentions one of the first of his many bouts with illness.*

EVD to James Whitcomb Riley

January 3, 1885
Terre Haute, Indiana

My dear Riley,

How is our dear Dr. Hays? Your telephone message and a letter from Mrs. Hays came in my absence. I came home ill and during the past several weeks have had the battle of my life with a complication of troubles that the most skilful doctors in our city have been unable to overcome. At the present writing I am still confined to my room with the grip, fever & the most violent and incessant headache that mortal ever suffered. The past year's work was too exacting for me & the cause of my trouble is nervous exhaustion which it will take some time to overcome. Under any other circumstances I should have hastened over on the very first train, for I remember the doctor's unwavering loyalty & love him as if he were a brother. I am worried much about the matter and beg you to drop me a line. Mrs. Hays did not answer my letter & this adds not a little to my distress. I never before so profoundly regretted my helplessness when a friend was in distress.

Hope you are in the best of health & full of joy.

Yours always,
E. V. Debs

ALS, InU, Lilly Library, Riley MSS.

☐ *As editor of the* BLF Magazine *Debs often found room for poetry and occasionally tried his own hand at it. Two samples follow, the first dedicated to his sister, the second to his father.*

EVD to Eugenie Debs

December 1886
Terre Haute, Indiana

> A nice little temper
> That is not always mild
> And gives her the appearance
> Of a spoilt saucy child
> > Has my Jennie
>
> A hand that can scrub
> That can finger the keys,
> Or make up the pie crust
> And do all with ease
> > Has my Jennie
>
> A neat little foot
> That can wear out the shoes
> Or can skip in the waltz
> If its owner but choose
> > Has my Jennie
>
> A flashing brown eye
> That shines like a star
> And that sparkles with anger
> When she is at war
> > Has my Jennie
>
> A pert little mouth
> That is saucy and neat
> As if made just for saying
> Things bitter and sweet
> > Has my Jennie
>
> A character as pure
> As the white driven snow
> And a will that is able
> To keep it just so
> > Has my Jennie

A heart full of sympathy
For those in distress,
Or that throbs in its rapture
At a loved one's carress
                    Has my Jennie

I pray that my love for her
May never grow less
That the Lord in his goodness
Will my home always bless
                    With my Jennie

T (poem). InTI, Debs Collection.

EVD poem

December 4, 1886
Terre Haute, Indiana

Dedicated to Daniel Debs on his sixty sixth birth-day

Yes, this is Grand-Pa's birth-day.
For sixty six long years
He has traveled lifes rugged pathway
Besprinkled with smiles and tears.
He is sixty six years old to-day
And he from us must learn
That we wish, for him, this birth-day
Would a hundred times return.

His life was not all sunshine
Yet many a pleasant hour
Has made more light his labors
Changed the weed into a flower.
This pleasant little party
Was selected, by the way,
To help Grand Pa enjoy the more
His sixty sixth birth-day.

We'll make Grand Pa forget his age
And once again be young
And mingle with us little folks

Who'se lives have just begun.
We will try to make him happy
And we wish for him the best
That for ever in the future
His life be richly blessed.

A faithful wife is Grand Ma
Who at every turn of tide
Has helped to share his burdens
Staid closely by his side.
They to-gether bear their sorrows
And every pleasure share.
Oh what a grand example
Is that good and noble pair.

Let us all congratulate them
And assure them of our love.
Give them all the admiration
Due the lion and the dove.
They are loved and much respected
By all who know them well
And we like to sing their praises
And on their virtues dwell.

Their lives have been a grand success
As one can plainly see
By glancing o'er their history
Since first they crossed the sea.
A monument more lasting
Than if made of copper plate
They have built where they resided
In the good old Hoosier state.

To the table now we will adjourn
And attend to the inner man
And out of compliment to the cook
Will dispose of all we can.
We will drink to the health of Grand Pa
With our glasses full to the brim
And disband with promises to reunite
When he reaches his three score ten.

T (poem), InTI, Debs Collection.

☐ *The new home mentioned in this letter to James Whitcomb Riley is now a state and national historical landmark. During Debs's life the house was the subject of periodic controversy centering on charges that it had been built by scab labor, that Katherine Debs would not admit working men and women to enter it, and that it was a luxurious mansion—proof of the shallowness of Debs's working-class roots.*

EVD to James Whitcomb Riley

April 1, 1890
Terre Haute, Indiana

My dear Riley,

I write to ask if it will be agreeable for you to be here Tuesday evening the 8th to participate in an entertainment to be given for the benefit of the families of the Indianapolis firemen who recently perished at their post. The undertaking is a most laudable one and *all Terre Haute* wants to see you.

Besides, I want you as my guest for a day or two, or as much longer as you can stay—We have lately moved into our new home and nothing would afford us more pleasure than to have you visit with us—Mrs. Debs joins me cordially in extending the invitation. The visit will do you good and we will enjoy ourselves together—please answer soon as I leave on Thursday night for the East, returning on Tuesday.

Yours always
E. V. Debs

ALS, EVD Foundation, Debs Home.

☐ *An immigrant from England, Samuel Gompers helped found the American Federation of Labor in 1886 and, except in 1895, served as its president until his death in 1924. The following two letters were written in the spirit of friendship and fraternal dedication to the cause of labor. Before long, however, the relationship between Gompers and Debs cooled and in time degenerated into one in which Gompers described Debs as an "apostle of failure" and Debs viewed Gompers as chief among the "labor fakirs" in the union movement. Their estrangement resulted in part from Debs's often-stated opinion that Gompers's role in the Pullman Strike of 1894 had contributed to its defeat and the dissolu-*

tion of the American Railway Union and, more important, from their basic dif-
ferences regarding the composition and role of labor unions, political action,
the acceptance or rejection of capitalism, and other issues.

Samuel Gompers to EVD

October 31, 1892

Dear Sir and Friend: —

The enclosed circular will remind you that the time is near at hand when the American Federation of Labor will again meet in annual session.

In transmitting this at this time I have a purpose in mind, which when I communicate it will I hope and feel certain touch a responsive chord. It is this. As your term as Secretary and Editor of the Official Magazine of the Brotherhood of Locomotive Firemen is about to expire, and you propose to enter the wide field of literature and the reform movement, the thought occurred that there could scarcely be a more fitting opportunity presented to embark in that wide field, than an address by you at the convention of the American Federation of Labor; not at an informal or an adjourned meeting but at one of its regular sessions.

I therefore extend to you a fraternal and sincere invitation to deliver an address upon any day of the sessions of the convention of the American Federation of Labor, and urge you to accept it in the interest of our great cause.

Of course if you consent you might choose any subject you might desire but I believe that one upon the subject of "Federated Labor; the Hope of Its Advocates, and Its Possibilities" would be of exceptional interest just at this time.

Sincerely hoping that you may find yourself in a position to accept the invitation and to comply with my request, and asking for a reply at your earliest convenience, I am,

Very Truly Yours
Samuel Gompers   President.
American Federation of Labor

TLc, DLC, Gompers Letterbooks.

Samuel Gompers to EVD

November 29, 1892

My Dear Debs: —

I am in receipt of your favors of recent date and owe you an apology, for not responding earlier. Need I assure you that had it been possible for me to reply earlier that I would have done so? I feel satisfied you will take it for granted.

I esteemed it a privilege to extend an invitation to you to address the delegates to the Philadelphia convention of the American Federation of Labor. That you cannot accept it gives me sincere regret, but I assure you it is heightened by the fact that you are not enjoying good health.

The few to whom I communicated my purpose of inviting you to address our delegates were simply delighted at the idea, and subsequent to my sending you the letter a number of others suggested the idea of my sending an invitation to you, among others, our old friend P. J. Mc-Guire.

I earnestly hope that you may soon be convalescent and be robust for the great mission beyond doubt you are to fulfil in the great labor movement.

By an oversight I was evidently led into the error that your official connection with the Bro'd. of Locomotive Firemen had entirely been severed, but I am pleased to learn that you are still directing the "Magazine."

In reference to the article you ask me to write let me say that I shall endeavor to comply with your request. Of course you understand that just about this time I am considerably crowded with work, but shall do the best I can under the circumstances.

I kindly ask you to send me a good photo of yourself as soon as possible, as I desire to place it with the photos of the officers of all the Nat. and Int. Union [sic] of the country in a frame to remain in the office of the A.F. of L.

Will you also kindly give me the name and address of the secretary of the new organization of Railroad Conductors, as well as its technical name upon receipt of this, and oblige,

Yours Sincerely
Samuel Gompers   President.
American Federation of Labor

TLc, DLC, Gompers Letterbooks.

☐ *The American Railway Union was organized on June 20, 1893, in Chica-*
go by about fifty dissident railroad labor leaders who shared Debs's disillusion-
ment with the aristocratic leadership and selfish interests of some of the rail-
road brotherhoods and their failure to remain united during strike crises. In
its first test of strength, in April 1894, the new union successfully carried out
an eighteen-day strike against the Great Northern Railroad. Debs's confronta-
tion during the strike with the Great Northern's president, James J. Hill, ele-
vated Debs to national prominence. In the following letter to Frank X. Holl,
leader of the ARU local in Minneapolis, Debs urges Holl to prepare for the up-
coming strike.

EVD to Frank X. Holl

[April] 16, 1894
Terre Haute, Indiana

Confidential

Dear Sir and Brother:

I am just advised of a carefully devised secret scheme to break up
the A.R.U. on the Great Northern System preliminary to sweeping
reductions of wages in every department. Some of our best men have
been discharged at various points for no other reason than that they
were active A.R.U. men. The scheme is to discharge our local leaders
at various points and thus demoralize and stampede the Order, re-
ducing the members to a headless, disorganized mob, a condition
under which it will be unable to resist the sweeping reductions of
wages that are to be made. Some reductions have already been made.
Others and greater ones are to follow.

There is but one hope. Everything depends upon immediate action.
Organize solidly at every point. Get every good man into your Union
at once. There must not be a moment's delay. The agreement with
the Company has been shamefully violated. Men have been indis-
criminately discharged. Wages have been reduced and unless prompt
measures are taken the men on the Great Northern will be reduced
to a horde of slaves. The issue will be pressed by the Company. We
must prepare to meet it. The reinstatement of the men discharged
without cause will be demanded. The A.R.U. will stand by them with
all its resources. Not only this, but if the case demands it I propose
to go over the Great Northern in person; hold popular mass meetings
at every point; appeal to the whole people to stand by us in this unholy

massacre of our rights. Get together promptly. Organize thoroughly. Stand up and be men. You may rest assured that you will not want for the support of courageous, manly men. Let me hear from you at once.

Yours fraternally,
Eugene V. Debs

TLS, TxU, Holl MSS.

☐ *At the first annual ARU convention held in Chicago in June 1894, the delegates, flushed with the recent victory in the Great Northern strike, unanimously approved a boycott of trains handling Pullman cars, in sympathy with the striking workers at the nearby Pullman Palace Car Company. Within days of the ARU boycott decision a strike paralyzed the western half of the nation, tying up the economic life of twenty-seven states and territories. The following exchange between Debs and Jane Lathrop Stanford, the widow of California railroad magnate, governor, and United States senator Leland Stanford, sheds light on the impact of the strike and on Debs's considerable power during its course.*

Jane Lathrop Stanford to EVD

July 1, 1894
[Dunsmuir], California

The trainmen offered their services to take me safely home. They have kindly brought me in my private car with 2 servants as far as Sissons. They have just telegraphed me that, while they are still willing to take me — desire that I obtain your permission & sanction. It is almost an absolute necessity that I should be in San Francisco on Tuesday July 3rd to attend to important business.

Most of the men in your organization are old & devoted friends of my husband, and it is to testify to their respect for his memory that they are anxious to take me safely ~~home~~ over the Road to my home.

I will be ready to leave Dunsmuir Monday morning and 8o'c & be taken to Sacramento. The next day proceed to S.F. — traveling only by daylight.

Kindly answer to Dunsmuir & oblige

Mrs. Leland Stanford.

ALS, CSt, Archives.

EVD to Jane Lathrop Stanford

July 2, 1894
Chicago, Illinois

THE TRAINMEN WILL HAUL YOUR CAR TO ITS DESTINATION ON PRESENTATION OF THIS TELEGRAM IF THERE SHOULD BE ANY FURTHER INTERRUPTION PLEASE ADVISE ME AND I WILL BE GLAD TO ASSIST YOU IN ANY WAY IN MY POWER IN SAFELY REACHING YOUR DESTINATION

EUGENE V DEBS

Telegram, CSt, Archives.

Jane Lathrop Stanford to EVD

July 2, 1894
Dunsmuir, California

I APPRECIATE MORE THAN I CAN EXPRESS YOUR KIND ACT. I ACCEPT IT AS A TRIBUTE & A MARK OF ESTEEM TO THE MEMORY OF MY HUSBAND, WHO FOR 25 YEARS WAS HELD IN VENERATION BY ALL OF HIS R.R. EMPLOYEES. IT WOULD HAVE PLEASED YOU TO HAVE SEEN THE JOY IN THE FACES OF THE REPRESENTATIVES OF YOUR ORGANIZATION HERE TO CARRY OUT YOUR SANCTION OF THEIR DESIRE.

GRATEFULLY YOURS.
MRS. LELAND STANFORD

Telegram, CSt, Archives.

☐ *Crippled by a blanket injunction against the leaders of the ARU and the intervention of federal troops to protect interstate commerce and maintain mail delivery, the Pullman strike collapsed and Debs and other officers of the union were indicted for conspiracy. From his Chicago jail cell Debs wrote the following letter to Henry Demarest Lloyd, whose* Wealth against Commonwealth *was*

one of the most widely read books in the reform literature of the Populist-Pro-
gressive Era.

EVD to Henry Demarest Lloyd

July 24, 1894
Chicago, Illinois

My dear Mr. Lloyd,

Your very kind and cheering letter of the 19*th* inst. has been received. A thousand thanks for your friendship and solicitude. We are
still in custody and our trial for "contempt of court" for violating a
drag-net injunction is now in progress. We spend the days in court
and the nights in jail. Having only acted in this matter in obedience
to the dictates of our consciences and our judgment we shall accept
with philosophic composure any penalties, however severe, the courts
may see fit to impose.

The one great result of this agitation has been to call the attention
of the country to the flagrant abuses of corporate power of which
working people have so long been the patient and uncomplaining
victims.

I am inclined to be optimistic and do not hesitate to believe that
all these things are working together for the emancipation and re-
demption of men from the thraldom that has so long held them in
slavery and degradation.

Rogers, Howard and Keliher, my fellow felons join in cordial
regard and greeting. We are not unmindful of the fact that your great
heart throbs in unison with every movement that has for its purpose
the regeneration of the children of men.

Thanking you again and again and hoping that you may be revived
and invigorated by your sojourn at the sea side I am

Very faithfully yours
Eugene V. Debs

ALS, WHi, Lloyd Papers.

□ *Debs believed that Samuel Gompers and the AFL, by refusing to endorse the*
boycott, contributed to the defeat of the ARU in the Pullman strike. In the fol-

lowing letter, written after the strike had ended, Gompers offers Debs financial aid for the costly court battle that followed.

Samuel Gompers to EVD

August 16, 1894
[unknown]

Dear Sir and Friend: —

You will remember the very interesting conference had between you, Mr. P. J. Mc-Guire and myself at the Revere House Chicago Ill. on Sunday afternoon July 15th. It has left a deep impression upon my mind. I am sure that the many important topics we discussed ought and will no doubt bring forth good fruit.

You remember our mentioning the fact that at the meeting of the Executive Council of the A.F. of L. an appropriation of $500.00 had been made to be contributed towards your legal defense before the courts, and that an appeal would be made for contributions towards a legal defense fund for you. In compliance therewith I enclose to you herein a check for $670.10 which in the name of the A.F. of L. and the other donors I ask you to accept with our best wishes.

In presenting this to you we desire to convey more eloquently than I can find words to express our unqualified disapproval of the attempts on the part of the governmental officials and the courts in throwing the weight of their influence in favor of corporate wealth and against the most necessary, useful and liberty loving people of the country — the wage workers. We offer it to you as a protest against the exercize of class justice, and as a further protest against the violation of rights guaranteed by the Constitution and the Declaration of Independence.

It would be superfluous to say to you in this letter that the end of the struggles of the masses is not yet, that the workers must thoroughly organize upon practical lines to maintain their manhood, to prevent their liberty from being filched from them, to achieve that success for which all previous contests were but preparatory to the attainment of that justice looked forward to by all lovers of mankind.

I kindly ask you to forward two separate receipts to Secretary Chris. Evans, one for the $500.00 donated by the American Federation of Labor, and another for the balance $170.10 at your earliest convenience.

Sincerely hoping that you may be successful in confounding the enemies of labor who are trying to secure your incarceration, and with kindest wishes, I am,

Very Truly Yours
Samuel Gompers   Pres.
American Federation of Labor

TLc, DLC, Gompers Letterbooks.

□ *On January 5, 1895, Debs reported to the McHenry County jail at Wood-stock, Illinois (about fifty miles northwest of Chicago), to serve a six-month term for violation of the federal court injunction handed down during the Pullman strike. He was released a few weeks later, pending an appeal to the U.S. Supreme Court by his counsel, which included Clarence Darrow. After the appeal was denied Debs returned to Woodstock on June 12, 1895. In the following letter he describes the jail facilities and seems intent on bolstering his father's morale.*

EVD to Jean Daniel Debs

January 14, 1895
Woodstock, Illinois

My dearest Father:

Your letter filled with kindness and cheer, characteristic of the stock, especially when the times are on that "try men's souls," is with me. I have immense satisfaction in knowing that you and mother, notwithstanding your years, are as proud, heroic and defiant as the rest of us and even our enemies admit that we have the courage of our convictions. My imprisonment is doing much to arouse the public conscience. No disgrace attaches to the family. You need not blush. In good time the right will prevail and then reward and vindication will come. A steady stream of letters is pouring in here from all parts of the country. No one can imagine what a wave of indignation is rising. Judge Woods is not so much at ease as [I am?]. My jail quarters are large, airy, clean and comfortable and I am perfectly at home with the sheriff's family whose residence adjoins the jail. Sunday

Charley Gould was here and we spent the afternoon in the Sheriff's parlors, regaling ourselves (after a good dinner of stuffed roast chicken) with a musical concert. Saturday Governor Waite of Colorado was with us from 11 till 2, taking dinner with us. He is a fine old man of about your age. He is chock full of fight and don't care what the plutocratic press say about him. We may get out pending the decision of our case by the U.S. Supreme Court and in that event I will see you before the close of the week. The signs of the times are all hopeful and the future is full of cheer. You and mother must carry yourselves like the Spartans of old. This is not the time for sighs or tears but for heroic fortitude which does not waver, no matter how trying [the?] ordeal. If the night is dark the dawn is near. Our day is coming. Just a little patience and we will celebrate our jubilee with becoming *eclat.*

My heart is with you always. Kisses to you both and to Eugenie. The jail but makes our attachment the stronger.

Your devoted son
Eugene

ALS, InTI, Debs Collection.

☐ *Samuel Huston was the prosecuting attorney in Terre Haute. In May 1894 he delivered the welcoming address on the occasion of Debs's return from the successful prosecution of the Great Northern Strike.*

EVD to Samuel Huston

August 15, 1895
Woodstock, Illinois

My dear Sir and Friend: —

I have received a very pitiable story from Ellen M. Lappin, now an inmate of the Vigo County Jail. She informs me she is but 16 years of age, a mere child I should judge and that she is in jail on a charge of larceny because of her failure to give bond. I, of course, know nothing of the merits of the case but have written her saying I knew you well and would write to you in her behalf. If her story is true, or but half true, it seems harsh to have imprisoned her under the circumstances. I know you will not suffer her to be subjected to a wrong and yet in your multifarious duties I thought the case might have escaped your personal attention and hence this letter. I am quite sure it is only necessary you should understand the case to insure justice being done. With cordial regards and best wishes, I am,

Yours Very Truly,
Eugene V. Debs

Dict. E. V. D.

TLS, EVD Foundation, Debs Home.

EVD to Samuel Huston

August 31, 1895
Woodstock, Illinois

My dear friend: —

Your favor of the 30th in answer to my communication in reference to Ella Lappin, has been received and I thank you for your courteous explanation in the matter. Since writing you I have noticed by the papers, which come to me from Terre Haute, that hers is a most curious case and I concluded from the public statements, which you now substantially verify, that she was probably demented and irresponsible. She has since written me another letter but I have not answered it. I felt and knew that if she was the victim of unfortunate circumstances and especially of tender age, that you would not suffer any wrong to be done her so far as undue or harsh punishment was concerned. My object in writing was to have the case brought to your personal attention and now that I know this has been done, I have no suggestion to offer, feeling perfectly satisfied that you will do what in justice should be done in the matter. Please accept my thanks for your kind words in allusion to myself personally and with kind regards and with best wishes, I am,

Yours very truly,
Eugene V. Debs

Dict. E. V. D.

TLS, EVD Foundation, Debs Home.

☐ *From the Woodstock jail Debs continued his efforts to keep alive the ARU. At the time, his brother Theodore ("Kude") began his life-long role as Gene's secretary, agent, manager, adviser, and most devoted friend.*

EVD to Theodore Debs

November 5, 1895
Woodstock, Illinois

My dear Kude:

Yours recd. No, don't send another dollar. I had just written Keliher refusing him money. All requests for money tell them you haven't got a dollar & that you have got to refer the requests to me. If the G.N. men want to fight let them put up their own money. We put up all the money we had for them in '94 and as soon as they got their pay raised they let the order go to the devil. Sorry you sent that hundred, but let it go. I told Keliher he would have to raise money enough to [support?] himself. Don't send another dollar to any of them unless I notify you to that effect. I have written them all & they must understand that they have got to do something themselves. We can't carry any dead-weights. Schwerzgen told me they took in 21 men in No1 a few days ago, all men that are working. Did you get their capita tax? If not tell Ben to write Burns & ask him why it has not been sent — tell Ben to write Burns that *I* wrote to inquire if it had been {received} ~~sent~~ & if not to call on him to know if it had been sent.

I sent you an order on Ben for $100. — Let me know how much more you will need *at once*. I have written you about this but you have not answered. Let me know immediately.

Tell Benedict to tell the committee that I will return via Indianapolis at 6-45, that I have business at latter place & will return that way.

Had a beautiful birthday. Schwerzgen has just left here. The "reception" will be an "eye-opener." There will be such an outpouring as to startle the natives. You come so as to reach here Wednesday evening. Leave there Wednesday 5 A M & get here that evening.

Love and kisses to all,

Your devoted brother
Eugene

ALS, InTI, Debs Collection.

☐ *Debs often cited the government's role in breaking the Pullman strike and his imprisonment following the strike as significant events in his conversion to socialism. The following letter, written shortly after his release from jail, suggests that he was thinking about the issue months before his formal announcement on January 1, 1897. Tom Watson of Georgia was a leader of the Populist party and that party's vice-presidential candidate in the 1896 election.*

EVD to Henry Demarest Lloyd

February 1, 1896
Terre Haute, Indiana

My Dear Mr. Lloyd:

Returning after several weeks absence I find your kind note of the 2nd instant awaiting me. I note particularly what you say in reference to the marked article in Thos. Watson's "People's Party Paper." I agree with you entirely that Mr. Watson has no rational conception of what "Socialism" really is, and it is not likely that his tirade will injure those against whom it is directed any more than it will help himself. I do not permit myself to be much disturbed by self-appointed censors. Permit me to thank you most cordially for your kindness in the matter. In my travels I meet very many of your friends and admirers to whom I am proud to be able to say that I number you among my personal friends. I feel profoundly grateful to you for many valued favors received at your hands and beg you to believe that I should esteem it a privilege to be of service to you at any time and in any way in my power. Believe me always,

Faithfully your friend,
Eugene V. Debs

TLS, WHi, Lloyd Papers.

☐ *In 1896 William Jennings Bryan was the presidential candidate of both the People's party and the Democratic party. Debs, who was urged, but declined, to have his name placed in nomination at the People's party convention in St. Louis, worked hard in Bryan's unsuccessful campaign.*

EVD to William Jennings Bryan

July 27, 1896
Terre Haute, Indiana

My dear Mr. Bryan,

With millions of others of your countrymen I congratulate you most heartily upon being the People's standard bearer in the great uprising of the masses against the classes. You are at this hour the hope of the Republic—the central figure of the civilized world. In the arduous campaign before you the millions will rally to your standard and you will lead them to glorious victory. The people love and trust you—they believe in you as you believe in them, and under your administration the rule of the money power will be broken and the gold barons of Europe will no longer run the American government.

With all good wishes
  believe me always

Yours faithfully
Eugene V. Debs

P.S.— Mr. Fitzgerald Murphy has just stepped in and joins in cordial greeting.

ALS, DLC, Bryan MSS.

☐ *Ignatius Donnelly served three terms as a Republican congressman from Minnesota (1863–69) before leaving that party to become, successively, a liberal Republican, a Granger, and a Greenbacker before helping to create the People's party, for which he wrote the famous preamble to the 1892 Omaha Platform. A popular orator and writer, Donnelly's* Caesar's Column *(1891) was compared to Edward Bellamy's* Looking Backward *and rivaled it in popularity.*

EVD to Ignatius Donnelly

August 17, 1898
Terre Haute, Indiana

My dear Friend:

Your esteemed favor of the 11*th* inst has been received. In reply I beg to say that for two months past I have been unable on account of illness to give attention to my usual duties and it is not probably that I will be able to leave here for several weeks to come. I note your kind and urgent invitation to attend the meeting to be held at Cincinnati on the 5*th* prox, but it is not at all probable that I can be present. To be candid with you I have little faith in the ability of the delegates to agree upon any definite plan of action. I am giving my whole time to the work of uniting Socialists and the task requires all the endurance at my command. When it comes to trying to unite Populists, Single Taxers, Labor Exchangers, Direct Legislationists etc etc it simply cannot be done and all time given to such efforts is wasted. The tendency is toward Socialism and I think it far better to make this fact clear and to unite those who grasp the true principles than to seek a union of elements who are at all the intermediary stages between capitalism and Socialism and who in this state are as difficult to harmonize as if they still adhered to the old parties.

But coming from you, the invitation is a strong incentive to my going and while unable to promise, if conditions are favorable I will do myself the pleasure of meeting you when the convention assembles.

Believe me always

Yours faithfully
Eugene V. Debs

ALS (in hand of Katherine Metzel Debs), MnHi, Ignatius Donnelly Papers.

□ *The many reforms introduced by Samuel Milton Jones, a successful business-man and mayor of Toledo, Ohio, earned him the sobriquet "Golden Rule Jones." His ideas were admired by reformers and denounced as socialistic by conservatives at the turn of the century. In the following exchange of letters Jones and Debs share some of their views on issues of common interest.*

Samuel Milton Jones to EVD

December 30, 1898
Toledo, Ohio

My dear Mr. Debs:

For a long time I have thought I would drop you a line. I do not like to use a war simile, because I do not believe in war, but for the want of something better I will say that it is a good idea for the sentinels to exchange words of encouragement occasionally between the firing. I am glad to note from the published references that I see of you now and then that the truth that you are standing and speaking for is taking hold upon the hearts of the people. I was especially pleased at the reception you received in the East and in Massachusetts particularly. I saw some very encouraging extracts from the SPRING-FIELD REPUBLICAN.

I enclose an editorial clipping from the NEW YORK JOURNAL having reference to my annual message to the Common Council, in order that you may see that it is somewhat socialistic. I also send you, under another cover, the Christmas literature that we distributed among the employees at the factory.

I am very glad to know that you are to be here in February, and can promise you in advance a royal welcome and good big house full of people to talk to. Socialism has made tremendous strides in Toledo in the past two years. I have announced that I am again a candidate for re-election, and in reply to the question, stated I would accept the nomination from the republican party if they chose to give it to me, but whether they did or not, I would be a candidate any way. I may be wrong, but I feel that the thing for me to do is to work for the truths of socialism where I am, in the church, in the lodge, or in the party; somehow I do not seem to be led into a new party just yet. I do not think the fact that I am not so led can be attributed to any selfish motive that I am nursing within my breast. You know I have stood here for non-partisan politics and I continue to stand so. Neither the republican machine nor the democratic machine, both of course purely capitalistic, have any use for me, or rather for the principles of equality that I advocate, and both are doing their best to defeat my re-election. I have no thought, however, that they will be successful; I believe that Socialism has gained tremendously in Toledo in the past year, and that the people will line up and vote for it at the poles [sic] when they have the chance.

I am going to Boston and New York and will make some addresses at both places during January. Anticipating with pleasure having the opportunity of talking these matters over at greater length when you come to Toledo, and again assuring you of a warm welcome, I am

Very faithfully yours,

S. M. Jones

TLS, OT, Jones Papers.

EVD to Samuel Milton Jones

March 6, 1899
Terre Haute, Indiana

My dear Mr. Jones:
Your telegram has been received and I am not surprised that you
have been defeated for the nomination. As I told you when last I saw
you I would have been surprised had you not been defeated. To be
candid with you I am glad you did not receive the nomination. The
Republican party is an organized conspiracy against the working class
and you have no place in it any more than it has use for you. So the
only way the Republican party could have honored you was by refusing
you a nomination and having done this, you have my congratulations.
You will, no doubt, run as an independent candidate. I need not say
that you have my best wishes for a triumphant re-election. Permit me
to express the hope that you can see your way clear to announce
yourself a Social Democrat and place yourself squarely as such before
the people of Toledo. You will not only strike terror to the Republican
machine, but your campaign against the brutality and corruption of
Capitalism will appeal to the whole country and inspire the people
everywhere with new hope and fresh courage in their sad and weary
struggle for emancipation from the thraldoms of the ages. Now, less
than ever before, should there be compromising or trimming, even
for the sake of high office. It is Capitalism or Socialism and I believe
that with the issue clearly and courageously made, you can and will
be elected in spite of all the power and boodle of plutocracy.
Believe me always

Yours fraternally,
Eugene V. Debs

ALS, OT, Jones Papers.

☐ *In the 1900 presidential election Debs was the candidate of the Social Demo-*
cratic party (Socialist Party of America after 1901), which had been launched
in 1898. In this letter to his brother Debs seems disappointed by the election re-
turns—he received about 100,000 votes—but ready to begin the 1904 campaign.

EVD to Theodore Debs

November 9, 1900
Terre Haute, Indiana

My dearest Theo: —

I have your letter of the 8th. You are as full of sunshine as a rabbit is of fur, and I'm with you with a whoop.

I must first make final report of my trip. The meeting at Toledo was a grand one and the comrades were greatly elated over it. At Evansville the hall was packed & intense enthusiasm prevailed. At Linton I spoke in the open air on Monday afternoon to a very large audience. A delegation of the Linton comrades, accompanied by their band, came to Terre Haute with me & cheered lustily for our ticket all along the line.

The Terre Haute meeting Monday evening was all that could have been expected. The crowd was large and appreciative from start to finish. Comrade Reynolds presided.

Thus closes the campaign — and the results show that we got everything *except votes.*

I am serene for two reasons:

1st. I did the very best I could for the party that nominated me & for its principles.

2d. The working class will get in full measure what they voted for. And so we begin the campaign for 1904.

I wish you to say to Stedman that I have his letter & have read it carefully. Let the conference be held without me for it is simply out of the question for me to attend. The convention should be held according to agreement & the call must appear in this week's issue. Otherwise we may get swamped — and above all, *prompt action* is what is wanted.

I am surprised at Stedman's intimation that we may have something to do with the other factions. Great heavens, haven't we got enough?

If there is any attempt to harmonize or placate, *count me out.* We must go forward on our own lines & those who don't choose to fall in need not do so. There must be no *wobbling* at this time.

I thought our plan of action was clearly understood & now I am overwhelmed with pleas to attend a conference etc etc etc etc.

Hell! Don't we know what we want? Or are we crazy?

We held a deliberate board meeting & went over the whole ground in detail & agreed to call a special convention within 30 days after election. I wrote the call & mailed it to you. Stedman should have written Herron all about it as he agreed to do. We could all reach

Chicago 2 or 3 days before convention & then hold the *conference*, but I don't see the necessity of a conference now & a convention in 3 weeks. It is simply a piece of damphoolism & reckless waste of time and money. If the conference is held then I suppose that does [a]way with the convention & in that case I stand branded as a liar before comrades of Iowa, Nebraska & comrades in the East to whom I confidentially communicated our line of action.

Stedman makes entirely too much of the "unaffiliated" & "{un}attached." I would not cater to them a damned bit. We have invited them to our convention & if they don't want to come let them stay out. A thousand men *organized* are better than ten times that number unorganized. Let us take care of those that are organized & the rest will take care of themselves.

I am well and in good spirits, but 20 hours a day for 6 weeks has told on me & I'm run down. I'll not go to Chicago, nor attend any conference till I'm rested. I would not be fit for service in my present condition. If the convention has been called *off* I feel {as} if I ought to pull out & let the whole thing go & attend to my own business, but I wont. I'll stick to the party, through the gates of hell, till it stands on rock and defies the thunderbolts of Jove.

Read this hasty letter to Stedman, Mrs. Brown Miss Thomas, Edwards & others interested. We are all right & all we want is a convention to make needed changes & above all to show that our party has nothing to do with other parties & that we mean business & propose to move straight along on our own lines & lose no time about it.

The Vigo County vote is small—about 325 The official returns are not yet in.

Note what you say about quail hunt & would be delighted to go, but first of all must dispose of the *mass* of letters etc etc etc which have piled up like Alps all around me.

Best love & kisses to you & Gertrude & Marguerite and to all our comrades beloved.

Yours without a flicker
Eugene

ALS, InTI, Debs Collection.

□ *Mary Harris "Mother" Jones was associated in one way or another with al-most every American industrial conflict of the late nineteenth and early twen-tieth centuries. She and Debs were allies in many of the nation's most contro-versial labor conflicts, especially those involving miners, but when Debs ran for Congress in 1916 Jones appeared in his district to campaign for his Demo-cratic opponent.*

EVD to Mary Harris Jones

January 28, 1901
Terre Haute, Indiana

Dear Mother Jones:

I am very sorry I could not be with you this afternoon, particularly on your own account. But it could not be otherwise and so I yield without regret. In a day or two I leave to fulfil my Wisconsin ap-pointments. When you get through at Indianapolis I wish you would drop me a line here and advise me of your address so I can write you about a little business matter in which we can be of mutual service besides helping the cause. I am trying to build up a little book business out of which to make a living so that I shall not have to accept anything from any source for any service I may render the cause. I feel confident you can help me a little and at the same time help yourself as well as the movement.

I have been reading the papers and as usual find myself the victim of calumny. I have no complaint to make, but it does seem as if there should be a limit to such cruel outrages. The press dispatches spread the report broadcast that the statement was made on the floor of the convention that a Pennsylvania delegate collected money from starv-ing miners for me and that I accepted it all. Of course the presumption is that a vast sum was paid me and that it was gouged from the lives of the famishing Miners. I can scarcely believe that such a villainous falsehood was uttered, and yet the effect with the general public is the same and I am once more freshly nailed to the cross. But I can stand it without a trace of resentment and if I can ever give a hand to the Miners in any struggle, if that hand is not freely extended as it has always been in the past, it will be because it is paralyzed.

You know without my telling you that I did not accept one dollar for my service from any one and that with the exception of a trifling part of my railroad fare, I paid all my own expenses besides. If any statement to the contrary is made it is maliciously false and in that case I desire you to ask the author of the statement how much money he gave me and if he names the amount, then challenge him to produce the receipt for it. If the press statement is correct the author of the statement is a self confessed criminal. He stands condemned out of his own lying mouth. What right had he to collect money from starving miners? and if {he did} so, is he not infamous to an extent that his word has no value? Next, is it likely that starving miners have any money?

Then again, on whom was he drawing for his own living expenses? Perhaps the operators might answer that latter question.

You have known me many years and you know if I would in any extremity take money from a striking, starving, miner. I would first destroy myself. I must correct you on a point touching the statement made by you as reported by the press in regard to the charges that were circulated about certain Labor Leaders receiving large sums of money for alleged services to striking miners in '97. Those reports originated at the Nashville Convention of the A.F. of L. held that year. The matter was discussed and charges and insinuations were made on the floor of that convention and they were exaggerated and telegraphed over the country. The files of the Nashville papers which were sent me at the time report the matter fully. Mailly, who was there at the time, will doubtless remember all about it. My name was included with the rest and not one was there to rescue it from the slander. I have had a number of personal apologies since in regard to it. The statements were made, not at the Columbus convention of the Miners but at the National Convention of the A.F. of L. I am writing this simply for your information and not because I desire any defense or vindication. That will come to me in good time. That I am on all occasions made the target for calumny is simple evidence of the fact that the capitalist press is aware that I cannot be bribed or bullied and that therefore I must be undermined by slander; and that delegates to Labor Conventions are the active instrumentalities in coining and circulating such calumnies simply shows that the capitalist class and their corrupt political bosses have their miserable tools in the councils of Labor to keep the enslaved workers securely manacled and to prevent any ray of emancipating light from penetrating their dismal dungeons.

Ah, but Socialism cannot be kept out [of] a Labor organization any more than the rays of the rising sun can be prevented from dispelling the lists of darkness. Hail to Socialism, in which the miner can lift his bowed form from the earth and stand erect, a new being throbbing with immortal life.

I thank you from a grateful heart for your kindness Mrs. Debs joins me. Our only complaint is that you are too generous by far.

Give Mitchell, Wilson, Scott and all the boys my cordial greeting and best wishes, and believe me ever,

Yours sincerely
Eugene V. Debs

ALS (in hand of Katherine Metzel Debs), PHi.

☐ *In 1881, Richard T. Ely was named the first professor of political economy at Johns Hopkins University. A critic of classical economics and Social Darwinism, Ely helped found the American Economic Association in 1885 and wrote sympathetically of labor's problems in a number of books and articles both before and after becoming head of the economics department at the University of Wisconsin in 1892, a position he held for thirty-three years.*

Richard T. Ely to EVD

April 24, 1903
[Madison, Wisconsin]

My dear Sir;

I am writing most of the articles on Socialism and Trade Unions for the New International Encyclopaedia, and I also wish, as soon as may be done, to revise my book "The Labor Movement in America" and bring it down to date. It has occurred to me that you very likely could assist me in procuring desired material. In the past you have sent me some things. You must receive an enormous amount of pamphlet material concerning the labor movement and socialism, and I should presume a great many labor papers. I am wondering if you may not have some things which would no longer be of any use to you, and which you would be willing to dispose of. Scarcely anything in the labor line would come amiss. Constitutions of labor organizations, files of newspapers and periodicals would be especially welcome. I have to say very frankly that my means are not such as to enable me to pay what are called fancy prices, and there is not enough in articles and books of this kind to make it possible. I can pay, however, something and especially could I remunerate anyone who would take the time to look over what you may have and arrange it and send it. I think the majority of men engaged in the socialist and labor movement do not keep things which they receive, but I am hoping that you may have done so.

I am just now about to write the articles on railroad labor organizations, but do not receive from the various Brotherhoods all that I would like in the way of annual reports, back numbers of their magazines, etc. It seems to me there must be members of the Brotherhoods who would have the annual reports and copies of the Brotherhood magazines which they would be willing to dispose of for a moderate sum.

Yours very truly,
[Richard T. Ely]

TLc, WHi, Ely Papers.

EVD to Richard T. Ely

April 29, 1903
Terre Haute, Indiana

My dear Sir:

Your favor of the 24" has been received and noted. I will with pleasure do what I can to assist you in gathering materials as requested, though my opportunities for doing so are at present quite limited as I am on the platform at present and almost continously absent from the city. I have a mass of matter which I have not time to sift, nor could I entrust the work to any one else; and I also have a good deal of material which I would not care to part with, although desirous that you shall have the use of it freely if it will help to serve the purpose you have in view. I will send you with pleasure a variety of papers and pamphlets and later on may be able to send additional contributions. My almost continuous absence will prevent me from placing myself as completely at your service in the very excellent work you are doing as I would be glad to do under other circumstances.

Let me suggest that you drop a line to the following:

F. W. Arnold. Grand Sec'y   Brotherhood of Locomotive Firemen, Peoria   Ill.
W S. Carter   Ed. Loco. Firemen's Magazine
                Indianapolis   Ind.
Clarence Smith. Secy American Labor Union
                Box 1067 Butte Mont.

All are personal friends and you can freely use my name if you wish. Each of them can be of service.

Yours very truly
E V. Debs.   K.

P.S. I am glad you are to bring your Labor Movement down to date.

ALS (in hand of Katherine Metzel Debs, including signature), WHi, Ely Papers.

☐ *In the following exchange of letters Henry Demarest Lloyd, a leading reformer of the Progressive Era, and Debs share their views on the issues of reform and the possibility of socialists joining in alliances with nonsocialist reformers.*

Henry Demarest Lloyd to EVD

June 8, 1903
Little Compton, Rhode Island

My dear Debs: —

Do you not agree with me that the present Traction question in Chicago affords an almost ideal opportunity for socialist propaganda and for the enlargement of socialist influence by procuring the union of progressive radicals of all the schools in a practical work? No solution of the Chicago Traction question can be halfway successful that does not come from the whole people. It must weave into one comprehensive scheme a plan for the cooperation through a long future of tunnels, surface, and elevated, with reference first and last to the public health and convenience and to the expansion of Chicago far into the country.

The fact that the administration is pledged to submit the ordinances to popular vote is our chance. We ought to begin at once to associate every radical and public spirited man we can get in an organisation that will prepare the people to reject any patch-work or hotch-potch. What do you say? Can the Socialists be brought to interest themselves in a question which tho' *immediate* can be made to illustrate their most ideal purposes? Can they be brought into cooperation with other organizations, like the unions, single-taxers, &c? I should be glad to hear from you, and would be happy to help in such a work.

Faithfully
H. D. Lloyd

AL (in hand of Caro Lloyd), WHi, Lloyd Papers.

EVD to Henry Demarest Lloyd

June 22, 1903
Terre Haute, Indiana

My dear Mr. Lloyd:

Your favor of the 8" inst. was received during my absence from the city. I have carefully noted all you say in your letter and also in your article in the Chicago Tribune in reference to the Municipal traction question.

I agree with you that the situation at Chicago is specially favorable for socialist propaganda and that the most should be made of the opportunity afforded by the agitation of the question, but I do not believe that more than a local issue can be made of it or that it will attract any considerable attention outside of Chicago and immediate vicinity.

It is true that as an object lesson it has its importance but it is also true that every community is having such lessons of its own every day in the week and yet the great mass of the people are ignorant or indifferent to their import.

No, I do not believe that single taxers, socialists and anti-socialist trade unionists can successfully harmonize upon any proposition whatsoever. In some exigency they may do so for the moment, but when it comes to formulating plans and platforms they are bound to separate for they are fundamentally antagonistic and every attempt to unite them, even temporarily, has resulted in failure and generally bitter feeling besides.

Experience has satisfied me of the futility of such an undertaking, however promising the prospect might seem.

I have long since determined to stick to the main issue and stay on the main track, no matter how alluring some of the byways may appear. Others may satisfy themselves better and serve the cause better by exploiting subsidiary issues as they arise, but there is nothing in this sort of thing for me. I am giving such time and energy as I have to the general propaganda of the socialist movement, taking due notice of such openings as you indicate and making the most of them in opening the eyes of the people, but never abandoning the main position, nor relaxing the main hold for a single instant to give special attention to any local or minor issue whatsoever.

I thank you for having been good enough to give me your views, for which, I need not assure you, I have the highest regard. Acting upon your suggestion and with such special and detailed information as the article in the Tribune has supplied I shall avail myself of every opportunity to exploit the Chicago traction situation in the interest of the socialist movement.

With all good wishes I am as ever,

Yours cordially
Eugene V. Debs

ALS (in hand of Katherine Metzel Debs), WHi, Lloyd Papers.

☐ *Clara Spalding Ellis was a journalist and the author of, among other titles,* What's Next? or, Shall a Man Live Again *(1906). Debs's letter to her contains one of the most explicit statements of his view of immortality.*

EVD to Clara Spalding Ellis

February 6, 1904
Terre Haute, Indiana

Dear Mrs. Ellis:

Your communication was received during my absence from the city. The question you ask is a large and serious one and it is doubtful if in the hurry of the moment I can make myself intelligible to yourself and readers. I am so busy with the affairs of this life, so much concerned with the wrongs that exist here, with the suffering that prevails now, and so profoundly impressed with the sense of duty I owe myself and my fellowman here and now that I have but little time to think of what lies beyond the grave; and but for the earnestness and anxiety so apparent in your letter, I should feel obliged to decline the attempt to answer a question which at best must still remain unanswered.

The most scientific minds have thus far failed to demonstrate the immortality of human life and yet the normal human being, the wide world over, be he learned or ignorant, wise or foolish, good or {evil, longs for, yearns for,} hungers and hopes for, if he does not actually believe in life everlasting, and this seems to me to present the strongest proof that immortality is a fact in nature.

There are many truths that are not demonstrable to the ordinary senses and yet they are so obvious and self-evident that it were folly to attempt to deny or contradict them.

Coming more directly to your question, as to whether I, my personal, identical, conscious self, shall continue to live after my body goes back to dust, I confess I do not know, nor do I know of any means of knowing; but as I, in that narrow capacity, am infinitesimally insignificant, it is a question which does not greatly concern me.

I believe firmly, however, in the immortal life of humanity as a whole, and as my little life merges in and becomes an elementary part of that infinitely larger life, I may, and in fact do feel secure in the faith and belief in immortality.

Men are small, but *Man* is tall as God Himself.

The universal life is eternal and will enrich and glorify the world with its divinity after all the planets wheel dead in space.

Yours very truly.
Eugene V. Debs

P.S. The above was written in the press of a busy day. If you put it in type I would thank you to send me a proof-slip that I may go over it again.

ALS (in hand of Katherine Metzel Debs), EVD Foundation, Debs Home.

☐ *This letter was written on the occasion of the fifty-fifth wedding anniversary of Debs's parents, affectionately known to the family as "Dandy" and "Daisy."*

EVD to Jean Daniel Debs and Marguerite Bettrich Debs

September 12, 1904
Memphis, Tennessee

My dearest Father and Mother:

No words of mine can express the love that goes with my greeting to you on your Anniversary day, a day that you will recall with mingled emotions of pain and joy and a day that we "children" have occasion to remember as hallowed and beautiful because of the wedlock that gave us birth. On this day we turn to you as naturally as the flower does to the sun and we cling to you as tenderly and as fondly as when in the years ago, in the flower of your own youth, you caressed our bruises, healed our little sorrows and guided our footsteps in the path of honor and duty.

On this day, too, we feel anew the sense of obligation that rests upon us for the many years of toil and agony you endured to bring up your brood in manliness and womanliness, that they might fare better than fell to your lot.

How well we know of your sacrifices and suffering, and how freely you bore it all because of your children, for whom you in fact suffered martyrdom; and it is not strange, therefore, that they lovingly cling to you in old age and would joyfully give their lives to save your own.

On this day, dearest and best beloved Dandy and Daisy, we realize that no children ever born had better parents, none more devoted, watchful and self-sacrificing, and our love and gratitude flow to you from the fulness of our hearts and most fondly do we hope that you may be spared to us many more years that we may have the joy of giving you increasing evidence that your children are mindful of their parental obligation and that they love and reverence the father and mother that suffered untold privation and pain for them without ever a word of complaint or a murmer of regret that martyrdom was their destiny that their children might reap joy and honor where they sowed in poverty and pain.

A thousand loving wishes to you and many joyous returns of the day.

Your most obedient son
Eugene

ALS, InTI, Debs Collection.

□ *Caroline Augusta Lloyd (Strobell), sister of Henry Demarest Lloyd, published a biography of her brother in 1912.*

EVD to Caro Lloyd

January 31, 1905
Terre Haute, Indiana

Dear Madam: —

Your note of the 21st. has been received. In answer I have to say that I have a very pleasant recollection of Mr. Lloyd, though I never met him personally but two [or] three times. During the great railroad strike in 1894 Mr. Lloyd was a staunch supporter of our side and I had several letters from him from his summer residence ~~from him~~ in Rhode Island, giving encouragement and advice, but these were in the files of the American Railway Union whose effects were scattered by corporate and governmental persecution. I remember that Mr. Lloyd advised us to employ Mr. Darrow to defend us and that he also subscribed $100.00 to our defense fund.

On my release from Woodstock Jail Nov. 22nd. 1895, there was a great popular demonstration at Chicago which included a mass meeting at Battery D which was packed with an enormous audience. On this occasion Mr. Lloyd delivered a very eloquent and stirring address which appears in full in the Chicago papers of the 23rd. inst., the day following. This address moved the audience to intense enthusiasm. I saw so little of Mr. Lloyd personally that I know of nothing that I could contribute that would add to the interest of the proposed biography. Mr. Lloyd proved himself to be in thorough sympathy with the railway employes during their greatest strike and I am sure they appreciated his attitude and held him in high personal regard. I am sorry I do not have any documents that would be serviceable to you in your very laudable undertaking. I can only say that Mr. Lloyd bore a brave and commendable part in the great struggle of labor against corporate {injustice} and that his memory will always be treasured by the weak and oppressed he so faithfully served.

Wishing you all success in this work I remain

Yours very truly
E. V. Debs

TLS, WHi, Lloyd Papers.

□ *Peter Damm was a member of the Wagon Workers Union in New York City. In the following exchange of letters the role of Samuel Gompers in the Pullman strike of 1894 is denounced by both Damm and Debs, the latter charging that Gompers and the AFL leadership "delivered one of the blows that crushed the strike."*

Peter Damm to EVD

April 16, 1905
New York City

Dear Sir and Comrade:—

I take the liberty to write you this letter—tho' Im aware that you no doubt have plenty of work on your hands—because I feel that you can advance the cause of Socialism considerable by supplying me with information in your possession. Guess I had better tell my little story from the beginning and then you see for yourself what is wanted and if it is in your judgement important enough to receive consideration at all.

Here it is: The recent strike on the Sub-way and L system was a failure. The officers—International Officers chiefly, gave the strikers the cold shoulder and denounced them publically. The matter came up in the central body—"C.T.U." Action: Com. of 5 app. to see Belmont to reinstate the old men. Result: Belmont turns down the com. The earnest & honest element of the C.T.U. "roasts" the Civic Federation, the president of the same as you know is Hon. Mr. Belmont. I and a few others go a step further and "roast" the labor leaders connected with it. I stated that Gompers could not [have] served the Belmonts any better if he was in their employ, that he could not {have} served the Pullmans any better neither if he had been paid by them, because at the time when the A.R.U. under the able leadership of E. V. Debs has practically its fight won, when a general strike had been declared by the union people of Chicago & vicinity, this Mr. Gompers came to Chic. went into conference with some labor leaders—quotation marks please—and as a result the general strike was broken. Etc. Etc Etc.

Now I was in Chic for many years, been out on sympathetic strike in question (am a carriage maker) and I remember all this to be true to my own satisfaction. But the conservative element of the C.T.U. squirmed, especially the org. of A.F. of L., Mr. Herm. Robinson[3] and a com. was appointed to "investigate the charges made by me and other against our highest official" I yan There! You have it in a nutshell! If you can & want to supply me with the detailed information as to exact happenings of the '94 affair, you surely contribut to the oustings of the unworthy Labor Leaders, or any way, the scales will fall off a good many honest trades-unionists. Hoping for an early reply, I remain

Yours most sincerely
Peter Damm
536 E. 89th Str
New York City

ALS, InTI, Debs Collection.

EVD to Peter Damm

April 22, 1905
Terre Haute, Indiana

Dear Comrade:—
Your favor of the 16th. has been received and noted. You are entirely right in your contention as to the attitude of Mr. Gompers

and his official associates toward the Pullman strike in 1894. First of all, Mr. Gompers was opposed to the A.R.U. from the start and did all he could in opposition to it. He did this in the interest of the old railway brotherhoods, expecting to get them into the Federation. These brotherhoods were and are entirely to his liking but the A.R.U. proposed to unite all railway employes to fight the railway corporations, not to be controlled by them, and this of course, made it necessary for such labor leaders as Mr. Gompers of the A.F. of L. and P. J. McGuire, his chief advisor and associate at that time, P. M. Arthur of the Engineers and others who are now hooked up with the Civic Federation and smiled upon by the corporations, to fight it and this they did every step of the way from the time it was organized until it was finally crushed by the corporations, reinforced by the labor leaders named.

As to the attitude of Mr. Gompers toward the strike, concerning which you particularly inquire, it was so notoriously hostile to the strikers, that he was openly denounced by his own followers in Chicago and among those who publicly charged him with both treason and cowardice for refusing to come to Chicago, in response to the practically unanimous demand of the organized workers, was Thomas I. Kidd, one of his present vice president's.

The whole body of organized labor at Chicago passionately supported the strike and the strikers. They demanded over and over again that Mr Gompers, their president, come to Chicago to give the weight of his official position to the strike. He utterly refused to answer the call until he was literally forced to do so, and when finally he had to yield to the increasing indignation, he was interviewed before leaving New York and said that he had to go to Chicago to attend a funeral. This was the death stab he gave to the strike when at last he was compelled by his own people to take some part in it. This interview was flashed over the whole country by the Associated Press and has since been repeated thousands of times and Mr. Gompers has never once denied it.

Mr. Gompers and his Executive Board finally convened at Chicago, after the whole country was aroused, and the whole body of organized labor at Chicago was clamoring to support the strike. These gentlemen did what they had made up their minds from the start to do. They decided against the strike and turned down the strikers and thus delivered one of the final blows that crushed the strike. So far as any help to the strike was concerned, Mr. Gompers and his associates had far better stayed away. They not only did no good, but did great harm. The whole capitalist press exulted over the decision of Mr. Gompers and his colleagues, commended their conservatism and pointed to them as final proof that the strike should be broken and as complete justification for the brutal ferocity with which they were maligning and outraging the strikers. These are the facts in the case, briefly stated, and they can [be] verified beyond all question of doubt. Every old member of the A.R.U. and thousands of other organized workers who were in the strike or in sympathy with it remember these facts and let me say in closing that they are just beginning to come home to roost. You are at liberty to use this letter in any way you may wish.

The strike of the New York Subway employees, disastrous as it turned out, will be fruitful of great results to organized labor. It had peculiar and immense significance and as an object lesson has had value to the working class of the whole country which it would be difficult to over-estimate. I very much appreciate the loyalty of the organized workers of New York to their struggling fellow-workers.

Yours fraternally
[Eugene V. Debs]

TLc, InTI, Debs Collection.

□ *Elbert Hubbard was the publisher of the* Philistine, *a widely read literary magazine, one of whose 1899 editions contained Hubbard's best-known work, "A Message to Garcia." In the following letter Debs urges Hubbard to take up the cause of Charles Moyer and William Dudley Haywood, officers of the Western Federation of Miners, and George A. Pettibone, a Denver merchant, who were being tried in Idaho for the murder of former Idaho governor Frank R. Steunenberg. The case attracted national attention, and Debs led the way in persuading the public that the three men had been denied their constitutional rights and were really being tried for their labor activities. Clarence Darrow was an attorney for the defense.*

EVD to Elbert Green Hubbard

April 15, 1906
Terre Haute, Indiana

My dear Hubbard:—

I am unable, I regret to say, to accept your extremely kind invitation. Thank you warmly and those who join you for the kindly feeling that prompts your loving words and generous expressions.

I am hoping that you will find it necessary and dutiful to say something in the Philistine, or otherwise, as you have the opportunity, in condemnation of the outrageous assault upon Moyer and Haywood and their associates who were recently kidnapped, thrown into dungeons and are now threatened to be hanged with no shadow of a charge placed against them except the alleged confession of a self-confessed criminal. I know these men personally and truer men never drew a breath. They are as innocent as I of the crime charged against them. The law of the land and the common humanities have all been violated in dealing with these men whose only crime is that they are true to labor and the Mine Owners have not gold enough to debauch them. This incident has in it the elements of a national crisis. If these men are hanged without a fair trial it will be the crime of the century. I feel for these men just as if I were in their places; my heart is with them and their wives and chidren, for I know what it is to have the hounds lapping for your blood for simply having served as best you could the cause of Les Miserables. It is the duty of every man who loves right to stand by these men and insist upon their having a fair trial, and you will therefore pardon me in bringing this matter to your attention for I feel that when such a tragedy is about to be enacted the men who "do things" must prove themselves worthy of the confidence reposed in them, and in this crisis Fra Elbertus can say some things in his own way that will strike terror to the conspirator[s] in the mountain states who are now plotting to put innocent men to death for daring to dispute their heartless sway.

I did not mean to write you at such length but I feel intensely upon this subject and I am calling upon every friend I have and every man I believe capable of rendering service in a critical hour to come to the front and do his duty by his fellow-men.

Believe me with all good greetings and the best of wishes

Yours faithfully
Eugene V. Debs

TLS, NNU Tam, Debs Collection.

☐ *Debs's mother died on April 29, 1906. In the following letter he replies to a letter of condolence from his cousin, Edouard Caspari, the son of Debs's aunt Marguerite Debs Caspari. Edouard was a professor of hydrographic engineering at the Polytechnic School in Paris and a noted author of books on chronometry and hydrography.*

EVD to Edouard Caspari

September 11, 1906
Terre Haute, Indiana

My Dear Cousin: —

Your good letter to father was duly received and since failing eyesight prevents him from answering in person, he wishes me to make {this} acknowledgment for him and to return his profound thanks for your expressions of affection and sympathy in our family bereavement, which are appreciated far more than mere words can convey.

The tribute paid by you to our dear mother was most touching to father and, indeed, to all {our} family. That circumstances were such that you could not see her more and know her better is to be regretted, for then you would have realized, as we have from our infancy, that father's life companion, the bearer of his children and the sharer of his joys and sorrows, was as true and faithful a wife, as tender and {loving a} mother and as self-sacrificing and noble a woman as ever lived, and that this earth is richer for her having been here. The most precious legacy she left us is the memory of her pure and blameless life.

Each word in reference to yourself and wife was noted with deepest interest by father and {by} us all. The life of usefulness you have led, the honors you have won and the rare and enviable fame you have achieved are indeed gratifying to father and to all our family and all of us join in loving regards and all {kind} wishes to you and your good wife and all beneath your roof.

Your devoted cousin
E. V. Debs

TLc, InTI, Debs Collection.

□ *Debs's father died on November 18, 1906. The following letter is Debs's reply to a letter of condolence from Stephen Marion Reynolds, a Terre Haute lawyer and long-time friend who published, during Debs's 1908 presidential campaign, the biographical sketch* Debs: His Life, Writings, and Speeches.

EVD to Stephen Marion Reynolds

December 13, 1906
Terre Haute, Indiana

My dear Stephen: —
   Your beautiful little message has a heart-throb in every word of it.
It is the voice of old Walt and I recognize it and feel comforted by
the message it brings of love and immortality. How deeply your pal-
pitant words enter into my soul and move me to a sense of thanksgiving
for having such a comrade, I shall not attempt to tell you for words
would not serve me and you understand me perfectly without formal
communication.
   I am so glad you remember father with {the} sweet smile of patience
and resignation on his dear old features. It is a picture sacred to us
which we shall carry with us into the realms beyond where he and
dear mother have been translated and are waiting for us, as your
loved ones are waiting for you. The old home is very still and desolate
and will never be the same again, but we are not lamenting and with
old Walt we will believe that all is good and all is well. Your dear
message is a poem of exquisite tenderness and aquiver with sympathy
and love. I thank you over and over again for us all. When you send
your love message to Chicago write my name in it. I often, very often,
think of Mrs. Reynolds and the little folks and send them my love-
thoughts over the invisible wires.

Yours always
E. V. Debs

TLS, InH, Reynolds Collection.

□ *The following letter was written soon after Debs joined the editorial staff of
the* Appeal to Reason, *a socialist weekly published in Girard, Kansas. At the
time, Claude Bowers was a young reporter for the* Terre Haute Star *whom Debs
had befriended when Bowers moved to Terre Haute in 1903. In his long career
Bowers gained fame as the editor of the* New York Evening World, *the author
of a number of widely read histories and biographies, including* The Tragic
Era *(1929) and* Jefferson and Hamilton *(1925), and as ambassador to Spain*

and Chile. Among other things the letter refers to correspondence dated Febru-
ary 7, 1907, in which Terre Haute mayor James Lyons informed a Crooked
Lake, Michigan, man that Debs was highly regarded by "all classes" of Terre
Haute's people and was a man who was "cultured, brilliant, eloquent, schol-
arly, and companionable, lovable in his relations with his fellow man."

EVD to Claude G. Bowers

March 28, 1907
Girard, Kansas

My dear Bowers:—
    Your note with enclosure has been forwarded to me here from
Terre Haute and both have been noted with interest and satisfaction.
I had already read your St. Patrick's Day speech and thoroughly
enjoyed it. You made a really eloquent speech upon that hackneyed
subject and I am not surprised that you aroused intense enthusiasm
among our Irish brethren. Let me congratulate you upon this happy
and inspiring effort.
    Accept my thanks for your appreciative words in reference to the
Appeal. I am only too glad to send it and feel fully repaid in having
you express your sympathy with our imprisoned fellow workers in
the West. Knowing you as I do, I am quite sure that nothing but
misunderstanding of this case could prevent the full measure of your
sympathy going to these men, and not only this, but your indignation
from finding expression in vigorous terms of denunciation of the
Mine and Smelter owners who are responsible for the crime. You
need not subscribe for the Appeal. It is quite sufficient that you will
find time to read it and I shall see to it with pleasure that you get it
regularly.
    I note with special interest what you say about the personal inquiry
in reference to myself from Michigan. Let me thank you and through
you Mayor Lyons with all my heart. Such personal fidelity of one's
friends when one is far away is a tribute of priceless value and I wish
you to know that I am not insensible to the obligation thus imposed
upon me. Mayor Lyons and I are moving along separate political lines
but he has always been my personal friend and I have always been
his and if I ever have the opportunity to reciprocate his kindness I
shall do so with the greatest pleasure. I need hardly say that these
same words refer also to yourself. You have shown me great kindnesses
in the past which I can never forget.

I often wish you were a Socialist and I somehow feel that you will yet be. However this may turn out, my personal regard for you will remain always the same.

I am here for a short time before going to Idaho on a staff of the Appeal to Reason to attend the approaching trial. Ryan Walker will be one of my associates. Ryan, you know, is a Socialist and will help do the trial for the Appeal. We will have a wireless telegraph service established and probably issue a daily during the trial. Last week over 14,000 new subscribers rolled in and the Appeal now has over 300,000 on its list, the largest of any labor paper in the world.

Roosevelt is largely responsible for the western situation. The people will sometime find out how base he is and how base and popular it is possible for a president to be at the same time. Only the ignorance of the masses makes this possible. It will not always be so.

Yours always,
E. V. Debs

Sending you a pamphlet worth reading through.

TLS (with handwritten note), InU, Lilly Library, Bowers MSS.

☐ *Eugene Debs and Katherine Metzel were married on June 9, 1885. This note marks their anniversary.*

EVD to Katherine Metzel Debs

June 9, 1907
[Girard, Kansas?]

To my bonny bride of
    Twenty-two summers ago.
        With all my heart.
                        Eugene
To Kate —
    The flower of my soul
                        Eugene

ANS (two notes), EVD Foundation, Debs Home, KMD Scrapbook No 3.

□ *Clarence Darrow, perhaps the most famous defense lawyer of his time, was part of Debs's counsel in the trial and appeal following the Pullman strike and played a leading role in many of the most controversial trials of the era. At the time of this letter the* Appeal to Reason *press was publishing a series of pamphlets based on Darrow's trial speeches.*

Clarence S. Darrow to EVD

November 1907
Rathdrum, Idaho

My Dear Debbs

Your nice letter came to hand some time ago & I assure you that I appreciate it and prize it. You are one who has never disappointed me & I know never will. I feel that I know you & you are always the same. I appreciate all you have done & all you have tried to do & wanted to do. I don't know as either of us are entitled to any sympathy for what we have lost for our convictions. We have likewise gained much & perhaps are better off than the rest.

I am just now trying the Adams case and am very hopeful about it. I shall try to go back through Girard & meet you all & talk business to you about my books.

How about the pamphlet of the Haywood argument. It ought to be out & I am getting a little impatient at the delay. If it is not coming right away I wish you would send me the proof as I never have had the full proof—but if it is coming quickly let it go.

I enclose some names to which please send copies.

Always with love & devotion

Your friend
Clarence S. Darrow

ALS, EVD Foundation, Debs Home.

□ *Charles Ervin joined the Socialist party in 1906, ran for Congress and for the United States Senate in Pennsylvania and for governor in New York on its ticket, and edited the socialist* New York Call *from 1917 to 1922. The first edition of the* Call *appeared on May 11, 1908, a few months after this letter was written. In discussing the upcoming Socialist Party of America presidential nomination, Debs refers to William Haywood, who was, along with Debs,*

*one of the founders in 1905 of the Industrial Workers of the World, often known
as the Wobblies.*

EVD to Charles W. Ervin

March 14, 1908
Girard, Kansas

My dear Ervin:—

Your letter of the twelfth is just received. Were I in condition and
had the opportunity I should gladly take hand in the campaign in
your district. The fight is the same everywhere and every comrade,
big or little, can serve about as well in one place as at another. Anyway,
I like you and if I can't speak for you I can at least wish I could and
cheer you on at long range.

I note with interest what you say about your visit to New York and
about the early appearance of the Socialist Daily. Like yourself I have
some misgiving. It is a big undertaking, and requires plenty of funds.
New York ought to be able to support such a paper and I am hoping
it will. It may be that just such a task is needed to engage the serious
thought and enlist the support of all to overcome the factional differences which now complicate and weaken the situation.

Too bad that Socialists must waste so much of their time and
substance in factional fighting. A certain amount of it may be inevitable but it seems as if we have a certain element which is not satisfied
unless there is a row on. I can never take a hand in that sort of
business and never do unless driven to it. I have no time nor have I
the disposition to engage in petty factional quarreling. I want to
reserve all I have for the enemy and it is little enough even at that.

I have noted what you say in reference to the approaching convention and the probable nomination for the presidency. I can only
repeat what I have said in the past and that is that I do not wish, and
for sufficient reasons do not think the convention should consider my
name in connection with, the nomination. I have discouraged the use
of my name and am still hoping it will not be presented to the convention.

I note with regret what you say in reference to Comrade Haywood.
I must confess that your letter is not the first of its kind I have received
touching this matter. I had hoped for entirely different results in his
impression upon the comrades of the east. But we cannot always

appear at our best or do our best, and even if we do we are apt to fall short and to this rule Haywood of course is no exception. I am quite sure, speaking of him in connection with the nomination, that he does not desire it and that he would only accept it from a sheer sense of duty to the party. He himself told me this and I am sure in all sincerity for Haywood does not dissemble. If the party thinks that his nomination would be an error he would be the very first to decline to have his name considered. If Haywood should withdraw his name or if the convention should for any reason deem another choice preferable I think that an entirely fresh candidate should be nominated. We have a number of comrades who are well-known and whose nomination would fairly represent the party and its principles and who would poll the full strength of the movement.

Referring again to myself, the party of course comes first and there is nothing in the line of duty that I would not do for the party, but I have no idea that the party will need me as a candidate this year, and since I have twice been honored with the nomination there is every reason why some other comrade should be chosen. For such a comrade, whoever he might be, I could work with all my heart.

Thanking you for your kind words and your frank expressions, I remain

Yours fraternally
E. V. Debs

TLS, MiDW, Archives of Labor History and Urban Affairs, Gould Collection.

□ *Ben Hanford was a New York City printer and editor who created the popular socialist folk hero Jimmy Higgins, the unsung party loyalist who did the necessary but seldom applauded work of selling tickets, printing leaflets, and organizing meetings for the party's leaders. Hanford was Debs's vice-presidential running mate in the 1904 and 1908 elections.*

Ben Hanford to EVD

May 2, 1908
Chicago, Illinois

Dear Debs—
Your faults are many. I have often discussed them, but never with other than your friends. Your virtues are great and they are countless.

It has been my privilege to uphold them before friend and foe. I do not know ~~that~~ the state of your health, but if you are not in your grave clothes you must allow yourself to be the candidate this year. We must make no mistakes. We cannot take chances on dark horses. This year we are to decide two things in America. First, we are going to conquer the right to make economic and political changes by orderly and peaceful processes. Second, we are going to make the Socialist Party the instrument of carrying out those changes. It is going to become the party of revolution—not merely in the educational and academic sense—but it is going to conquer so much new ground, and make so much new growth, that there will be no room for any other party of labor. The Socialist Party is going to show itself competent to carry out its programme. This means, face to face with these great opportunities, that no mistakes can be made. *You,* and no other, are the man to head the army. I do not know the condition of your throat. I have heard all sort of stories. But if you are not able you need make few speeches, and those only in halls. Note the size of our party, and note its finances. If you are not able to speak, you can write, and the party can *print,* and circulate. Besides, look at our Socialist press. See the powers in the hands of the Movement now. To me it seems that I have no right to consider any other man unless you tell me that you positively decline, and in the event that you do so you are in duty bound to give me your reasons, and I have a right to weigh them as well as yourself. We differ in opinion on many party matters, but in purpose we are one, now as aforetime. I inclose a letter from Fred Long. Please read it and return it to me, There is no man in our movement of broader knowledge or sounder judgment. Do not mind what he says of me. But to my mind, you must be moved by the confidence of such a man as you know him to be. Please let me hear from you—and let me be able to say that now as always, Debs is ready and willing to answer to any call that is made upon him. Do not consider me personally for a moment. Physically I am all to the good. I shall work in the movement once more, and believe me, it is the work and the Movement I love, and not the place. Debs, *you are the man,* and it is your duty to let it be known that you can and will respond when called upon.

With a comrade's love,

Yours truly
Ben Hanford

Address me c/o Barnes.

ALS, InTI, Debs Collection.

□ *Joseph Labadie played an active role in organizing Knights of Labor and, later, AFL locals in Michigan and was the first president of the Michigan Federation of Labor. He embraced philosophical anarchism in the 1890s and printed scores of tracts and pamphlets advocating anarchism. Called the "Gentle Anarchist," Labadie in 1911 donated to the University of Michigan his collection of labor and radical materials, which formed the nucleus of the Labadie Collection, one of the most important archives of its kind in the United States. In this letter Debs notes his disagreement with anarchist philosophy but expresses admiration for individual anarchists such as Voltairine de Cleyre, a well-known anarchist author.*

EVD to Joseph A. Labadie

May 5, 1908
Girard, Kansas

My dear Joe:—

Some days ago a letter came from you which I had but time to glance at and meant to answer later, but to my regret I am now unable to find it. In the thousand and more letters which pour in here daily yours seems to have gone astray. I remember, I think, the substance of your letter and regret that you felt that you had cause for writing it. It is quite probable that there is good ground for your complaint. I do not justify nor attempt to justify any misrepresentation of anarchism or anarchists. But this sort of thing has been engaged in on both sides. At Chicago and some other places there are those who call themselves anarchists who are to be found in every election with the money of the capitalist politicians in their pockets and doing the service of ward-heeling politicians, denouncing Socialists and visiting their wrath on the Appeal to Reason and other Socialist papers. Between elections, of course, they have no use for politics and denounce all politics as corrupt but when there is an opening to make a few dirty dollars they are in the thick of the vilest kind of politics. But I know you do not defend this and I am simply mentioning it to show that there are those on both sides who are engaged in the reprehensible work which you and I both condemn.

I have had a letter from Voltairine de Cleyre on the same subject and have just answered her. Of course you know that I am not an anarchist and do not agree to the anarchist philosophy. but I can none the less admire such a comrade as Voltairine de Cleyre, in whose letter which lies before me there is everything that is commendable and not one word to which any fair and decent person could take exception.

I have often defended anarchists and I think no one more fully appreciates the moral heroism of the Chicago anarchists who were legally murdered than I. Certain anarchists have at times treated me unfairly but I have rarely paid any attention to them for the very reason that I do not wish any personal controversy with those who are opposed to capitalism. So far as we can work together well and good. Where we cannot do this we can each pursue his own course with all due respect for the other. I number some anarchists among my warmest personal friends and the only change I could wish in them is that they were Socialists.

I appreciate the kindly spirit in which you have written me and you may rely upon me to do what I can to prevent any misrepresentation of anarchism on the part of Socialists.

I am glad your mail has been held up by the government. This gives you fresh credentials and increases, if possible, my personal regard for you. In any such fight, if it became serious, I need not assure you that you could count on me without fear of disappointment.

I hope you are well and cheerful, and with all good wishes, remain as ever,

Yours faithfully,
E. V. Debs

TLS, MiU, Labadie Collection.

□ *Debs was nominated for the third time as the Socialist party's presidential candidate at the Chicago convention on May 10–11, 1908. In the following letter he describes the celebration of the event in Girard, Kansas, where he was working for the* Appeal to Reason.

EVD to Theodore Debs

May 17, 1908
Girard, Kansas

My dear old Pard:

Yesterday Saturday afternoon was one of the rarest most beautiful and touching occasions of all my life. It was a *complete* surprise. At 3 o'clock I was casually invited by Warren and Eastwood to walk uptown. Mayor Ryan met & walked with us. On the court house campus a stand had been newly created, a great crowd of men women & children were assembled A band, a magnificent one, brought here for the occasion began to play, then Richardson, one of the rarest of souls, made a beautiful address and paid me a most touching tribute and for the first time it flashed upon me — the *people* of Girard, regardless of party, creed or color, had assembled to compliment me upon my nomination. I spoke — and said little or nothing for my emotions overmastered me. Then a large number of little girls in white came forward, each with a huge basket of beautiful flowers. No words can describe it. The people surrounded me. The Mayor, a Democrat, paid me a beautiful tribute and all the people applauded and every [*sic*] they came to my room and shook hands and spoke kind words. My room was *packed* with flowers all around the walls a solid mass that the biggest wagon would not have held. One magnificent basket, so beautiful as to excite pity that it must wither bore amidst its many colored ribbons and decorations the inscription "From those who love you" —

This day — and how I wish you could have been here — drew ~~the curtain~~ aside {the curtain of the future} and for a brief {moment} ~~day at least~~ I caught a glimpse of the fine, sweet, beautiful, *human* society *that is to be*. My love and kisses to you all.

Your brother and pard
Eugene

ALS, InTI, Debs Collection.

☐ *Lincoln Steffens's articles on the "Shame of the Cities" established his reputation as one of the leading muckrakers of the time. During the 1908 presidential campaign he interviewed Debs and wrote a widely read article on the socialist candidate for* Everybody's *magazine. In the following letter Debs comments on a draft of the article.*

EVD to Lincoln Steffens

August 12, 1908
Girard, Kansas

My dear Mr. Steffens: —

Having read your article I feel that I should write you a few lines in regard to it. In returning the copy to the Editor I took occasion to say that your work was magnificent and that I was greatly pleased with it. I desire to repeat this to you now, with the reservation, however, that there are some things in the article which I wish were otherwise. Of course I did not expect it would be possible to produce an article of such importance and under such great difficulties which would be entirely free from objections. But such objection as I do find I make to you and not to the Editor, for I know how conscientiously you did your work and I would not have you feel that I am lacking in proper appreciation.

When the copy was submitted to me it was under circumstances that made any change or revision practically impossible. The time was exceedingly short as was indicated by both telegrams and letters received at Terre Haute a day or two before the copy reached there. I was instructed to return the copy with the least possible delay and also to make no changes unless absolutely necessary and to wire those changes so the copy could go to the printers on time. All of which indicated a strong desire to avoid changes.

To add to the disadvantages, I was obliged to leave Terre Haute before the copy reached there to meet imperative engagements in Kansas. I left word with my brother to have the copy rushed to me by immediate delivery on the very first mail. After reaching Girard I was on the alert, knowing that my having to leave would add at least three days more to the delay and as the time of going to press was overdue I felt that I must rush the copy back from here on the first mail by immediate delivery, which I did. This allowed but a hasty reading of the article and no time to deliberately consider or revise it. For this reason but two slight alterations were made.

I shall not now point out the particular things which I should have had otherwise, but one or two may serve. You have me say that I expect sometime to do some very foolish thing. That surely must have been an error on your part, for I made no such statement. Not that I may not do a foolish thing, but the statement was used to indicate that I would do a very foolish thing at a very critical time when it would have disastrous effects; but at any rate it is not the kind of a statement that I would give place to in such an article.

In the matter of the difference between Berger and myself, as to compensation to the class which has confiscated the wealth produced by the working class, I was quite familiar with the literature on the subject and with the opinions of certain prominent Socialists, but, if you remember, I asked you to entirely omit that part of the interview, or at least to say that bridge would be crossed when we got to it and that the question of compensating the present owners of the means of production would be determined by the people at the time they were taken over. This is the way in which this point should have been presented. It is purely a matter of conjecture at this time. The people, especially those who have amassed their fortunes by confiscation, are exceedingly sensitive upon that subject when the same method is to be applied to themselves

But I am not writing to find fault, but only to be candid with you and to indicate what changes I would have made if I could have done so without marring the article or causing delay, against which the publishers so persistently and pressingly urged me.

In my hasty reading of the article I did not fail to observe that to make the changes here suggested and one or two others would have mutilated the article and necessitated the rewriting of certain parts of it, and I readily understood your request therefore that no change be made unless absolutely necessary.

Permit me to assure you that I appreciate fully the difficulties under which your work was undertaken and also the conscientious desire to do justice which you brought to the task. You produced a really wonderful article and I made no mistake in saying to the Editor that it was a piece of magnificent work. From my point of view it has its objections, but, all things considered, it were strange if this were otherwise. As for myself personally you have treated me generously indeed, more so by far than I deserve, and I am deeply sensible for every kind word your article contains. It is not myself, however, that I am concerned about, but the great Cause of which I am but a very small part, and my whole object in the interview was to have that Cause so presented to the people that it should be rightly understood, knowing that nothing but their ignorance in regard to it keeps them from supporting it and hastening the day of its triumph. If the article serves that purpose in such part as our comrades expect, as I believe it will and hope it may, it will fully justify all the labors required to produce it and the objections I have pointed out will detract but little from it and not at all from the commendation it will evoke from our friends and sympathizers.

Permit me to thank you in my own name and for my comrades for the service you have rendered and for the sympathetic interest which animated you, and believe me, with all kind regards and good wishes,

Yours faithfully,
Eugene V. Debs

TLS, NNC.

□ *An immigrant from Riga, Latvia, Morris Hillquit became a leading writer
and spokesman for the Socialist party and, as an attorney during World War
I, often defended socialists accused of violating espionage and sedition laws.
In the following letter Debs seems to apologize for his performance in New York
City during the presidential campaign and, at the same time, reveals something
of the rigors of the so-called Red Special campaign (named for the train that
was chartered by the Socialist party to carry Debs to both coasts and across most
of the Midwest and Rocky Mountain regions). Altogether, the Red Special made
it possible for Debs to reach an estimated half million people in three hundred
communities in thirty-three states, but the results were a disappointment:
420,793 votes, an increase of only 20,000 over his 1904 total.*

EVD to Morris Hillquit

October 15, 1908
En route to Reading, Pennsylvania

My dear Hillquit: —
    Your letter of the 7th. was duly received. Thank you for it warmly.
No trace remains of that incident. It is closed and forgotten. I have
but one regret in connection with it and that is not having been able
to attend the banquet and thus serve the Call and receive the splendid
greeting so kindly planned for me.
    Some strange fatality has attended me at the New York meetings
and my part in them was as insignificant as the meetings themselves
were magnificent. It was there I wished to be strongest and was
weakest. Fortunately the meetings did not need me and my strength
was reserved for other places where it was needed. The kindness of
the comrades in spite of my almost contemptible showing touches me
deeply and never can be forgotten.
    The day I was on the East Side I was little more than a portable
corpse. I had an attack of grip which all but paralyzed me and it had
to come at a time of course when I ought to have had all my powers.
Today, thanks to the goodness of my comrades and a little rest, I am
quite myself again and for the rest of the trip I shall be able to meet
every demand. There is no trouble with my bodily powers. In all my
life I was never so strong as now. The trouble is that I cannot speak
worth a minute's listening if I do not speak with all the intensity of
my nature. The result is that when I am through I am drenched with
perspiration and there is hardly a dry thread in my clothes. I then
have to be more or less exposed to the drafts and the cold with the
result that I am chilled through with the usual consequences. Last

Sunday afternoon and evening I addressed at length three packed audiences in Philadelphia and Camden and believe I did justice to them all. At the close of the last I was wet with sweat from head to foot and in that condition was taken out into an open auto and for forty minutes whirled along through a cutting wind, being delayed for a time at the ferry. My clothes were glued to my body and when I got to the car I had a violent chill until my teeth chattered. This was followed by an intense fever and it was this that put me in the condition I was in on the day following and the next day when we met at the East Side in New York. This trouble was not due to any physical weakness but would have occurred under the same conditions to the strongest man on earth. I cannot resist this bit of explanation for my devotion to the cause is such that when I appear weak at a meeting, especially one of such stupendous importance as the New York meeting, I feel a sense of personal guilt which neither the kindness of my comrades, the indulgence of my friends, nor any possible self-explanation can condone. I have been informed by my brother of your insistence upon my having a three days' rest and of you and Comrade Stokes having provided for it and assumed full responsibility for so doing. A thousand thanks to you both! Fortunately I am almost recovered and in another day or two will be as strong as the day the campaign opened, {but} I feel just as grateful for your thoughtfulness and solicitude as if I were obliged to take advantage of it.

Let me thank you also for your extreme kindness in the matter of the box at the Hippodrome for Mrs. Debs and her party for which you decline to permit me to share any part of the expense. Mrs. Debs was delighted as well she might be with your gracious hospitality and that of Mrs. Hillquit and in her name and for myself and all of us I thank you both with a deep sense of gratitude.

Earnestly hoping that you may be elected to a seat in Congress where you are so much needed, and wishing you well in every way I remain

Yours faithfully
Eugene V. Debs

TLS, WHi, Hillquit Papers.

□ *Charles Sandburg, who had not yet changed his first name to Carl, had attracted more attention as a socialist lecturer and orator than as a poet when*

Debs wrote the following letter to him. In it Debs agrees to write a testimonial, in which he would describe Sandburg as "one of the most brilliant young orators in the Socialist movement in the United States."

EVD to Chas. Sandburg

November 27, 1908
Terre Haute, Indiana

My dear Comrade:—
Your letter with enclosures has been received. I shall examine the latter a little later as I am just leaving for the West. Of course I can give you a testimonial for your circular and I enclose it with pleasure. If anything further is needed command me. I regard it as a duty to serve a comrade and particularly when he happens to be one as worthy as yourself. I remember and shall always remember the service you so freely rendered on the "Red Special" and your fine spirit amd wholesome presence. May you find many to engage your service and give you the chance—all you ask or need—to deliver your message and do your work.
Count me always

Your loving comrade
Eugene V. Debs

P.S. If the enclosed should need any change of wording for your particular purpose you are at liberty to make it say what you wish.

TLS, IU, Sandburg Papers.

☐ *Robert M. La Follette, governor of Wisconsin and congressman and U.S. senator from that state, was a leader of the reform impulse of the Progressive Era. In the following letter Debs seeks the support of Senator La Follette for the defense of a group of Mexican revolutionaries who were working for the overthrow of the Mexican dictator Forfirio Diaz but were being held in American prisons for violation of the neutrality laws. In the pages of the* Appeal to Reason *Debs kept up a steady demand for the release of the Mexicans, and in 1910 La Follette joined others in the Senate in passing a resolution calling for an investigation of the "Mexican cases."*

EVD to Robert M. La Follette

March 7, 1909
Girard, Kansas

Dear Senator La Follette:

I do not know how closely you have been following what are known as the Mexican cases. For nearly two years the leaders of the Mexican Liberal Party have been in American jails. No one seems to be able to get any information as to when they are to be tried. The Appeal to Reason has through its own special correspondents made a study of these cases. It is almost impossible to conceive the enormity of the outrages of which these patriots have been the victims, both in their own country and in the United States. I beg of you to take the time, busy as you are, to read the statement made by Ricardo Flores Magon, President of the Mexican Liberal Party, who has been in jail upon the alleged charge of having violated the neutrality laws, for almost two years. It is shocking and revolting beyond words, and I am convinced that it is absolutely true in every harrowing detail. It is enough to make the blood of Americans who are not yet themselves vassals burn with indignation.

Not to be too long, I am writing to ask if you can not introduce a resolution in the senate demanding an investigation of these cases. The whole working class is vitally interested and a large section of it is conscious of that fact. There are fourteen million peon slaves in Mexico, and there is a billion of American capital invested in that country. The average wage is 37½ cents a day in Mexican money. The railroads, mines, smelters, cotton industries, etc. are mainly owned by American capitalists. They are having their industries developed and operated on the basis of peon labor. That is one of the reasons why there are over two millions of idle workingmen in the United States, and why millions of others are getting such miserable wages.

You will no doubt recall Root's visit to Diaz while he was Secretary of State. An ovation was given him, and for good reasons. He was the emissary of the capitalists in negotiating a secret treaty of peace. Anyone with the least insight can comprehend it at a glance. Diaz is a devil in human form. A meaner mercenary does not exist. The bloody butcheries he has been guilty of would put a hyena to shame. He is getting his full share of the plunder that is being wrung from the peon slaves by American capitalists. This accounts for Mexican patriots rotting in American jails. During their preliminary hearing when it was found that there was no evidence against them, and they were about to be dismissed, Attorney General Bonaparte wired the

District Attorney: "Hold them on any account. They are wanted in Mexico." Of course they are wanted in Mexico. They are the fearless and incorruptible leaders of the Liberal Party and the sworn enemies of tyranny and of peon slavery, and Diaz wants to get them into his bloody claws to murder them as he has murdered thousands of others for the same cause.

Magon, Villareal, Rivera, Sarabia, Araujo, and other leaders of the Mexican Liberal Party, who are either in our jails or penitentiaries, along with scores of others of their countrymen, are all patriots in the loftiest sense of that term. Each of them is a cultured, high-minded gentleman, who loves his fellowmen too well to allow the present bloody tyranny to exist without protest. All of them have sacrificed their material interests, their liberty, and have repeatedly risked their lives in the cause of freedom.

Is it not the concern of the American people that such men are allowed to lie in our jails for two years without being granted a trial? If they are guilty, why are they not tried? If they are not guilty, why are they not released? Is the United States Government the catcher of the escaped refugees of Diaz? It must be confessed that it looks very much that way. Government officials of the United States, high and low, are cooperating heartily with the Diaz despotism to imprison and murder patriots whose crime is their love of liberty, and their abhorrence of peon slavery.

But apart from all these considerations, fourteen millions of human beings are writhing in the fetters of peonage at our very doors. They are struggling to be free. Is our government to crush their aspirations with an iron heel; to destroy their hopes by conspiring to imprison and murder their leaders?

I venture to say that if the American people knew of the atrocities that are being perpetrated at this very hour upon the patriots of Mexico who have sought refuge under our flag from the bloody tyrant across the Rio Grande they would rise in revolt all over the land. If we honor the memories of Jefferson, Paine, Sam Adams, Franklin, and other patriots of our own country, we cannot but honor Magon, and his compatriots who are fighting to deliver their own unhappy country from the Diaz despotism based upon force and plunder, and steeped in the blood of innocents.

This surely must constitute a proper subject for investigation by the American Congress. A speech in the Senate upon this subject would do more to bring the attention of the people to this vital question than any other one thing I can think of at this time. I am sending you by even mail the papers which contain the latest accounts in reference to the more important cases. Mr. Warren, the managing editor of the Appeal to Reason, has just returned from Texas where he instituted a personal investigation. The judge who had just tried one of the patriots at San Antonio, Araujo by name, sending him to the Federal Prison at Ft. Leavenworth for two years and a half, declared at the time he pronounced the sentence in open court, that he was prejudiced against the defendant and that he was bound to break up the opposition to the Diaz administration. This is truly a fine state of affairs.

Warren and I have just returned from the Federal Prison at Leavenworth where we had a personal interview with Araujo and we found him to be one of the finest, most cultured, educated and refined young men we have ever met anywhere.

If you do not see your way clear to introduce a resolution demanding an investigation, perhaps a resolution calling upon the secretary of state to furnish the senate with the papers and essential data and information in these cases might be in order. You know better in regard to this, but in any event, I hope you will see your way clear to take some action. You are the only member of the United States Senate to whom I would make this request.

With all kind personal regards, and hoping I may have a line from you, I remain,

Very sincerely yours,
Eugene V. Debs.

TL transcript, NNC, Steffens Papers.

☐ *Robert Hunter, a native of Terre Haute, lived only a few blocks from Debs. His best-known book,* Poverty, *was based on his experiences in New York City and Chicago settlement house work. Hunter believed that the Socialist party should cooperate with, and seek to convert, AFL unions to socialism. In the following letter Debs discusses Hunter's strategy and warns him against cooperation with the leadership of the AFL unions, especially Samuel Gompers.*

EVD to Robert Hunter

February 4, 1910
En route, Ohio

My Dear Robert: —
Yours of the 27*th* ult. has overtaken me here and I have read it carefully. Unfortunately I am under such pressure on this long ex-

tended speaking trip that I cannot begin to answer as I wish. Time forbids. I must come straight to the point. If my letter to Simons was a blow in {your} face your mixing with the fakirs at Toronto was a blow in the face of the whole Socialist movement. Understand me, I not only do not object to your working on the rank and file of the {A.F. of L.,} but I would encourage you in every possible way and on a thousand occassions I have commended you and your work, quoted you in my speeches and given you full credit for your splendid services. But I draw the line sharp and clean on the traitors and fakirs who are running the A.F. of L in the interest of the capitalists. As now constituted the A.F. of L. does not run its officers but its officers run it. Gompers is the boss and he is kept where he is by the capitalists whose slaves dumbly do their masters' bidding and it is made unanimous, sad to say, by a few Socialists whose antics {at} each convention, in slobbering over Gompers and being puked on in return by him, would make angels weep. Berger's performances in this connection have been disgraceful and contemptible beyond words and you are at perfect liberty to use this statement as you wish for I have no private opinion in these matters that the rank and file are not entitled to know.

It is only necessary for Gompers, the miserable traitor and coward, to say to the other fakirs at a convention that the capitalists tried to bribe him to have them shed their regulation tears, the size of horseballs, and on the inner circle of this group are the Socialists, arch-suckers that they are, the first and freakiest in raising Gompers' salary and making his election unanimous. If this is not contemptible and disgusting to the last degree, to put it mildly, I don't know what it is unless it is treason to the working class. For alleged revolutionary Leaders {to} honey around and mix up with such arch-traitors as run the A.F. of L. conventions is absolutely inexcusable and the time is near when they will be held accountable for it. It is this very thing that confounds and confuses the rank and file, muddles the situation and makes our already difficult task next to impossible; and it is this very thing that will result in the launching of a union labor party and when it comes such Socialists as attend A.F. of L. conventions and mix with Gompers and his gang will be largely responsible for it.

When you and Simons go to an A.F. of L. convention you are identified with and become a part of it and you have got to take the consequences. I have heard you both condemned over and over again by party comrades who have hitherto held you in the highest esteem. You maintain at least a semi-friendly relation with Gompers, Mitchell and other tools of the capitalist class and in that you cannot justify yourself as a revolutionist to save your life. Gompers is the deadly enemy of my class and so is Mitchell, and I am theirs. Between us there can be nothing but war and I want them to distinctly understand it and when they launch their Civic-Federationized fake labor party, which they have just announced, I will hit it just as hard as I can and as often, and I will make Gompers and Mitchell face the issue or drive them off the platform, and the rank and file will trust me because I have not been hand in glove with them, not affiliated with them at their fakir conventions as you and Simons have done, thus at least implying some degree of tolerance and sanction for their attitude and policy.

I am for clear cut action and uncompromising tactics. I do not propose to try to win the intimidated rank and file of the A.F. of L. by publicly pandering {to their} corrupt bosses. For you personally my feeling remains unchanged but you have made a mistake, and so has Simons, and the time will come when you will realize it.

Yours aye
[Eugene V. Debs]

TLc, InTI, Debs Collection.

☐ *Two of Debs's favorite poets, often quoted in his speeches and writing, were Walt Whitman and Robert Burns. In this letter to Claude Bowers, who had recently given a lecture in Sullivan, Indiana, on "The Religion of Robert Burns," Debs shares his view of the poet.*

EVD to Claude G. Bowers

April 13, 1910
Terre Haute, Indiana

My dear Friend: —

I read your beautiful lecture on Burns and wish to send you this word of thanks and appreciation. A marked copy of the paper containing the lecture was sent to me by my brother while I was East and I felt then that I should drop you a line but the passing days were all so crowded that I could not find the time. Your interpretation of the character of Burns and of his democracy is not only clear and illuminating but truly poetic and if his spiritual ears are attuned to what is now said of him he must have smiled indeed when your lecture was delivered. So many well meant but stupid apologies have been made for Burns because of his so-called infirmities of character that it is refreshing to hear of him exactly as he was by one whose own poetic nature enables him to understand that if Burns had not been exactly as he was, singing or sighing, in love or in liquor, he could not have been Burns at all.

With thanks and congratulations I am as ever

Yours cordially
Eugene V. Debs

TLS, InU, Lilly Library, Bowers MSS.

□ *George Brewer was on the staff of the* Appeal to Reason *and regularly accompanied Debs on his lecture tours. In the following letter Debs discusses his plans for the upcoming off-year campaign in the broader context of his own health problems. Soon after the letter was written Debs went to the Mayo Brothers Clinic in Rochester, Minnesota, to have a tumor removed from his side.*

EVD to George D. Brewer

July 7, 1910
Terre Haute, Indiana

The intense heat and humidity of the past few days have so enervated and depressed me physically, that I have not felt like writing, or you would have heard from me sooner. I have thought the matter of the fall campaign all over and have arrived at a pretty definite conclusion so far as my own activities are concerned. Personally, I would prefer to entirely quit the platform for a year at least, and there are strong inducements to this course which need not be discussed here. But there are also strong reasons why I should be in the field this fall and I believe I have taken them all into account, especially the Appeal to Reason and the great work upon which its success so largely depends, and I have also to consider that this [is] a campaign year, a national campaign at that, and so I have concluded to give myself to field work as far as I can do so consistently with my health and strength and with other duties I owe to myself and family.

I have been an exile from home on account of the labor movement nearly all of my active life, and especially since I have been married, giving up all the comforts of home to serve the cause. I have now reached a point in life when I can do so no longer and where I would be unjust to myself and cruelly so to my wife if I attempted it. For this reason and without going into further details I should not be away from home more than one third of the time, but I am willing to make it half the time to carry out our plans. But this is all the time I can put in on the road, at least for the present and until I am mentally and physically recuperated. Nor do I wish any trip to be longer than two weeks. Beginning with September you can book me for two weeks at a time, and for every two weeks I am out speaking I want to be home two weeks, during which I can rest and at the same time write for the Appeal and keep up my correspondence and meet other demands, so that no time will be lost.

Of course if this arrangement will not be satisfactory to Comrades Warren and Wayland I would not think of pressing it for an instant, nor would I have it accepted. They have both treated me with the greatest kindness and consideration and never since my connection with the paper have I had the least cause for complaint. They, of course, have to look out for the interests of the paper and I am expecting them to do that, and to give the paper preference, and if the arrangement I have suggested is not considered a suitable or satisfactory one to the paper I shall expect to be told so frankly and I shall have only the same good will for the paper and every one connected with it that I always have had and continue to commend and support it as I always have done.

I cannot stand the long stretches of travel and the continuous round of work and excitement I did for so many years, and to attempt it and appear before an audience jaded and fall flat would not help the Appeal, nor myself, nor any one else. I believe I appreciate my limitations and within these I wish to serve and shall serve to the full extent of my ability and power.

In this connection I want to suggest that Irvine, in my opinion, is the man for the Appeal to press into service. With a ringing announcement in the Appeal showing how he came to quit the church, the church of which the Belmonts and Astors are communicants, I believe there would be applications for him from all over the country and that he could be readily booked and be a decided help in developing the Appeal Bureau, which I am more and more convinced will prove to be the greatest circulation-expander and paper-builder ever brought forth in the socialist movement. Irvine would pave the way for another and there are several available people who could and would make good in the field. Kier Hardie, who was suggested by Fred in your previous letter, would make an excellent man and if we decide upon plans herein outlined I will gladly write to him in regard to a tour of the country under Appeal auspices and I do not in the least doubt it would prove a great success.

I had hoped to be out to see Fred and Wayland ere this but my going to the hospital has prevented. Just at present we have a number of visiting relatives here but I expect to be able to leave for Rochester soon so as to be have the operation over with as soon as possible. Let me hear from you as soon as convenient. It goes without saying that if I am in the field this fall it will rejoice me to have as heretofore your co-operation and support, of which I have the fullest possible appreciation.

Yours always
E. V. Debs

TLS, MiDW, Archives of Labor History and Urban Affairs, Brewer Collection.

☐ *Debs regularly lamented and denounced the internal divisions and dissension that plagued the Socialist party and eventually contributed to its decline. In the following letter to Carl Thompson, a Congregational church minister in Milwaukee who embraced socialism and became a strong supporter of Victor Berger, the leader of the SPA in Wisconsin, Debs reveals a strong distaste for what he considered Berger's "autocracy" as a socialist leader.*

EVD to Carl D. Thompson

November 26, 1910
[Terre Haute, Indiana]

My dear Carl Thompson: —
    I have been trying ever since I acknowledged the receipt of your letter of the 5th. inst. to answer it but I have been pressed so hard that I have found it impossible to do so, and even now I am compelled to hurry through it without doing it more than half justice. There has been a perfect flood of letters in here since my return, and matters of all kinds have been awaiting attention, and to cap it all I have had to let go of everything to take hold of the Warren case which will probably make it necessary for me to entirely change my plans and go to Girard, leaving affairs here to take care of themselves until I can get back again.
    I am in hearty accord with every word your letter contains excepting alone on the subjects of trade unions and immigration. If the performance of Berger at St. Louis at the convention of the fakirs, where

he makes himself the annual laughing stock, is not sufficient to disgust socialists I do not know what else would be required, or what further were possible. But we will not now discuss trade unionism and immigration. We will put these off for some other time.

You are absolutely right when you say that at heart Berger is an aristocrat and {not} a socialist. He holds the common run in as much contempt as did Alexander Hamilton or as does Theodore Roosevelt or any other rank individualist. Berger really feels that he is made of superior clay and that the tremendous responsibility of making the socialist movement rests upon his shoulders, and his egotism increases and his vanity inflates as he progresses in power. But I have not the least fear that he is going to foist himself upon the national movement as a dictator. Not the least in the world. In that I disagree with you, and that constitutes the only difference between us except as to the two subjects above named.

Like yourself I appreciate all there is of ability and energy there is [sic] in Berger, all that merits good report in a true socialist—and Berger has his full share of all these qualities, and he is especially gifted with mental powers—but I am unalterably opposed to the toleration of his autocracy in the socialist movement, and I am strongly inclined to find fault with you and others at Milwaukee for allowing him so long to have unbridled sway and to really function as a boss in the Socialist party.

To me there is something shockingly abhorrent about the boss in the socialist movement. He belongs to capitalism and its exploiting mechanism and rotten parties. There is no earthly place for him in the democratic party of the working class.

It is urged by some of the friends of Berger that he is clean and free from corruption. That makes him all the more repugnant and indefensible. There is consistency in a corrupt boss; there is no excuse for a clean one. Corruption is the only possible excuse for a boss. In the socialist movement men are supposed to be enlightened enough to boss themselves and if they are not they are out of place and an element of weakness and to the extent that the party depends upon them it will crumble and collapse and have to build all over again.

Let me make this point clear: To the extent that the Socialist party of Milwaukee and Wisconsin depends upon Victor Berger as a boss, instead of a mere comrade counting one, all of one but no more, it is not a socialist party at all. All of it that hangs upon the influence of a boss will collapse and should in truth be battered down to a substantial basis, the sooner the better.

I discovered [his] true nature long ago, but I was indulgent with him to the verge of cowardice. I have heard him talk to Fred Heath in a room full of people as I would not talk to the mangiest cur, and Heath took it all meekly and without protest, and Berger took it for granted that it was his right to exact such servile and debasing obeisance from comrades. He tried it on me but there he struck a snag. I yielded and submitted until self-respect moved me to call a halt, and I did. Berger was determined that I had no right to differ with him and insultingly commanded me to act the part of a lackey to him, and then our relations came to a very sudden end. I told him that I was a man and a socialist, that I had opinions of my own and the right to express them and that I would permit neither man nor god to boss or dictate to me in the vulgar spirit that moved him to turn purple as he tried to bulldoze me into docile subjection to him as he had done to so many other comrades.

Now the thing for you to do is, in my opinion, to summon those comrades who are agreed with you and formulate a program of resistance to Berger's boss rule. Do if you have to resign your office and leave Milwaukee. The issue has got to be faced and it is the part not only of cowardice but of treason to evade it. If the socialist movement tolerates a boss, be it Berger or Jehova, it is false to its professed principles and the lightening should strike and will strike it just as certain as we invite it. I will back you up when the time comes for me to take my part. I want some time to face Berger upon that very issue before the delegates of a convention, or better still, the rank and file, and he may then have full opportunity to exploit his power as a boss, but if I don't strip him nakeder than he ever was before as a boss it will not be my fault.

And all this is written without a shadow of ill feeling toward Berger. As for envy I know not the meaning of the term. I rejoice with all my heart when I hear of a comrade who can do more than I can for the socialist movement. But for the boss, if he appear in the form of my best friends or my dearest comrade I can have only scorn and contempt.

This is not a confidential letter. You can treat it as you may think proper. What it contains I am ready to stand by. I am only sorry that I have had to express myself in such haste and risk making myself misunderstood. Perhaps at a later time I may have a chance to talk over the matter with you. I hope so. The fine spirit and the manly tone of your letter appeal to me very strongly. I want to get closer to you and work with you in every way I possibly can to build up a truly democratic movement without a boss and without a sycophant. With love and good wishes I am

Yours always
[Eugene V. Debs]

P.S. You have seen {what} happened to Roosevelt, haven't you? Well, Berger will ride to just as hard a fall if the swelling continues.

TLc, InTI, Debs Collection.

☐ *William Allen White was, through his editorials in the* Emporia Daily *and the* Weekly Gazette, *one of the most influential rural spokesmen for liberalism in the Republican party and throughout the nation. Debs and White shared not only a strong suspicion of the role of the federal courts as a bulwark of conservatism but also a wide popularity among rural readers and voters.*

EVD to William Allen White

January 27, 1911
Corpus Christi, Texas

My Dear Mr. White:—
   Your kind note has just reached me. I shall be happy to see you at the earliest opportunity. I have been following you as best I could with deep interest and full appreciation. Your recent article on the courts especially attracted my attention. If I can be of any service to you of course I am at your command. But my movements for the next few weeks will be very uncertain. I have now been away from home six weeks and after closing this speaking tour at Austin on the 30th I shall go directly to Terre Haute. On the 12th prox. I speak at Chicago. Beyond that I am not quite certain. All I am really sure about is that I am having to revise my program on very short notice and with increasing frequency in these days of rapid changes.
   If there is no particular hurry about the matter you have in mind I will arrange to see you as soon as I can possibly do so, although I cannot say at this moment when that may be. I am to make a speaking tour of the southern states in March but I shall quite likely be out to Girard before that time. You can always reach me by addressing me either at Terre Haute or Girard. I would like very much to sit heart to heart with you for an hour or two. I see the fine flame from the altar-fires of your soul in your writings.

Our meetings down here are all crowded to the doors and the more radical the speech the greater the enthusiasm and the heartier the approval.

Love to you and all kind wishes!

Yours always,
Eugene V. Debs

TLS, DLC, White Papers.

□ *On January 28, 1912, a grand jury in Los Angeles indicted Clarence Darrow for attempted bribery in the James and John McNamara trial (the McNamaras were charged with, and eventually pled guilty to, the bombing of the* Los Angeles Times *building). Attacked by much of the labor and socialist press for his strategy as chief counsel—namely, guilty pleas in exchange for reduced sentences—Darrow was defended by Debs in the* Appeal to Reason. *In the following letter, however, Debs tries to explain to Darrow the grounds for criticism being leveled at him by former staunch friends and supporters.*

EVD to Clarence S. Darrow

February 19, 1912
Girard, Kansas

My dear Darrow:—

I have your note of the 12th just received here, forwarded from Terre Haute by my brother. I feel exceedingly touched and pained by your words and have just had a long personal talk with Warren. I shall not attempt to tell you what was said except that Warren assured me and I know he meant it that he had not one bit of personal resentment or bitterness now against you. He explained why from his point of view the Appeal could not say the things he would personally say for you and in defense of you in your present situation. At the same time he felt keenly what is expressed in your note in reference to being deserted by your old friends and supporters in this crisis of your life.

It is not for me to utter a word now to add to your pain in this bitter trial you are now undergoing, but there is undoubtedly a strong feeling against you among Socialists which it is doubtful if even the Appeal and all other papers could succeed in overcoming at this time to any considerable extent. I would make no mention of this except that I would have you understand my own personal position. From my own point of view it is not now the time to point out what you did or did not do, or might have done or should have done, but it is the time to stand solidly behind you and back you up in your fight for vindication against the wolves and hyenas into whose clutches you have unfortunately fallen. I know something about how it feels to be in your situation and to be deserted by the very ones who ought to be most loyal, and the only reason I know it is because I have had the same bitter experience.

You may think it very cruel on the part of your former staunch friends and admirers that they are now lacking in sympathy when you most need it, but perhaps you are not entirely blameless and they are not wholly at fault. I know you will allow me to be as candid with you as I would be with a brother. It appears that there was some investigation at Chicago recently as to certain facts in your record, conducted with a view to getting at the truth, and that the report was anything but flattering to you. Among other things it is charged that in consideration of a fee you went over to the Harvester Trust in some case in which a school fund was involved and that you succeeded in beating the school fund out of a large sum due it for the fee you obtained for such service from the rich owners of the trust. I do not know anything at all about the case and do not now care to know about it, but I only give it to you that you may not be in ignorance of why so many of your former friends have lost confidence in you. It is claimed that this is only one instance of your having gone over to the other side purely for money, and probably your espousal of the cause of Merriam the republican in the recent municipal campaign had about as much as anything else to do with the Socialists and others having concluded that you loved money too well to be trusted by the people.

But for myself I can't understand why you should care for money for I know you to be anything but extravagant in the use of it. It is true that I have noticed some things in you that I have wished might have been otherwise but the same is no doubt equally true in some things you have seen in me. The thing that surprised and in fact shocked me was that you should employ such a notorious corporation corruptionist and all around capitalist retainer as Earl Rogers. I have never met the gentleman personally but I am familiar with his record and know where he stands. When I read that you had retained him I first concluded that it surely was a mistake but upon second thought

I saw in this report what seemed to me the seriousness of your situation and the extent to which you were driven to engage the lead-wolf to escape the pack.

I am more than glad that you also have Judge McNutt to defend and stand by you. The Judge is a lawyer and judge among ten thousand. You know I have no respect for the legal profession but if lawyers and judges were of the type of Judge McNutt I would uncover in the presence of the bar and the bench. I know Judge McNutt thoroughly and you can count on him to the extent of his ability to serve you against all the influences that could possibly be brought to bear upon him to desert you. You may be sure that all my heart is with you and that I am going to see what can be done to set the tide moving in your direction. Let me entreat you not to take this matter too seriously. The good there is to your credit no amount of ingratitude or indifference can wipe out. You have fought on the right side and I am sure with your heart in the right place even if you have made mistakes and in the end the summing up will be to your everlasting credit. I know how keenly one feels neglect and indifference in such an hour and I know too what superhuman power is required to rise above such demoralizing influences and triumph over such a crucial situation. If it were the penitentiary or even the gallows for serving the cause of right it would be easy enough but to be deserted and neglected by the very ones for whose sake these bitter penalties are imposed, that is the supreme test. To that test you are now being subjected and you are going to prove equal to that as you have been to all others in the past.

The thing of most vital concern to you now is that Darrow, above all others, shall stand by himself and {be} strong enough, even in his present situation, in which he is being tried by fire, to stand alone and to face the world unafraid.

Hoping from the very depths of my heart that you will triumph over your enemies and emerge from this ordeal completely vindicated, and with all loving regards and good wishes to both yourself and Mrs. Darrow, I remain,

Yours faithfully,
[Eugene V. Debs]

TLc, InTI, Debs Collection.

☐ *During the course of his career Debs was troubled by health problems of one kind or another. In the following letter he describes one such episode to his brother.*

EVD to Theodore Debs

April 21, 1912
Girard, Kansas

My dear old Pard:

Have just written Kate fully about last 2 weeks. Go to our house when you have time & she'll tell you about it. I haven't time to write. This is first day's work I've done for 2 weeks & I'm tired. Easter 2 a m was seized with spasm of lumbago — fell on floor & was helpless & suffered all the tortures of damnation until 2 or 3 days ago. Thought I was done for. Resigned but Warren would not accept. Did not let you know because I didn't want to worry you. Am on my feet again. A scientific osteopath is making me new again. He has already done wonders. Will be here 3 weeks yet & then go home. In that time he will put me in better fighting shape than I've been for 20 years. I can already feel it. Each treatment lasts 1½ hours and its drastic & from scalp to toe-nails. He has already about cured my catarrh & my throat — my voice already rings like new. He's going to give me new digestion & circulation & he's already done wonders. Before I had this attack my blood was so cold that I couldn't get warm in bed under 6 inches of quilts & blankets. He understands thoroughly. The attack of lumbago that came near being my finish was a collapse due to my run down condition. I'll never again be caught in that condition. It's a clear but never to be forgotten lesson. To-morrow I begin to take systematic exercise & air — no medicine — but every nerve, muscle & tendon in me set to work.

I was on the verge of wiring or writing you but glad I didn't. Would have resigned but Warren wouldn't listen to it. The kindness of these people I never shall forget. But I'm on top again — thank God & all the world's beautiful once more.

Love & kisses to all
Gene

ALS, InTI, Debs Collection.

□ *Debs was nominated as the Socialist party's presidential candidate at its Indianapolis convention held on May 12–18, 1912. Emil Seidel, socialist mayor of Milwaukee, was his running mate.*

EVD to Theodore Debs

May 18, 1912
Girard, Kansas

My dear old Pard:

The nomination has come despite everything I have done to prevent it. It is well. Destiny regulates these things & we have only to acquiesce & go forward with our duty. I am prepared. Physically I am 500 per cent stronger than I was four years ago. I feel *perfect*— better than I have felt for 20 years. The rest here & the scientific treatment & air & exercise & diet have made me brand new. Will see you next week & the joy will be great. With love to you and Gertrude & Marguerite I am always, old pard,

Yours to the last breath
Gene

ALS, InTI, Debs Collection.

□ *J. Mahlon Barnes, Debs's campaign manager in the 1908 Red Special campaign, was also named campaign manager for the 1912 election—a decision that created a storm of controversy in the Socialist party ranks due in part to charges of sexual promiscuity that had led to Barnes's resignation as national secretary of the party in 1911. Debs was obliged during the course of the 1912 campaign to devote considerable time and energy to "the Barnes Affair," as it was called. In the following letter Debs explains his ideas regarding the 1912 campaign and recalls the killing schedule made for him four years earlier.*

EVD to J. Mahlon Barnes

May 31, 1912
Terre Haute, Indiana

Dear Comrade Barnes:—

The only two appointments I have, as I understand it, are the ones at Chicago and New Castle. Please do not make any more until we meet at Chicago. I do not think that I shall fill any appointments at all during July or August. I have sufficient reason for this which I will make clear to the committee when we meet.

I am receiving many letters from comrades asking me not to make a long campaign. Warren insists that it should not be over six weeks. A long campaign sags and drags. I believe in concentration and in bringing all our forces to bear within the six weeks or two months preceding the election. Of course the local campaigning will go on continuously but I have reference now to the presidential campaign and to its management.

I have always put into every campaign the very best there was in me and I shall do the same this year, but I shall want a voice in determining what the program shall be. Four years ago the campaign was organized for me and I was never invited to attend a meeting of the committee, or to offer a suggestion. The only two requests I made of a very modest nature were declined. It will be different this year. I wish no arrangement made which involves me without being consulted.

I shall not be wanting in physical and mental powers to do my full duty, but I shall object to any arrangement under which I am taxed beyond the powers of any human being, and the many letters I am receiving show conclusively that the comrades who nominated me do not want a load put upon me such as no one can reasonably be expected to bear.

Four years ago I was booked 68 straight days without one single day of intermission and in that time I made about 560 speeches. No man has ever made a campaign like it before or since. Not even Bryan or Roosevelt has ever spoken over six days a week. When I returned from my long Western tour of thousands of miles and hundreds of speeches not even one day was allowed me before being rushed off to the East in {a} car so foul that {it} was not fit for an animal to be shipped in. From the start to the finish not a single day was allowed me to nurse my voice or to rest my body and at many of the places, Philadelphia among the rest, three and {four} big {evening} meetings were arranged after a hard day's speaking along the road, and that I did not break down utterly, as most men would have done, is simply because of my love for the socialist movement and because I have a constitution of iron.

It is now thirty-six years since I began to speak for organized labor and to fight the battles of the labor movement and I am 56 years of age, but I have never been fitter for a campaign, never better qualified for service than now, and I shall not disappoint my comrades, but I wish my dates arranged and program made with the same consideration for the limitations of human capacity and endurance that every comrade expects for himself. I anticipate no misunderstanding in this matter and am confident that we shall be able to decide upon arrangements that will be entirely satisfactory to all concerned.

You need not take the time to answer this. I understand we are to be in Chicago on Saturday the 15th. We will then have ample time to talk matters over.

I am with all good greetings and kind wishes,

Yours fraternally
[Eugene V. Debs]

TLc, InTI, Debs Collection.

□ *During the Progressive Era many sincere Americans believed Prohibition was a fundamental reform that would lead to the solution of most of society's ills and evils, and this point of view was eventually embodied in the Eighteenth Amendment. In this letter to Charles Jones, chairman of the Prohibition party, Debs explains his opposition to that party's goals.*

EVD to Charles R. Jones

June 1, 1912
[Terre Haute, Indiana]

Dear Mr. Jones: —

Your communication addressed to me at Girard has been forwarded to me here and I have given it careful reading and now beg to thank you for having taken the pains to express yourself so fully and for the kindly spirit in which you have written to me. But I cannot agree with you as to prohibition. I do not in the least question your integrity. On the contrary I have perfect faith in your sincerity and I can read in all your lines how deeply you feel upon this question, but still I am unable to accept your conclusion. I regret not having time to write to you as fully as I would wish, but after three months' absence from here and on the edge of a national campaign I have so many hundreds of letters pouring in and am so besieged that it is utterly impossible for me to do justice to such letters as you have written to me.

As a socialist I am for the suppression of the liquor traffic but I am convinced that it will never be accomplished by prohibition. I have been in Kansas too long to be deceived as to what prohibition means in-so-far as the liquor evil is concerned. Not until capitalism is overthrown and the profit is taken out of the whisky business will that business be destroyed. When the workers are economically free and when they get what they produce and can live decently and when the present parasitic and idle elements have to work for what they get and produce what they consume, intemperance as it now curses society will disappear.

Frances Willard understood this after years of careful study and investigation and it was this that made her a socialist.

I admit all you say about the liquor evil and we differ only in the way this evil shall be destroyed. Prohibition will never do it. Besides, there is but one way to get at the root of the evil and that is by abolishing the profit system of which intemperance, like prostitution, is the legitimate fruit. The socialists are right in refusing to be led away from the main issue and to give attention to the thousand and more of ills that flow from capitalism, private ownership, profit and exploitation, to the neglect of the main, fundamental issue and the weakening consequent thereupon, if not the destruction, of their revolutionary movement.

For reasons of my own I am constitutionally opposed to the principle of prohibition. Theft and murder are prohibited but it is to be doubted if these crimes are lessened to any appreciable extent on that account. The world pays too much attention to effects while it ignores causes and this is as true of the liquor evil as it is of any of the rest of the evils that afflict society.

Pardon these hasty and inadequate lines. I am under such stress on account of the accumulation consequent upon my long absence and the many other demands upon my time that I cannot send you a more worthy answer to your very sincere and appealing communication.

I thank you from the depths of my heart for your more than kind and generous personal words and beg to assure you of my deepest respect and appreciation.

Yours faithfully
[Eugene V. Debs]

TLc, EVD Foundation, Debs Home.

□ *Fred Warren was the editor of the* Appeal to Reason, *which was the most powerful supporter of Debs's candidacy in the 1912 campaign, reaching some half a million subscribers. In the following letter Debs explains the origins of and identifies the contributors to a testimonial pamphlet, "What Debs's Neighbors Say about Him," that was published during the campaign. In the November election Debs received 901,873 votes, or roughly 6 percent of the total votes cast, running fourth behind Woodrow Wilson, Theodore Roosevelt, and William Howard Taft.*

EVD to Fred D. Warren

August 2, 1912
Terre Haute, Indiana

My dear Fred;—
  The Rev. J. H. Hollingsworth, a fine old minister who gave up his church and the brightest wordly prospects on account of Socialism, and now a member of the Socialist party, and a warm personal friend of mine, has for some time been quietly at work getting an expression of the people of Terre Haute as to my character and standing in the community in which I have lived all my life. I knew nothing of this until the work was completed and placed in my hands. These testimonials have been reduced to eight and these representing the various elements that make up the community and among the oldest, best known and best respected citizens.
  One of these is from Hulman and Co., my former employers, one of the largest wholesale grocery establishments in the United States. Another is from Max Ehrmann, the famous author and poet whose home is here. Another from Prof. Curry, professor of literature in the State Normal School which is located here. Another is by Clarence Royse one of the most brilliant young lawyers in this section, and when you have read what he has written, entirely apart from the personality he treats, you will get a fine idea of the high character of this exceptionally elevated mind and soul. He is one lawyer in ten thousand, one it is a delight to know and some time you and Jake Sheppard must personally meet him. His personal character is as spotless as that of any man I have ever known and he commands the respect of every one in the community.
  Still another is by Viquesney, of the Viquesney Printing company, successors of Moore and Langen, to whom I paid a printing bill of over $3,000. owed by the A.R.U. out of lecture proceeds, and this fact is set forth in his statement. There has been a good deal of lying about my having become rich out of my lecture proceeds and this will help to set matters right. This is but one of the many debts of the A.R.U. I paid, aggregating a good many thousands of dollars,

and it took me about twelve years and all I earned in that time on the platform and otherwise over and above living expenses to pay these debts and save the A.R.U. free from reproach.

Another is by the oldest physician in Terre Haute, another by the oldest clothier, another by a leading manufacturer who happens also to be my neighbor.

I am reluctant to send you this matter myself but Comrade Hollingsworth felt that I should do so on account of your not knowing him and I did not feel as if I could decline him after his more than kindly interest and his trouble in the matter.

I wish you would take the time to read these over personally so that you may have a better idea of them. They are more than mere testimonials and they are free offerings from non socialists and will, I think, serve to prevent a repetition of a good many of the falsehoods that were put in circulation in the last campaign.

You have perhaps noticed that the Catholic priests are systematically spreading the falsehood that I have accumulated immense riches and that my only interest in the working class is to take advantage of their ignorance and fleece them of their earnings. This is especially true in Pennsylvania where reports of my enormous income are being spread and where it is also being said that my reputation was poor where I was known and that I was without standing among reputable people.

There is considerable of this matter and yet I am inclined to think that it will be worth while to give it space. It is not on my own account that I think this but on account of the harm that will come to the party if the false reports that are being and will continue to be more and more circulated as the campaign proceeds are not met and discounted in advance such as is here effectually done.

If the matter could all be inserted in a single issue it would show up best, especially if it could be done in the Appeal's regular sized type so it would be clear and readable.

In almost every mail we get there is a letter from some comrade who writes in to say that in his community there is some fellow who is circulating the report that I sold out the A.R.U., or that I have a million dollars deposited in New York, or that I am coining money on my investments, or some other lie, and wanting something to enable him to meet and deny these slanders. For this purpose there could hardly be anything better than the matter that is herein enclosed. I am sure that in almost every town and city this lying is going on and having a certain effect, and if the enclosed matter is published in the Appeal it will enable the Appeal workers and readers to take this issue of the Appeal and put it before these falsifiers and slanderers and effectually silence them.

You will note that I have stricken out some of the lines to reduce it as much as possible.

You are soon to begin to run the ten propaganda numbers of the Appeal and I am wondering if it would not a good idea to run this matter in the issue just preceding these numbers or perhaps in the same number that contains my propaganda article the first in the series. The copy for this, by the way, will be with you on time.

Use your own good judgment in the handling of this matter and anything you may see fit to do with it will be appreciated by

Yours always
E. V. Debs

TLS, Warren Papers, Schenectady, New York.

□ *Henry Mayer Hyndman was an English journalist, social reformer, and founder of the Social Democratic Federation (1891), which was the nucleus of the socialist movement in British politics. In the following letter Debs discusses the internal dissension in the Socialist party created by the decision at its 1912 national convention to expel members who opposed political action or advocated "sabotage or other methods of violence."*

EVD to H. M. Hyndman

January 31, 1913
Terre Haute, Indiana

My dear Hyndman: —

I have just read your splendid editorial in the current issue of Justice and I wish to drop you this line of thanks and appreciation not only for myself but in behalf of the many thousands of socialists on this side who love you and hold you in highest respect for your uncompromising loyalty to the socialist movement through all the years of your active life.

It is wonderful what a clear understanding you have of the situation on this side; much clearer I must admit than that of many of our own comrades.

Syndicalism has swooped down upon us and the capitalist papers and magazines are giving it unlimited space but the Socialist party is in no danger on account of it. Just at present there are some sharp divisions and some bitter controversies on account of it but the Socialist party will emerge all the stronger after syndicalism has had its fling.

The anarchists are all jubilant over the prospect that syndicalism may disrupt the Socialist party, but they will again be disappointed. There are many of our socialists who favor syndicalism and sabotage, or think they do, but the party is overwhelmingly opposed to both and will stick to the main track to the end. We are with you in your position and in due time you will be once more triumphantly vindicated. Revolutionary political action and revolutionary industrial organization will finally win out against all opposition both from without and within.

With love and greeting and warmest wishes I am, my dear old comrade,

Yours always
E. V. Debs

TLc, InTI, Debs Collection.

□ *William English Walling, a "millionaire socialist," became one of the Socialist party's most respected and influential writers and public speakers. In the following exchange of letters he and Debs discuss the impact of the party's decision to expel those members who opposed political action or who advocated violence, particularly the recall of William Haywood as a member of the party's national executive committee in February 1913.*

William English Walling to EVD

March 2, 1913
Cedarhurst, Long Island, New York

Dear Comrade Debs,

Items like the enclosed (from Perkins organ) have appeared in *every one* of the Capitalist papers of New York. Does this not show that Haywood's recall is taken as a victory of capitalism within the Socialist Party?

Do you approve of the statement on the recall ballot that Haywood was guilty of an untried charge against the Socialist Party (repudiation of political action)? Is not Montana right in demanding a new ballot? As we Socialists approve of proportional representation, ought it not to apply to party affairs? Even if Haywood only represents a third of the party is not this third entitled to some voice?

Do you not advocate {or approve} *some* of the practices that now go under the name of sabotage? Do you not approve of law-breaking under certain exceptional circumstances?

I have consulted with nobody in writing this and shall mention it to nobody. I am confident that your own judgement and initiative will lead you to the right action. I only trust that letters like mine may help to hasten any public statement you have in mind.

I sent you my "Socialism As It Is" and received no acknowledgment. Enclosed find some press notices. If you have not received it I shall send another copy.

Fraternally,
Wm English Walling

P.S. Are you aware that Haywood's supposed repudiation of political action lay in the exact use of your words "I do not ask the workingman for his vote"?

ALS, InTI, Debs Collection.

EVD to William English Walling

March 5, 1913
Terre Haute, Indiana

Dear Comrade Walling: —

It does not matter to me what the capitalist papers think is going on in the Socialist party as long as we can keep the party as it ought to be.

I regretted to see Haywood's recall but it was inevitable. He brought it on himself. I should not have put section 6 in the constitution but it is there and put there by the party and Haywood deliberately violated it. Is this not the fact?

The question of what sabotage means has nothing to do with the matter. Its advocates have shown that it means anything, everything, or nothing at all. If I had been in Haywood's place and had felt bound to advocate sabotage as he did I would have withdrawn from the party to do it. If I had deliberately violated the constitution I would have expected to be called to account for it. Else why a constitution at all?

The constitution also prohibits fusion with other parties. Suppose certain members fuse with other parties, would they have any fault to find if they were expelled from the party?

I am not now judging Haywood, I am answering your questions. I am free to confess, however, judging from some of the reports I have seen, that Haywood has been talking a good deal more like an anarchist than a socialist.

The I.W.W. for which Haywood stands and speaks is an anarchist organization in all except in name and this is the cause of all the trouble. Anarchism and socialism have never mixed and never will. The I.W.W. has treated the Socialist party most indecently to put it very mildly. When it gets into trouble it frantically appeals to the Socialist party for aid, which has always been freely rendered, and after it is all over the I.W.W. kicks the Socialist party in the face. That is the case put in plain words and the Socialist party has had enough of that sort of business and I don't blame them a bit. There are I.W.W. anarchists who are in the Socialist party for no other purpose than to disrupt it and the Socialist party is right in taking a decided stand against them.

Answering your questions specifically, (1) The statement on the recall ballot you refer to should in my opinion {have been} omitted. (2) I have not seen Montana's demand but so far as the right of it is concerned, whatever it may be, that is for the party to decide. (3) Certainly I approve of some of the practices that now go under the name of sabotage, for almost everything goes under that name. (4) The same answer as to law-breaking. There are certainly circumstances under which I advocate it but I must know what the circumstances are. (5) I think you know there is a very wide difference between the kind of political action Haywood advocates and the kind I advocate, even if we happen to use identical words.

I received the copy of your book and sent you quite an extended acknowledgment of it from Girard where it reached me. Sorry this letter did not get to you. Allow me to thank you now for it.

Pardon these hurried words as I am extremely busy. This letter is not private and you can use it as you wish.

Yours fraternally
[Eugene V. Debs]

TLc, InTI, Debs Collection.

□ *In this letter to Robert Sims, one of the framers of the Arizona Constitution and at the time warden of the state prison at Florence, Debs answers Sims's request for his opinion on capital punishment.*

EVD to Robert B. Sims

May 23, 1913
Charleston, West Virginia

Dear Mr. Sims: —
Pardon this belated acknowledgement of your favor of the 14th inst. which has been forwarded from Terre Haute and has only now reached me here.

I regret that in my present situation it is not possible for me to make such answer to your communication as I would like to do under more favorable circumstances.

The measure now pending in the State of Arizona providing for the abolition of the death penalty is one that should appeal to every just and humane person in the State. Capital punishment is simply a relic of barbarism. There is absolutely no justification for its survival in our present civilization. The taking of human life through criminal impulse or in an hour of passion by an individual is not to be compared to the immeasurably greater crime committed by the State when it deliberately puts to death the individual charged with such crime.

Society may not consistently condemn murder as long as it is itself red-handed with that crime.

We are now sufficiently enlightened to understand that what is known as crime is in a large measure due to unfortunate environment; that crime is in fact a disease, an infirmity, and that every consideration of humanity demands that the unfortunate victim of society's weakness or maladjustment, shall be treated with the same degree of patience, and with all the skill that science has made available, that is bestowed upon other human derelicts and infirmitives.

The people of Arizona have shown themselves to be so progressive and so entirely abreast of the enlightened spirit of the times in so many other matters that I feel safe ~~confident~~ in predicting that she will follow the lead of other progressive States and blot this insufferable stigma from her fame.

Thanking you for your kindness and with all good wishes, I remain
Yours sincerely,
[Eugene V. Debs]

TLc, InTI, Debs Collection.

☐ *In May 1913 Debs led a Socialist party committee that investigated and is-*
sued a widely circulated report on a bloody West Virginia coal strike. In June
the United States Senate launched an investigation into the strike, and Debs
was asked by Idaho's William Borah, chairman of the Senate committee, to share
his knowledge of conditions in the West Virginia mine fields.

EVD to William E. Borah

June 26, 1913
[Terre Haute, Indiana]

My dear Senator Borah:—

Your favor of the 23rd. inst. has been received and noted. Answering your inquiry I beg to say that there are a number of witnesses
who should in my opinion be heard by the Senate committee but who
were not given the opportunity to present their testimony at the
Charleston hearing. It appears that some of those participants in the
strike who were most relentlessly persecuted and suffered the greatest
wrongs were for some reason I am unable to understand not permitted
to appear before the committee at all. I have reference to Mother
Jones, who could undoubtedly give testimony that would have weighty
influence with the committee and be of interest to the country; also
John Brown, W.H. Thompson, C.H. Boswell, Fred Merrick and others,
some of whom were seized outside of the military zone and tried
and sentenced under martial law in violation of their constitutional
rights. It seems to me that all such testimony as this which comes at
first hand from those who were active participants in the troubles
under investigation would be of value in arriving at a just conclusion
and clearing up this unfortunate situation.

I have taken the liberty in some correspondence with Brown and
Thompson in the last day to suggest that they write to you in regard
to being heard by the committee. I can give you all their addresses
if you should wish to communicate with them, or with any of them,
direct.

I have wondered why none of the state and county officials of
Kanawha county were placed upon the stand and questioned as to
their participation in and knowledge of certain acts and facts in connection with the strike and the trials and convictions under martial
law which have been so bitterly condemned and have provoked such
widespread resentment.

Complaint has been made in letters I have received that powerful
influences have been brought to bear to shield Governor Hatfield,

Sheriff Hill and other state and county officials. What foundation there is, if any, for this charge I do not know but certainly I hope that before the Senate committee has concluded its labors it will have brought before it every person of whatever rank or degree, official and otherwise, whose testimony is necessary to have every essential fact brought out that the responsibility may be placed where it properly belongs and that such measures may be taken as may be deemed necessary to prevent a recurrence of the terrible wrongs which the miners of West Virginia and their wives and children have suffered during the past fifteen months.

If there is any well grounded suspicion that any person or set of persons, be they whom they may, are shielding from the consequences of their acts, the confidence the people now have in the fairness, fearlessness and rigid impartiality of the committee will suffer and the effect of its findings and the value of its work will be correspondingly impaired.

I have no reason to believe that the committee has been other than fair and conscientious in reference to the desire to hear all material testimony and this I am certain {is true} in a special sense of yourself and Senator Martine.

I take this occasion to call your particular attention to the case of W.H. Thompson and his associates and the suppression of his paper, The Socialist and Labor Star, at Huntington, the looting and destruction of the newspaper property and the burglarizing of his home and the carrying away of his private papers by a squad of soldiers after midnight. I think this one of the most outrageous affairs that ever occurred under a civilized government and that every one who had to do with it should be ferreted out and punished to the full extent of the law. The soldiers in this instance carried on their work of destruction and pillage over the protest of the sheriff and this can be proved beyond any question of doubt.

And yet I am informed by Mr. Thompson that after vainly waiting for four days at Charleston he was turned away and denied the opportunity to tell his story.

If there is any act of cruelty and outrage and of utter defiance of constitutional and lawful rights in connection with the West Virginia strike it is the wanton destruction of this newspaper property and the midnight sacking of the editor's home after being thrown into jail without warrant and without the least knowledge as to the reason why.

Huntington, bear in mind, was far beyond the military zone when Thompson and his associates were seized and thrown into jail at midnight by a squad of soldiers, their property which was a general publishing concern, destroyed, smashed, torn into shreds and scattered about for blocks, including orders to the general trade ready for delivery, and when Thompson's home was entered, after he was jailed, and his wife, who was ill, subjected to the terrors of such a barbarous attack, while the soldiers went from room to room, searched every drawer and ransacked and carried away with them private papers and letters, with all the brutality and bravado of Russian cossacks. I avouch that I know enough of this particular case to warrant my saying to you that every material fact here stated can be substantiated by incontrovertible testimony before your committee.

Let the members of the Senate committee imagine if they can just how they and their wives would feel if they were seized and torn from their homes at midnight by a squad of soldiers without knowing why, thrown into jail without warrant, their homes sacked and their private letters and papers stolen, what they would think of the United States constitution, and what sentiments of patriotic devotion to their country would be inspired in their breasts!

Enclosed I beg to hand you an article I have written in which this matter is more fully presented.

Pardon me for having written you at such length. I well know how busy you are and I should not have ventured to intrude upon your time under any other circumstances.

Thanking you for your kind and considerate attention and with all good wishes for the success of your work and for you personally I remain

Yours very sincerely
[Eugene V. Debs]

TLc, InTI, Debs Collection.

□ *Debs spent the month of October 1913 in the "clear, cold atmosphere" of Estes Park, Colorado, drawn there by the hope of "getting well."*

EVD to Theodore Debs

October 2, 1913
Estes Park, Colorado

My Dear old Pard:

Arrived here at 3 PM yesterday after a fine ride through the mountains in a steamer—auto. Left Denver at 8 AM—arrived at

Loveland, 60 miles north, at 11. left at 11 in steamer—auto with 6 passengers & arrived here at 3—we passed through a grand canyon & I wished often that you were with me to enjoy it. Am 30 miles from railroad, 7500 ft high & a clear, cold atmosphere. Feel like I shall be greatly benefited. I am temporarily at a nice little hotel here where the Sweets have secured a room for me. Have a cozy room, clean bed, electric light, hot & cold water, closet in house & yet there are hardly 50 people in the little village at present. Thousands come in here in summer months. Yesterday just after leaving Boulder saw a lone prairie chicken—it lit close to the train & seemed very big to me. Shortly after saw a beautiful pheasant & it was a winged glory. The latter are protected by law all the year around.

The people have left the ranch I was to go on so I must find another. Mrs. Sweet gave me several names.

Heavy frost last night & every night. It has already snowed here. The snow-covered mountains are all about me. Wish you were here. Have but one thought here & that is to *get well & strong* & want you to do the same. Don't write much, nor will I. *Get out & get well!* All depends on that. Tell everybody I'm away from railroad & mails, cut off everything *as short* as you can & *answer nothing* that does not positively have to be answered. I shall work early & late every minute, to get into condition. *I can & by the eternal, I will.* That's sure. When I get home we'll make things hum—but we can't do it as *corpses.* Dead men cut sad figures in live roles.

You old hound I shall beat you to a pulp on sight. Kisses to you and Gertrude and Marguerite.

Enclosed find some stamps. Begin sending letters & papers & all my mail here Estes Park P.O.   Colo.

AL, InTI, Debs Collection.

EVD to Theodore Debs

October 30, 1913
[Estes Park, Colorado]

My dear Kude:
Just read a lovely letter from Reynolds. He is indeed a fine loyal soul.

To-morrow I'm to leave here for the village. I have grown to love my little cabin so that I am truly sorry to think that to-morrow I will sweep it out and tidy it up for the last time. You must some time see this place & we'll come together next time.

Mr. Mills took me out to the beaver colonies again & I saw a beaver, the first I ever saw, & was intensely interested in him.

I feel better, clearer, stronger, cheerfuler and more confident, self-reliant and hopeful than for the last five years. This life in the wilds has done me a world of good. My blood is turning red again and I can once more feel it tingling & bubbling in my veins & the old enthusiasm kindling in my soul. As I'm to leave to-morrow we're to have a farewell at the cabin of Mrs. Sherman & her son John, whom I have grown to love as dear old friends. Mrs. Sherman's husband is editor of the Chicago Inter-Ocean.

The secret of health, bodily and mental, is to eat moderately, eat slowly, anything you please, chew it well, & spend every minute you can *out-doors.* Rain or shine, snow or sleet or hail, go out, stay out, take long walks, *breathe in deeply* the fresh air & health is bound to come & stay. If [you can] sleep outdoors all [the] better. *Oxygen is [life-giving & the]* body could not live [five?] minutes without it. The blood & tissue hunger for oxygen & must have it. You & Gertrude must go out daily for long walks & keep it up *every day.* Let nothing prevent. *Neglect everything to be outdoors.* Every minute out in the fresh air is a blood-builder & a life-preserver.

Have just called on Mr. Mills to settle my bill. The regular rate for the accomodations I had would have been $115.00 for 23 days. Mr. Mills said *Nothing* is the amt of your bill. I protested & insisted & finally he agreed to accept $20. to at least cover the cords of fuel I burnt up. Mr. Mills is one of the noblest souls I've ever met & you too must know him. From now on we're friends in the closest bonds and I'll tell you he's a friend worth having.

Can now split wood hours at a time without getting tired—when I first came here 10 minutes used up all my wind & strength & left me limp as a rag. See? My muscles now stand out like whipcords. This means that there's a damn slim prospect for your hide. Do you follow me?

Sunday evening I speak on Socialism at the only church in Estes Park & all the folks will be there.

Friday morning.

Last night Mr. Mills & Mrs. Sherman gave me a little farewell dinner here, one of the sweetest occasions of my life. Mrs. Sherman is an expert cook & you ought to have seen the dinner. A delicious leg of mutton, mashed potatoes, peas, radishes, fruit salad, honey, cakes, coffee etc. etc. After dinner we went to Mrs. Sherman's lovely log cabin & had Grafanola music, stories, etc. etc. Again coffee was served and then we all said a happy good night. All meet here on common ground—pure democracy. The men all had our pants in our boots & were dressed in our corduroys & overalls. The help, including the cook, carpenter and others were as one with the host & hostess. That's my style of society. Never in my life have I spent a happier evening.

At 4 this A.M. I go down to the village —9 miles & there I will stay till I leave for Denver. They will all come down to hear me speak Sunday evening.

Love & kisses to all!

Gene

ALS, InTI, Debs Collection.

□ *Helen Keller, who overcame the effects of an illness that left her blind, deaf, and mute at the age of nineteen months to graduate cum laude from Radcliffe in 1904, entered a career of writing and lecturing that took her around the world many times and led to her recognition as one of the world's great women. This letter was written shortly after Keller had given a lecture in Terre Haute, accompanied by her life-long teacher, friend, and companion, Anne Sullivan Macy.*

EVD to Helen Keller

December 23, 1913
Terre Haute, Indiana

My dear Comrade Keller:—

Very sorry am I and so is Mrs. Debs that we missed you on your recent visit here. We are just returned after several months absence and among the first things we heard was of your wonderful address here and its profound impression upon our people. It was a complete conquest and you seem to have captivated the entire community. Please let me tender my hearty congratulations to both you and dear Mrs. Macy.

This morning I met Mr. Gwinn and he was all aglow with enthusiasm over your visit here. He told me of how you had touched the hearts of all your hearers and won their instantaneous love and admiration. And then he told me of the more than kind words you had spoken of me and coming from no other source could such an expression have touched me more deeply or afforded me greater satisfaction. I need not say to you that the sentiments of appreciation and regard so kindly and generously expressed by you are heartily reciprocated by me, and some good day I hope it may be my pleasure to take you by the hand and make personal acknowledgment of the sense of obligation I feel for the incomparable struggle you have made, in the face of a thousand disheartening obstacles, to serve the cause of humanity.

Mrs. Debs and the comrades here join in hearty greetings to you and Mrs. Macy and in wishing you a right joyous and prosperous New Year. Believe me always

Your loving comrade
Eugene V. Debs

TLS, American Foundation for the Blind, Keller Collection.

□ *Debs ended his editorial work and public speaking for the* Appeal to Reason *at the time of the 1912 presidential campaign. His editorials in the* Rip-Saw *continued until that magazine, a monthly published in St. Louis, was suppressed during World War I.*

EVD to Fred D. Warren

January 19, 1914
Terre Haute, Indiana

My dear Fred:—

I have made an arrangement with the Rip-Saw, to write their editorial etc. and speak under their auspices, and I think I ought to tell you about it. I had intended and was preparing to organize a little bureau of our own when I got strong enough to work again, believing that I could do my work better, be at home more, and get better results all around. But Phil Wagner and Harry Tichenor came over here and made me a proposition and terms that were so favorable in every way that I concluded to accept them for a time at least. I could not possibly have asked for anything better or more satisfactory than the conditions they proposed and I accepted.

I shall always have the same warm feeling for you personally and for all of the Appeal comrades and workers. All of them treated me at the very best and I can only think of them with feelings of thankfulness and affection.

Hoping that I shall get to see you occasionally and that we can continue to help each other in doing our work as we have in the past, and with kindest remembrances to Mrs. Warren and to the little Warrens who always greeted me so lovingly, I remain as ever

Yours in the cause

E. V. Debs

TLS, Warren Papers, Schenectady, New York.

☐ *The hierarchy of the Roman Catholic church played a leading role in the attack on American socialism in general, and on Debs in particular, in the period before World War I. At the same time, many of Debs's best friends and strongest supporters were found among Catholics, including some priests. His opinion of the church hierarchy is plainly stated in the following letter.*

EVD to Claude G. Bowers

April 22, 1914
Terre Haute, Indiana

My dear Friend Bowers: —

Returning here I find the copy of your eloquent and poetic address at Boston on St. Patrick's Day awaiting me, for which please accept my thanks. I have gone through its pages and have found it to be beautiful and elevated in the sentiments expressed as is everything that comes from your pen or tongue, but I fear that addresses and occasions of this kind will be of little real help to the poverty stricken and suffering people of Ireland. The one thing they are suffering from is priestcraft and superstition and as long as they are ruled as they now are by the Roman political machine masquerading as a holy religious institution they will remain where they are and where they have been all these centuries, and no amount of glorification of Irish history and eulogy of Irish patriots will alter their slavish lot.

Look into Italy and Spain, the Philippines and Mexico, where the Roman church has ruled for centuries in holy partnership with the robber kings, barons, plutocrats and other ruling and exploiting classes and you will see what is the matter with Ireland, and this is what ought to be said at a gathering of Irish on St. Patrick's Day but which, if said, would be resented by the Irish politicians of whom there are many in Boston and who are in fact the enemies and not the friends of the oppressed and long suffering Irish people.

As to Irish Home Rule, so-called, about which there has been so much fuss, it is ninety-nine per cent pure humbug and if established tomorrow would be of no earthly help to the peasants and toilers of Ireland, nor make their lot one particle more tolerable than it is today.

Priestcraft is the curse of Ireland, priestcraft in alliance with king-craft and landlordcraft, but the orator who would dare to make this true statement of Ireland's woes at a banquet composed of Irish gentlemen would quite likely be handled pretty roughly by way of applause and appreciation. That smooth and smug cardinal at Boston and that other at Baltimore who are hand in glove with Tammany Murphy, with "Jim" Hill, Andrew Carnegie, Thomas Fortune Ryan and that gang of brigands are the real enemies of the Irish people and they and their hypocritical ilk who hobnob with the rich while they roll their eyes heavenward, perched piously like the blood-sucking leeches they are, on the backs of the suffering poor, will have to be gotten rid of once and for all before poverty and misery, born of ignorance and superstition, relax their grasp upon the toiling and producing masses.

"The Irish Dawn" is in the class-conscious awakening of the Irish toiler class and their marshalling beneath the banner of International Revolutionary Socialism and this thank God sows with stars of hope their otherwise black and starless night.

Thanking you and with all kind wishes I am as ever

Yours sincerely
E. V. Debs

P.S. There are two books I venture to suggest that you ought to read. You will doubtless find them in the Washington library. They are "The Call of the Carpenter" and "The Carpenter and the Rich Man," both by Bouck White. You will thank me for making the suggestion.

TLS, InU, Lilly Library, Bowers MSS.

☐ *Daniel De Leon was one of the most influential American socialists of the pre–World War I era, leader of the small Socialist Labor party, and frequent critic of Debs and the Socialist Party of America. At the time of De Leon's death in 1914, Debs wrote a widely reprinted "Tribute to Daniel De Leon" and, in the following letter, asks that the essay be included in the* International Socialist Review. *Charles Kerr, the editor of the* Review *and a leading publisher of socialist books and pamphlets, chose not to print the tribute.*

EVD to Charles H. Kerr

July 11, 1914
Xenia, Ohio

Dear Comrade Kerr:—

The enclosed article on DeLeon was written for the Rip-Saw but in making up the forms it was omitted, to my regret. I shall see that it goes in the August issue and in the meantime I am sending it to the New York People. But I have a personal reason for wishing it to appear in the International Socialist Review and I am hoping you can find room for it in the August issue without imposing on your space. I already have an article with you but you may be able to accommodate this also without asking too much.

A good many members of the Socialist party will not like this article at all and will in fact resent it, but no matter. I think that what I have said is due to DeLeon and therefore I am saying it. Personally I have as good ground as anyone, probably more, for grievance against him, as the paper he edited lied about me outrageously for a long time after the Socialist party was organized; these lies were proven to him to be lies and he knew they were lies but he never retracted a word he had slanderously published about me. He had, moreover, as Lucien Sanial said, "an extraordinary talent for intrigue" and he was anything but scrupulous and honest about a good many things, but when all this is said there still remains his great work for the movement for which we are bound to give him credit and I cannot permit the recollection of any personal wrong he did me interfere with my duty to him and to the cause for which he lived and died. I therefore hope you can do me the kindness to give space to the enclosed article in your August issue.

Yours fraternally,
Eugene V. Debs

TLc, InTI, Debs Collection.

☐ *Debs was one of the most popular (and highly paid) public speakers of his time, but the long lecture tours took their toll, as he explains in this letter to Frank O'Hare, business manager of the* Rip-Saw *and the person who scheduled Debs's tours.*

EVD to Frank P. O'Hare

February 14, 1915
Pocatello, Idaho

Dear Frank:—

Whatever possessed you to put Tooelle into this schedule? The place is almost inaccessible—no earthly way to get from there to Burley and the latter is lost to us, notwithstanding I have been up all night and am about half dead in the vain struggle to get there. There is but one train to Burley and that leaves Salt Lake City at midnight and it is humanly impossible to get back there from Tooele to make that train.

The snow was so deep and the roads so bad that no auto owner would let us have a machine at any price—the only thing we could get was a light open buggy. Naylor of Salt Lake went down with me. I cut off my speech at 9.40 and got into the buggy, steaming hot, in the vain hope of getting to Salt Lake in time to make Burley. In 15 minutes I was half frozen, chilled to the marrow, and my feet soon became like ice. The snow and half-frozen mud from the horses hoofs covered us and we were till midnight on the road—then we had to wait in the cutting cold no depot—for the train—and all for nothing because there was no possible train connection. The buggy was hardly big enough for two, yet three of us were jammed into it taking turns sitting on one another. It was another Kennett ride —enough to kill an ox—and today I'm sick, my throat is raw, my whole body aches, and Burley, where there is to be one of the biggest meetings on the route, sacrificed—no possible way of getting there. I have just wired them a long and detailed explanation expressing regrets etc. etc.

I have now been on the road five weeks and have averaged 18 to 20 hours daily on trains, in the hotels at work, meeting visitors, interviews, comrades etc., but last night alone came nearer knocking me out than the whole rest of the trip. Today I am unfit for anything and ought to cancel the rest of the dates and go home. Must I have such a damned killing dose as {this} administered to me on every trip? I am willing to be killed for the cause but I don't want to die a fool's death. Kennett and Toole each set me back six months. I can stand the work as well as any one but I can't go out of a hot hall, covered with sweat, and climb into an open buggy on a bitter cold, raw night and ride 17 miles over half-frozen roads and then stand waiting for a train until I'm frozen numb—nor can anybody else— and it seems that the only way I can stop it is to do my own booking and that's what I'd better do.

I am so constituted, foolishly perhaps, that I would have taken that ride and made every effort in my power to reach Burley if I had died in my tracks.

They have written me several letters from Burley telling me they were to have the biggest meeting ever held there—people coming in from miles around—and now they are to be disappointed. It cuts me to the quick and makes my heart bleed for those comrades. I feel like a criminal although I am not to blame and have risked my life and outraged my health in the vain and desperate attempt to prevent their disappointment.

I'm not angry and I don't want to find fault—but I can't help but feel keenly the trials of the present hour. To disappoint an audience is to me a crime. It seems that I am fated to be punished and perhaps I ought to be glad that I can stand it. I've had nearly 40 years of it and I'll try my best to be thankfull for it all.

With love,
Gene

P.S. There was no train out of Tooele until Sunday afternoon and if I hadn't taken that midnight ride I would not only have missed Burley but Twin Falls also.

TLc, InTI, Debs Collection.

□ *Following the outbreak of World War I in Europe in 1914, American so-cialists found an increasingly divisive issue that would eventually become a near-fatal one: could socialists, committed to internationalism, support their country in a war? Allan Benson, who would become the Socialist party's presi-dential candidate in 1916, was a leader in the War Referendum movement, which called for a popular vote of approval before any declaration of war. When the following letters were exchanged, Benson was engaged in an effort to secure a Socialist party referendum on the issue and sought Debs's support.*

Allan L. Benson to EVD

March 19, 1915
Yonkers, New York

Dear Debs:

I have your letter of the 19th and have read it with interest. I did not know that the German Socialists had ever demanded the democratization of the war-making power. I do not care if they did. I am not trying to be a hero. I am trying to end war. If the German Socialists beat me to it in advancing this idea, I am going to try to beat them in something else. I am going to try to make this idea take root in the popular mind. The German Socialists did not do that. *I am going to do it.* I have the goods. I know how to dress windows. I am going to keep at the job until it is done. I shall make the facts of this so plain that even Socialists will see them. I know that thousands of Socialists already see the facts. You speak of the improbability that I will ever be able to put the question to a vote of the party. Nothing is more certain than that I shall put this to a vote of the party. I am going to come within an eyelash of it this spring. I shall probably fail at that, but I shall not fail in the days that will follow this spring. Nine thousand votes are necessary to put it to a national referendum. I had 7,000 votes last week. I could go out now and speak in a few cities in the middle west and get the votes. I should have won anyway if Hillquit had not upset New York. But I am not going out after votes because I know my book will do the job in the next year or two and do it thoroughly.

I ask you if you detect any sign of party inability to grasp the idea when one man, in a few months, without the help of anybody who could help, and with the opposition of Hillquit, could start a movement that could command 7,000 votes in so short a time? The slightest breath of approval from you or from anybody who had power, could turn the scale toward victory now. I don't expect help from anybody who doubts the expediency of the plan, or who does not believe in it. But with or without help, I am going to make the rank and file see it, and I hope even to make the leaders see it. I should have liked to win this spring, but if I can't, I'll win when I can.

I shall keep the letter I have just received from you, as well as the other one in which you made certain observations about the war-referendum and, in a week or two, will endeavor to meet the points you make in a chapter in my book. I shall answer them to your perfect satisfaction. I can see the answers as plainly as I can see this typewriter.

You are entirely too generous in what you say about my work. I have worked under a tremendous inspiration and have done the best I could, but what the effect has been and will be, God only knows — at least I do not.

Whatever you do, don't get the idea that I am in the least irritated because you could not see your way to help. I know that in whatever you do or don't do, you are on the square, and that is all I ask of any man.

Yours Truly,
Allan L. Benson

TLS, InTI, Debs Collection.

EVD to Allan L. Benson

March 22, 1915
Terre Haute, Indiana

My dear Benson: —

Your communication of the 18th. inst. has just been received and carefully read. In the closing paragraph you assure me that you are not in the least irritated and yet I must conclude that you must have been at least a bit "heated" in what you had to say in answer to my letter. If there is not a distinct rebuke in what you have written then I certainly misunderstand you. If, as you say, "the slightest breath of approval" from me would give you victory, my refusing you that breath would certainly justify your rebuke.

Now I am not in the least sensitive when I am dealing with a comrade in whom I have confidence such as I have in you, even though he speak his mind plainly, as you have done, and find fault with me for any real or fancied shortcoming on my part. In fact, I think all the more of him for being frank with me for I would rather be frankly criticised, even condemned, than to be hypocritically commended.

In the scores of times I have commended you and your work against war from the public platform and in the articles I have written and the letters I have sent out to the same effect, it seems to me that I have given you that "slightest breath of approval" which you deny me in the letter now before me.

It would be not only strange but a miracle if you and I were in perfect agreement on this great question upon which scarcely two can be found who hold identical views. You have concentrated all your splendid abilities in the war against war, while I have concentrated the little strength I have in the war against capitalism, the breeder of war, refusing steadily to abandon the main issue and to give myself wholly to secondary issues under any circumstances whatsoever. This has not prevented me, however, from devoting a considerable part of my time to the question of war in every speech I have made not only since the European war began but many years before.

I have never had occasion to criticise you but I am going to do so now for I think you have given me for the first time license to do so. I do not like this last letter from you at all and I excuse it on the ground that notwithstanding your protest to the contrary you were in a state of irritation when you wrote it. You doubtless preserved a copy and if you will look it over and note the number of I's in it you may understand that while such {a} large personal claim might be expected in a letter written by Berger, it appears to me strangely out of place in a letter from Benson.

Reading your letter the conclusion is forced upon one that you feel that this whole anti-war agitation and the responsibility for it has fallen upon your shoulders, and that the whole tremendous task of converting the nation had devolved upon you, that you have been abandoned, deserted of everyone who should have given aid, that you have done and are doing it all, that all others have fluked and that you are going to carry the banner single-handed to victory.

Now I think that an unfortunate mental attitude, to say nothing of the exaggeration of the indictment, and I fear that Hillquit has so lodged in your craw for the moment that you have become splenetic in your attitude toward those who do not agree in toto with your program. You give credit to no single person for a particle of aid or encouragement or co-operation.

Do not understand me as objecting to egotism or to a man's profound faith in himself and his capacity, such as is expressed in your letter, for I know that there are times when even the most intense self-importance and fanaticism are essential in the accomplishment of a task, but in the present instance I do not think you are justified in flouting all others impatiently and asserting the claim that they have done nothing, and that you and you alone are going to put an end to war. In your letter you say very positively, your words underscored:

There are personal as well as other reasons why I would be among the last to detract from the value of your service in this crisis or to under-estimate its importance, but when you say that you "have not had the help of anyone who could help" and proceed upon that assumption to claim that you stand alone in the war against war you are saying that for yourself which, if it be true, were better left to be said by others.

You will note by enclosed letter that I have an article with the Appeal on your anti-war crusade. In this poor expression you will see what I have said and have tried to do to help you in all my travels.

This is all. It was my duty to be frank and I have been so. My confidence in your integrity is absolute; my faith in your judgement is great. You are a man and not a god and therefore have a man's liability to err. I know, having erred a thousand times. It may be that you are right and that I am wrong. In either case my respect and affection for you remain undiminished, and when you see a flaw in me I shall expect you to point it out to me and set me right.

It may be that you have been denied support you should have received but I prefer to believe that all good comrades and true, each working along his own line and in accordance with his own ideas of his particular part, are co-operating as efficiently as may reasonably be expected, to put an end to war and to the system that produces war.

With all wishes for your success and all personal regards I remain as ever,

Yours fraternally,
[Eugene V. Debs]

TLc, InTI, Debs Collection.

☐ *In 1915 Debs wrote and spoke frequently on behalf of Joe Hill, a Swedish immigrant whose Wobbly songs—"Preacher and the Slave," "Casey Jones—The Union Scab," "There Is Power in a Union," and "Nearer My Job to Thee"— became permanent parts of labor-song history. In January 1914 Hill was arrested in Salt Lake City on a murder charge, in June of that year he was tried and convicted, and for the next seventeen months he remained in prison while a massive campaign to secure a new trial for him was carried forward. Eventually the Swedish government, Samuel Gompers, and President Woodrow Wilson joined the campaign, but Governor William Spry and other authorities in Utah denied Hill a new trial and he was executed by a firing squad on November 19, 1915.*

EVD to William Spry

August 20, 1915
Terre Haute, Indiana

Dear Governor Spry:—

Please allow me to say a word in behalf of Joseph Hillstrom (also known as Joe Hill). From the reports that have come to me from those in position to know the facts and whom I regard as entirely trustworthy, I am convinced that there is more than a reasonable doubt as to the guilt of this unfortunate brother of ours in the cause of labor. He was convicted upon circumstantial evidence, denied the right to choose his own counsel, while at the same time there was unquestionably a strong prejudice against him on account of his activity in the labor movement.

Joe Hill is a poet, a writer of songs, a man of soul, a tender and sympathetic nature and the crime of murder is as foreign to him and as unthinkable as it would be to any other man of like temperament. For this reason and others I will not trouble you with I beg you to give serious consideration to the case of Joe Hill and if you do I am confident you will grant him executive clemency. Joe Hill is not a murderer; he is a man and the great state of Utah where murder is so abhorred cannot afford to take his life.

Thanking you sincerely for myself and for the working people in whose behalf Joe Hill has labored and suffered and made many sacrifices I remain,

Yours very truly,
[Eugene V. Debs]

TLc, InTI, Debs Collection.

□ *William E. Sweet was the son of one of Debs's closet friends, Channing Sweet of Denver, Colorado. An investment banker in Denver and later governor of Colorado (1923–25), William Sweet was a member of Denver's Mile High Club, which included many of Colorado's business and professional leaders. The following exchange of letters involves Sweet's proposal that Debs speak before the Mile High Club.*

William E. Sweet to EVD

August 26, 1915
Denver, Colorado

Dear Mr. Debs:

I understand from father that you are comtemplating a trip to Denver next Fall. Would it be possible to make a date for the Mile High Club? We have slipped up on this once or twice before.

With kind regards and awaiting your prompt advices, I am

Very truly yours,
Wm E Sweet

ALS, InTI, Debs Collection.

EVD to William E. Sweet

August 28, 1915
[Terre Haute, Indiana]

My dear Mr. Sweet:—

Your note has just come and replying I have to say that I have not yet, so far as I am advised, any engagement in Colorado. All my dates, so far as the route sheet shows are in Oklahoma and Texas. It is possible however that negotiations are pending for dates in Colorado as the booking is done in St. Louis.

You know of course that {for} you personally I would gladly do anything but to be candid with you I do not think it would be well for you or for the Mile High Club or myself to speak before that Club at this time. I understand that the officials of the coal companies are members of the Club and if so I should certainly have to denounce them to their faces as arch criminals and conspirators, debauchers of the state's politics, committers of murder and of other crimes too numerous to mention. I am filled with the reports being issued by the Federal Board of Industrial Relations exposing these rich men as the vilest criminals that ever went unhung and I could not be true to myself if I stood in their presence without telling them so. I certainly would not deliver myself of a lot of polished platitudes and go away from there with their applause ringing in my ears and despising myself for my hypocrisy. I assume that you are reading the reports being issued in installments by Frank Walsh and his Federal Commission and if you are you know beyond any question of doubt that these mine owners and their official hirelings are the coldest-blooded murderers, woman-ravishers and baby-roasters that ever figured in the annals of crime. They are wholly responsible and the Commission brands them for exactly what they are. Every drop of my blood is hot with indignation as I read the positive proof, the unimpeachable evidence of their crimes against the state and against the men, women and children of the suffering poor who by their labor and sacrifice produced every dollar of their wealth. I cannot think of these crimes against the unfortunate and weak; I cannot think of the criminal conviction of Lawson, the passing of a measure through a rotten legislature at the instigation of these rich and respectable criminals to put a low shyster on the bench by special appointment of a degenerate governor, the tool of these criminals, to send innocent men to the gallows; I cannot think of these brutal and disgraceful outrages upon civilization and humanity and everything of decent report among men without feeling every drop in my veins running hot and there is only one way I could deal with them and shall deal with them and that is to denounce them with all the passion that fills my soul and seek by all the means at my command to arouse the people against these modern pharisees and the corrupt and inhuman system that enables them to drink the life-blood of the toiling slaves and then despise them and shoot them down like dogs for protesting against conditions against which animals would revolt.

Allow me to thank you for the kindness intended which I appreciate fully and to subscribe myself as ever,

Very sincerely yours
[Eugene V. Debs]

TLc, InTI, Debs Collection.

☐ *In November 1915 President Woodrow Wilson announced a "Preparedness Program" that called for the addition of 156 ships to the navy, doubling the size of the army, and enlarging the National Guard and the merchant marine. For many socialists, including Debs, "preparedness" was merely a code word for "war mobilization," but others, like Charles Edward Russell, a leading muckraking journalist and socialist, accepted "preparedness" as a safeguard of democracy.*

New York Sun to EVD

November 28, 1915
New York City

E V DEBS.

IN SPEECH AT PHILADELPHIA C E RUSSEL SAYS ALTHOUGH A SO-CIALIST. HE BELIEVES WE CANNOT KEEP OUT OF WAR AND MUST PRE-PARE NOW   QUESTION IS'NT WHO IS TO MAKE PROFITS   WE MUST HAVE GUNS AND HAVE THEM NOW, WILL YOU WIRE OUR EXPENSE THREE HUNDRED WORDS YOUR VIEWS.

                                                    THE SUN

Telegram, InTI, Debs Collection.

EVD to *New York Sun*

November 29, 1915
Terre Haute, Indiana

NEW YORK SUN,

REPLYING TO YOUR INQUIRY, CHARLES EDWARD RUSSELL HAS HIGH STANDING IN THE SOCIALIST MOVEMENT, BUT IF HE IS CORRECTLY QUOTED IN HIS PHILADELPHIA SPEECH IN REFERENCE TO WAR, I DO NOT AT ALL AGREE WITH HIM, AND HIS VIEWS ARE AT VARIANCE WITH THE ATTITUDE AND PRINCIPLES OF THE SOCIALIST PARTY.

IT IS MY CONVICTION THAT WE CAN KEEP OUT OF WAR, BUT NOT BY PURSUING THE COURSE INDICATED BY MR. RUSSELL. EUROPE IS TO-DAY A FLAMING EXAMPLE OF WHAT PREPAREDNESS FOR WAR MEANS TO CIVILIZATION.

A LARGE STANDING ARMY, A POWERFUL NAVY, AND A STUPENDOUS MILITARY ARMAMENT SUCH AS PRESIDENT WILSON WITH THE BACK-ING OF WALL STREET PROPOSES, MEANS A MILITARY AUTOCRACY AND IT CAN MEAN NOTHING ELSE, AND IF THE AMERICAN PEOPLE AC-QUIESCE IN SUCH AN OBVIOUSLY PLUTOCRATIC PROGRAM THEY MUST NOT BE SURPRISED IF OTHER NATIONS TREAT IT AS A CHALLENGE TO WAR, AND IF THEY THEMSELVES ARE CONSCRIPTED TO FIGHT AND DIE TO MAINTAIN PLUTOCRATIC SUPREMACY IN THE UNITED STATES.

IF THE PEACE OF THE WORLD CAN BE MAINTAINED ONLY BY A RACE OF ARMED MURDERERS THEN THE RACE SHOULD PERISH FROM THE EARTH FOR IT IS NOT FIT TO SURVIVE.

SOCIALISM MEANS INTERNATIONALISM AND SOCIALISTS, IF THEY ARE TRUE TO THE FUNDAMENTAL PRINCIPLES OF THEIR CAUSE, ARE

OPPOSED TO WAR AND TO "PREPAREDNESS" AS THAT TERM IS UNDER-
STOOD IN THE PRESENT DISCUSSION. IT IS THE RULING CLASSES WHO
INSTIGATE AND DECLARE WAR WITHOUT CONSULTING THEIR SUB-
JECTS, AND SO FAR AS THE SOCIALISTS ARE CONCERNED, THE ARIS-
TOCRACIES, BUREAUCRACIES AND PLUTOCRACIES WHO ARE RESPON-
SIBLE FOR WAR MAY ALSO FIGHT THE BATTLES.

WE ARE LIVING IN THE TWENTIETH CENTURY BUT THE RULING
CLASS STILL HAS THE BARBAROUS SPIRIT OF THE MIDDLE AGES. THE
UNITED STATES GOVERNMENT IS TODAY IN POSITION TO STRIKE A
DEATH-BLOW TO WAR BUT UNDER ITS PRESENT CONTROL IT MAY NOT
AVAIL ITSELF OF THE SUPREME OPPORTUNITY.

IF IN THE PRESENCE OF THE APPALLING CONFLAGRATION THAT IS
NOW DESTROYING THE OLD WORLD THE GOVERNMENT OF THE UNITED
STATES WERE TO PROVE IN GOOD FAITH THAT IT IS OPPOSED TO THE
BARBARISM AND BUTCHERY OF WAR BY ISSUING A PROCLAMATION OF
PEACE, AND ITSELF SETTING THE EXAMPLE OF DISARMAMENT TO THE
NATIONS OF THE WORLD, ITS PREPAREDNESS WOULD BE, NOT ONLY IN
ACCORDANCE WITH ITS VAUNTED IDEALS, BUT A THOUSANDFOLD
GREATER GUARANTEE TO THE RESPECT OF ITS NEIGHBORS AND TO
ITS OWN SECURITY AND PEACE THAN IF IT WERE LOADED DOWN WITH
ALL THE IMPLEMENTS OF DEATH AND DESTRUCTION ON EARTH.

                                                          EUGENE V. DEBS

Telegram, InTI, Debs Collection.

□ *Upton Sinclair hoped that his novel* The Jungle, *which was commissioned by and appeared serially in the* Appeal to Reason, *would convert workers to socialism, whose cause he served not only as an author but also in the political arena, as an unsuccessful candidate for Congress, for the United States Senate, and for the governorship of California. As the following letter indicates, Debs disagreed with Sinclair's proposal for "the defense of democracy throughout the world," described by Sinclair in the pamphlet "Democratic Defense."*

EVD to Upton Sinclair

January 12, 1916
Terre Haute, Indiana

Dear Comrade Sinclair:—

Your note of the 7th. inst. enclosing a copy of your proposed military or anti-military program has been received and the latter has been carefully read. Replying, I regret not being able to sign the document as requested for the reason that I do not coincide with the views therein set forth. I appreciate fully the spirit and intent of your undertaking but I know of no reason why the workers should fight for what the capitalists own or slaughter one another for countries that belong to their masters. Any kind of an army that may be organized and any kind of a military establishment that may be instituted under the prevailing system and under the present government will be controlled by the ruling class and its chief function will be to keep the working class in slavery. I have not the least fear of invasion or attack from without. The invasion and attack I want the workers to prepare to resist and put an end to comes from within, from our own predatory plutocracy right here at home. I do not know of any foreign buccaneers that could come nearer skinning the American workers to the bone than is now being {done} by the Rockefellers and their pirate pals. The workers have no country to fight for. It belongs to the capitalists and plutocrats. Let them worry over its defense and when they declare wars as they and they alone do, let them also go out and slaughter one another on the battlefields.

I am with all kind regards,

Yours fraternally,
E. V. Debs

TLS, InU, Lilly Library, Sinclair MSS.

□ *In a January 8, 1916, letter to the* Terre Haute Post *Debs denounced the widely hailed motion picture* Birth of a Nation *as a "studied insult to the black race" intended to "revive and intensify the bitter prejudices that grew out of the war." "For every white woman raped in the south by a black fiend," he added, "a thousand black women have been seduced and outraged by white gentlemen but no hint of this is given . . . in The Birth of a Nation." Debs's letter was widely reprinted and he received a flood of correspondence not unlike the following from Charles Bailey, a Connersville, Indiana, banker and building and loan company official.*

Charles A. Bailey to EVD

ca. January 16, 1916
Connersville, Indiana

Dear Sir—:

I see in the Indianapolis Ledger, one of the greatest Negro journals of the United States, under the date of Jan. 16, 1916 a double header in large black a word of kindness from the famous Socialists orator Eugene V. Debs setting the famous play, "The Birth of a Nation," in its true light. I only wish that the speaker would allow that article to be published in pamphlet form that the twelve million Negroes in the United States could see for themselves a true and tried friend of the oppressed race of the United States. And if such a character was placed in the hall of Congress and by him being elected to that exalted position that the world could see the right man in the right place. Or if men of his caiber and his conviction speak the whole truth and all of the truth as our friend Eugene Debs did in his letter dated from Terre Haute, the prejudice against our people would melt as the frost on a May morning.

I have this day subscribed for, "The Appeal to Reason," as I hope the same will be done by every colored family in the United States.

This letter is only to show how the Colored people in this part of the state appreciate those sledge hammer blows from a free and fearless advocate of "Rights to the Many."

No more at present. May all your Efforts be crowned with success. I remain

> Yours Truly
> Chas. A. Bailey
> Connersville, Ind.

ALS, InTI, Debs Collection.

☐ *As the war in Europe dragged on, the issue of preparedness intensified in America and "Preparedness Parades" became common civic events. That the issue placed great stress on the unity of the Socialist party was made clear in the following exchange between Debs and Daniel W. Hoan, who was elected as the socialist mayor of Milwaukee in 1915 and served in that capacity until 1940.*

EVD to Daniel W. Hoan

August 11, 1916
Terre Haute, Indiana

Dear Comrade Hoan:—

The press dispatches reported some time ago that you headed a military preparedness parade at Milwaukee. I denounced it at the time as a falsehood. Since then it has {been} repeatedly charged

against you and I now drop you this line to get the denial from you
direct. I simply cannot believe anything of the kind.

Awaiting your reply I am as ever,

Yours fraternally,
E. V. Debs

TLS, Milwaukee County Historical Society, Hoan Papers.

Daniel W. Hoan to EVD

August 15, 1916
Milwaukee, Wisconsin

Dear Comrade: —

I was very much pleased to get your inquiry of the 11th. In reply
will state that I did parade here in what one or two of the newspapers
continued to call a "Preparedness Parade" to the end. However, what
the citizens committee in charge of the same and most of the papers
here termed "A Patriotic Demonstration." At the outset the Security
League attempted to organize a regular preparedness parade, but
thru up their hands in despair, consequently the Citizens Committee
made an endeavor to hold a preparedness parade, but all of us socialists
declined to participate, as did the federated trades council.

About three weeks before the parade was held, however, the committee saw perhaps that such a parade would be a fizzle and announced
that the parade, which they would hold would not be a military
preparedness parade, or for more munitions but merely a demonstration of national loyalty. It may not be easy to understand why the
socialists should have anything to do with such a parade, but when
the committee announced that the demonstration was not one in favor
of militarism, the Caucus, with one exception, voted unanimously that
I participate, and the County Central Committee as well, felt that
while the socialists generally could remain out of the parade that for
me to decline would be to deny any national feeling whatsoever, and
probably cripple the party locally for years.

I will state, moreover, that all the documents which have been
published, including the announcements of the committee, the letter
of Mr. Potter, inviting me to parade, my answer announcing my
acceptance, and the proclamation declaring a half holiday, particularly
the latter two, strongly emphasized that the parade was not military.

Anticipating some inquiries from the outside, I have requested Mr.
Osmore R. Smith, a local comrade, on the staff of the Milwaukee

Leader, to write up a history of the affair as he had learned it as a newspaper man and I am sending you herewith a copy of the article he wrote for the purpose of publication, if it were found necessary and and which you may use as you see fit.

We appreciated fully just what the position was, and what the outside party members and others might think, but rather than set the party back a number of years and deny any loyalty to the American Nation what ever, it was agreed that I march. While demonstrations originating from capitalistic sources are hypocritical and more or less disgusting, I submit that careful thot will lead any thinking socialist to the conclusion that every socialist is imbued with a genuine patriotic spirit, and that we are devoting our lives to make this nation a better place in which the men who toil may live, as well as displaying an international patriotism. I feel that it is surely preferable, rather than scoff at the word patriotism, to seize upon it and make it a word to express our ideas and popularize our thots.

Yours fraternally,
Daniel W. Hoan
Mayor

TLS, InTI, Debs Collection.

□ *In 1916 Debs resisted considerable pressure to run again as the Socialist party's presidential candidate, but he did agree to run for Congress in his home district in Indiana. In the following letter to his friend Stephen Marion Reynolds he discusses one of the party's 1916 campaign platform planks calling for "an independent department of health."*

EVD to Daniel W. Hoan

August 17, 1916
Terre Haute, Indiana

Dear Comrade Hoan:—

Your communication of the 16th. inst. with supplementary statement by Osmore R. Smith attached came to hand this morning and both have been carefully read.

I cannot but express my surprise and regret that you were placed in any such position by the socialists of Milwaukee, and I shall be mistaken if you do not find yourself under the necessity of explaining for a long time to come. I cannot at all agree to the views regarding patriotism expressed in your communication. Socialists are not required to demonstrate their patriotism for the benefit of the capitalist class and that class will not only not thank them for it but hold them in greater contempt.

The parade at Milwaukee from your own account of it was a capitalist parade and intended to serve capitalist ends and for myself I would have been eternally damned before I would have marched in it. The capitalist politicians were just a little too shrewd for the socialist politicians of Milwaukee and their press was not slow to spread the news over the country that the socialist mayor of Milwaukee had marched at the head of a preparedness parade.

The socialists of Milwaukee who are responsible for this perversion of principle may think it good vote-catching politics, but in my opinion it is an insult to militant socialism and it is just because of such vote-seeking, office-hunting political practices that hundreds of red-blooded socialists quit the party in disgust.

When we of the Socialist party have to march in capitalist parades to prove that we are patriots then I shall quit the party, and if that be a test of socialism then I shall deny that I am a socialist.

I can but repeat my surprise and regret, and if the socialists of Milwaukee expect to win for socialism by such methods they are doomed to bitter disappointment.

With all kind personal regards I am,

Yours fraternally,
[Eugene V. Debs]

TLc, InTI, Debs Collection.

EVD to S. M. Reynolds

August 17, 1916
Terre Haute, Indiana

My dear Stephen: —

I have just finished reading your letter and you are very near to me this morning. Thank you from my heart for each kind and loving word. You are always the same loyal, sweet-souled Stephen.

I knew that your heart would be in the campaign in this district and I need not say to you that your kindly interest is sincerely appreciated. The comrades are all working together earnestly and energetically and they seem to think that there is a chance for election.

But whether it is or not we shall do our best just the same and when we do that for the cause we are winning even when we lose.

I note what you say in objection to the clause in the platform relating to health. Upon every other point in your letter I am in hearty agreement with you, but I do not interpret that clause as you do. I cannot see why a department of health would not be in order and why it should not be organized and maintained upon a sound and scientific basis and do good work. Its control by the medical trust is another matter. I do not see why that should follow. As well might we assume the same in the case of every other proposition and refrain from creating a board for any good purpose for fear that it might be controlled by some private monopoly. But I am glad to have your views for your vision is clear, and when we meet, which I hope may be soon, we will go over the matter together.

I am sorry that I shall not be here on Sunday. I have already accepted an invitation which will take me away from here or I should be only too glad to see you. Perhaps you can come at some later time and I shall very likely be at Chicago soon.

You have had no letters from me lately because I have been too busy to write. But the hours are never so busy that I do not send you and Jessica and Marion my love-thoughts. We often regret that we cannot see you oftener. But you are not far away and we are always looking forward to seeing you again. Meanwhile the miles that lie between do not in the least divide us. You are always with us and we are always with you.

Katherine and her mother and Theodore and his family all join in greetings of love and good wishes to you all.

Ever faithfully,

Your comrade,
E. V. Debs

TLS, InH, Reynolds Collection.

□ *Carlo Tresca, an Italian immigrant, became a Wobbly and played a leading role in the IWW's most famous strikes, including the 1916 miners' strike on the Mesabi Range in Minnesota, during which he was arrested as an accessory to the murder of a sheriff's deputy. While confined he wrote the following letter thanking Debs for* Rip-Saw *editorials and speeches on his behalf.*

Carlo Tresca to EVD

ca. September 18, 1916
Duluth, Minnesota

Dear comrade Debs,

I have taken notice of your valuable, powerful, brotherless support to my case with very much pleasure. I am tankful to you. If, battling for the liberty and the emancipation of our class, we expect any premium or rewards, I have the best anyone cant have because I have the support of Gene, the noblest, the greatest, the valiant leader in the field. Let your voice go, go everywhere, in every town and city, go to the heart of all the workers, calling, comrade Debs, not only for the necessary solidarity with all of us in jail, but, and most, for the necessity of uniting in one front only, in one army all the rebels of America for the coming great battle between the master and the slave, between the reactionarie force and the force of libertarian. We are at the point, right now: our banner most arised signifying our victory. Help, Gene! You are the heart, the brain of the worker in America and your voice is the voice of labor. Not make difference what well be, in this fight, the consequence for me and my felloworkers in cell, arise, comrade Debs, arise the workers and let them realize the necessity of the stand, one for all and all for one, unite against the Steel trust, the red blood thirsty monster.

Tank you, comrade! With greatest and heartest salutation.

I am, yours for industrial unionism
Carlo Tresca

P.S. Excuse me for writing with many mistakes this a first attemp for me to write in english.

ALS, InTI, Debs Collection.

☐ *In the campaign in Indiana's Fifth Congressional District, Debs ran third with 8,886 votes, behind winner Everett Sanders, the Republican candidate, who got 20,977 votes, and Ralph W. Moss, the Democratic candidate, who got 20,270 votes. Daniel Hoan was one of several nationally—and internationally—known socialists who came to the district to help in Debs's campaign.*

EVD to Daniel W. Hoan

November 7, 1916
Terre Haute, Indiana

My dear Comrade Hoan: —

It was certainly very kind of you to take the time out of your busy hours to come down here and make the splendid speech you did in behalf of the Socialist party and of myself as its candidate for congress in this district. The comrades have told me that you made one of the most effective appeals of the campaign and that your coming here stimulated them to renewed activity in the campaign. Please accept my hearty thanks and the assurance of my sincere appreciation. I am exceedingly sorry and so is Mrs. Debs that we both happened to be out when you called. Mrs. Debs found your card on her return. I need hardly say that we should have been happy indeed to have had you break bread with us and visit our home.

I do not know what the outcome here will be but the comrades have all done their best and we shall be satisfied with whatever fate or fortune has in store and go on working with unabated energy for the cause.

If I had not been kept so extremely busy I should have looked you up but unfortunately there was not time enough to go around and some claims upon my attention had to suffer neglect. But you have been through all this and I am sure you understand. I only wish you to know that I am deeply sensible of your kindness and of your splendid service in our fight. Believe me with warmest wishes

Yours faithfully
Eugene V. Debs

TLS, Milwaukee County Historical Society, Hoan Papers.

☐ *At the turn of the century George Herron was a leader of the Christian Socialists in America and played an important role in uniting socialists in the new Socialist Party of America. Since his controversial marriage in 1901 to Carrie Rand he had lived in Italy but maintained his interest in American socialism in general and in Debs's career in particular. In the following exchange of letters Debs and Herron discuss the present status and future prospects of socialism against the background of World War I.*

EVD to George D. Herron

November 16, 1916
Terre Haute, Indiana

My dear Comrade Herron,

You will not think me remiss, I know, for not acknowledging sooner the very fine letter received from you in the early part of September and which I have taken occasion to read several times to friends and comrades, whose tear-filled eyes attested their heartfelt appreciation of its sad and pathetic contents. Your vivid description of the victims of war fills us with sorrow and we cry aloud in protest and horror against this shocking butchery of humanity.

How your great, tender, loving heart must be wrung daily, nightly, incessantly by the scenes of suffering you are fated to witness all about you! I can well imagine your own keen suffering and your outraged sensibilities as you medi[t]ate upon these awful crimes and the accursed system responsible for them. I am with you absolutely in the matter of militarism. I am opposed to any shadow of compromise with the God-damned institution and I would see myself in hell for all eternity before it should receive a word of encouragement or a particle of support in any form from me. Militarism has not a solitary redeeming feature and war is an unmitigated crime and I shall fight both un-compromisingly just as you are doing while there is breath in my body.

Well, our election is over and while we secured no office we won in every other way in this district. We more than trebled our vote and we now have an organization under way that promises much for the future.

The results of the national campaign as a whole are sorely disap-pointing to many of our comrades. For myself I never suffer myself to be disappointed or discouraged. Blessed are they who expect noth-ing for they shall not be disappointed. I simply do my little utmost as well as I can and take what comes without complaint and without regret.

I wish I could see you, dear comrade, and have a heart to heart talk with you over things in general. I would so love to counsel with you about plans for the future. Our party here needs to make some changes or it will certainly face deterioration if it has not already done so. There is too much time and effort given to vote-catching and office-seeking. If the politician can thrive in the Socialist party it is because its revolutionary spirit is dead and itself is doomed.

Pardon these incoherent lines. I am so far behind with my work in consequence of the campaign that I am unable to write you decently as you deserve. But you always understand and to you, beloved comrade, I need never apologize or explain.

Theodore and I have sent you papers from time to time but I doubt if they were allowed to reach you. Our own matter has often been intercepted on account of the war and yours no doubt even more. We often, often think of you: we always love you.

We all unite in heartfelt greetings and most earnest wishes that your cruel banishment may soon be ended.

Your brother in life and death,
(signed) Eugene V. Debs.

Transcript, CSt-H.

George D. Herron to EVD

January 10, 1917
Geneva, Switzerland

Dear Brother Debs:

The chief of the Propaganda Bureau of the French Government has been to see me, and we have had three serious conferences concerning the situation in America and the advisability of a French Educational Agitation and Propaganda to bring understanding to the American people, and to counter-act the profound and wide pro-German influence. He has asked me if I would undertake a mission to America on behalf of France and I have replied in the negative, although I have placed myself at his disposal to render every possible service I can from here. I have told him frankly that I believe, both my past personal conflicts and revolutionary socialist attitude, would militate against my undertaking such a mission. It is possible that Bergson will be persuaded to go. Indeed, he is now thinking quite favorably of it. But, in any case, there must be an American also. I have told the chief that I believe you are in a position to inform him, better than anyone else could inform him, of the common feeling of the people throughout all the interior part of the United States. He returns to Paris tonight, and will write to you at once. Will you give him as complete a report as you can, of the pro-German influences at work, both in the general public and in the socialist party, and also as to what portion of {our} people, if any, understand the significance of this supreme human hour, and what it is the Allies are fighting for. You can render no greater service to the great Cause than this. For I can assure you, from personal knowledge as well as conviction, that the result of the victory of France and England will mean a speedy coming of the Co-operative Common-Wealth and the abolition of militarism in both countries.

I have just written a little book, entitled, "The Menace of Peace," which is being published simultaneously in London, Paris, Geneva and Florence. I think its appeal will interest you and I will send you an English copy as soon as it has appeared.

Please give my affectionate greetings to Mrs. Debs and to Theodore as well as take my eternal love for yourself.

Affectionately yours,
George D. Herron

TLS, InTI, Debs Collection.

EVD to George D. Herron

January 23, 1917
Terre Haute, Indiana

Dearest of Comrades,

The letter from you under date of the 19th ult., enclosing copy of a letter from you to Simons, reached here this morning and both have been carefully read. It appears that a letter I wrote you about the holidays did not reach you. I do not remember the exact date nor have I a copy of it. I am sorry you did not get this letter, not that it was specially important, but that you might have known we were thinking of you and feeling for you and wishing ourselves able to share fully the terrible ordeal through which you of all others seems to have been marked by fate to pass through.

The letter from you just received arrived here cut open at the end by the censor, and not resealed, so that it came really open for the inspection of anyone that might choose to inspect its contents.

As I am just back from a speaking tour and am having to leave here soon again, with many matters here awaiting attention, I shall not attempt to review your letter to Simons which I am very glad you have allowed me to see. I share fully in your indignation but I fear that in the stress of the terrible position in which you have been placed, and with your keen sense of what should have been and your super-sensitive nature you have allowed yourself to become embittered and unduly pessimistic. All the vital and essential elements of the international movement are intact and I apprehend no such trouble about reviving the movement with all the cowardly and betraying elements eliminated. In the enclosed article from the current Rip-Saw you will see what I think of Liebknecht and of the miserable traitors calling themselves socialists who are defaming him.

There are some things in your letter that set me thinking seriously along new lines. I wish to feel as keenly as you do, though I fear that is impossible, the sense of shame and outrage socialists ought to feel for the failure of their movement at the time of its greatest opportunity and in the supreme crisis of the world. But is it not possible that too much was expected from the socialist movement under all the conditions that surround it? I am, like yourself, utterly opposed to excusing treason, but there are times when moral weakness is not a crime.

I cannot see my way clear to your view that the class-struggle is to be abandoned in the future realignment and program. I cannot imagine a socialist movement that does not incarnate the principles of the struggle, the warfare going on all about us and continuously between the exploited and exploiting classes of society.

But your views and opinions are always of the deepest concern to me and I need not say command in advance my most serious consideration. You write as does no other and if you are open to any criticism it is that you are what in capitalistic ethics is called "absurdly honest."

A thousand loving wishes!

Yours always,
(signed) E. V. Debs

Transcript, CSt-H.

☐ *Charmian Kittredge London was the widow of Jack London, who commit-*
ted suicide on November 22, 1916.

EVD to Charmian London

February 25, 1917
Terre Haute, Indiana

My dear Comrade London:—
  Thank you warmly for your very appreciative letter just received.
I can only regret that it is not better deserved. I have been suffering
with the grip these several weeks past and my work has been but
poorly done during that time.
  Your beloved husband was very dear to me as he was to many
thousands of others who never had the privilege of laying their eyes
upon him. I often wondered why I was among the unfortunate who
were never permitted to see him. I felt the great heart of him, loved
him, read nearly everything he wrote, and rejoiced in applauding his
genius. But I never happened to be in the same place with him at
the same time and I hoped that some good day in the future I might
meet him and have the chance to tell him how much I loved him and
how glad I was that he was in the world. But the chance never came,
and there is not another in all the world to take his place.
  Mrs. Debs and I thought of you with the deepest sympathy when
the painful and shocking news came and we wished ourselves near
enough to speak to you our word of loving sympathy. But you did
not want for friends and comrades in that solemn hour and I hope
that by this time you have become reconciled and that the sun again
shines into your life.
  Our dear Jack is with you and us still and will abide with us for
the great soul of him cannot die.
  Thank you for the very excellent picture you were so thoughtful
as to enclose. It is just what I wished and I prize it far more than
could be expressed in words.
  Mrs. Debs joins me in affectionate greetings and warmest wishes
and I am always,

                                        Yours faithfully,
                                        Eugene V. Debs

TLS, CSmH, London Papers.

□ *Senator Robert La Follette voted against the declaration of war against Germany and was bitterly denounced in a broad spectrum of the press as pro-German and lacking in patriotism. Debs sent the following telegram to La Follette after the Senate vote on the arming of merchant ships.*

EVD to Robert M. La Follette

March 7, 1917
Providence, Rhode Island

HON ROBERT M LAFOLLETTE
    LET THE WALL STREET WOLVES AND THEIR PROSTITUTE PRESS HOWL. THE PEOPLE WILL SUSTAIN YOU AND HISTORY WILL VINDICATE YOU.

                                                        EUGENE V DEBS

Telegram, DLC, MSS. Division, La Follette Family Collection.

□ *Debs wrote the following letter to Bruce Rogers, who had worked with him for several years on the* Appeal to Reason, *after receiving a letter in which Rogers suggested that Debs had not fully supported the victims of the "Everett massacre" of November 5, 1916, in which five Wobblies were killed and scores wounded by the county sheriff and several hundred "deputies" at Everett, Washington.*

EVD to Bruce Rogers

April 9, 1917
Terre Haute, Indiana

Dear Bruce Rogers:—
    Your letter of the 1st. is at hand and coming from you I am surprised at it not a little. Since when have you discovered that I have done nothing for the Everett victims? You are the only one I know to lay claim to that distinction. I have appealed in their behalf in nearly every speech I have made, have appealed in their behalf for funds and support through the Rip-Saw and other papers, in my correspondence and every other way I have known how, and I have their

grateful acknowledgment of my fealty to their cause and the service I have rendered them.

You think me slow to help them because they belong to the I.W.W. I have good reason not to feel kindly toward some of them but I have never in a single instance refused them aid and support and it seems strange to me that you appear to be in utter ignorance of this fact. So far as I know you are the only one to bring this complaint against me.

Who was the first man appealed to by the I.W.W. victims at Lawrence and especially the leaders on trial? And who was the first to respond? Ask Ettor, ask Giovannitti. They know.

I raised more money than anyone else to defend them and have the written expression of their thanks and gratitude. The same is true of the Paterson strike and its arrested leaders.

Who issued one of the first appeals for funds to save Joe Hill, wrote personal letters to the governor and did everything in his power to save his life?

To whom did the Mesabe strikers turn first when they were arrested and who issued the first appeal for funds and support in their behalf? Ask Ettor, ask Carlo Tresca. If you do not know they can tell you.

I fought for them to a finish through the papers and in every way I knew how and I have letters from both of them expressing the deepest thanks and sincerest gratitude in their own behalf and in behalf of their organization and the cause they were fighting for. I even had myself bitterly criticised in socialist circles for charging in some of my articles that the strike on the Mesabe range was not being supported because it was led by the I.W.W.

You seem to mourn over the alleged fact that I am withholding myself from the "Revolution's physical phenomena." I challenge you to name a single instance in which your I.W.W. has fought a fight of any account in which I have not given encouragement and support by all the means in my power. I have been trying for years to keep {up} with all the demands that have been made upon me and so often have I exceeded my physical strength that twice recently I have been on the verge of a complete nervous and physical collapse from overwork, and at this writing I am barely able from the same cause to stand on my feet and yet Bruce Rogers thinks the revolution is being "cheated" out of my services. In the name of God, what do you want? I have given my life to the working class and its struggles drop by drop, and almost to the last atom of my strength, and if this is not enough to satisfy you then I have absolutely nothing more to offer or to give.

Yours fraternally,
[Eugene V. Debs]

TLc, InTi, Debs Collection.

□ *Immediately following the U.S. declaration of war on April 6, 1917, the Socialist Party of America called an emergency convention, held in St. Louis from April 7 to April 12, and adopted a strong antiwar resolution. Adolph Germer, one of the socialist leaders of the United Mine Workers, was national executive secretary of the SPA.*

EVD to Adolph F. Germer

April 11, 1917
Terre Haute, Indiana

Adolph Germer,

Greetings of love and loyalty to my comrades in convention assembled. I had intended being with you but am too ill to leave home. You have met at the most crucial hour in history. The future of our party, the hope of the workers is in your hands. I have full faith that you will rise to the demand and declare to the world in clear and unmistakable terms the attitude of the party toward war and toward the ruling class system which has forced this frightful catastrophe upon mankind.

Now is the time for the Socialist Party to prove itself and to make revolutionary history for the working class. There must be no fear, no evasion, and no compromise. The crisis forced upon us by the ruling class must be faced squarely by an aroused and determined working class. Our enemy is not abroad but within our {own} borders. The American plutocracy with its prostituted press and pulpit, wrapped up in the stars and stripes, and hypocritically proclaiming its hostility to Prussianism in Germany is at this very hour straining all its mighty energies to Prussianize the United States. Its program for the future is one of absolute military domination.

Conscription, enforced military service, a rigid censorship, espionage, military training of children in public schools, the guarding of industrial plants by federal troops, compulsary arbitration, the penalizing of strikes are all embraced in this arch-conspiracy of capitalist preparedness, which must be exposed, denounced and resisted to the limit if every jail in the land is choked with rebels and revolutionists.

The Socialist party as the exponent of international working class solidarity can have no concern in any ruling class war. To be consistent with its revolutionary character and true to its international principles and pledges it is morally bound to stand squarely against every war save and alone the war against war, the war of the world's enslaved and exploited workers against the world's enslaving and exploiting masters.

The convention, I feel confident, will not fail to give all possible consideration to the case of Tom Mooney and his associates and to the victims of the Everett massacre now on trial at Seattle. I beg that no measure of sympathy or support to these outraged workers be overlooked. The infamy of the conviction of Mooney and his associates and of the cold-blooded murder of the union workers at Everett at the behest of the Lumber Trust must stir to hot resentment the blood of every delegate who sits in a socialist convention. Everything within the power of our party and our press must be done in behalf of these martyrs to our own class. To them we owe all loyalty and all support, but not one particle to the brutal exploiting class of which they are the victims.

Praying devoutly for the success of your deliberations and the future of our party, I am with heart and soul

Yours for the Revolution,
Eugene V. Debs

TLc, InTI, Debs Collection.

☐ *Debs's antiwar stance was bitterly attacked by the vast majority of the American people, including many of his friends in Terre Haute. In the following exchange of letters, Debs's attitude and that of a close Terre Haute friend, Clarence Royse, are set forth.*

Clarence A. Royse to EVD

May 21, 1917
Terre Haute, Indiana

Dear Gene:

I am sending you a copy of the book by Andre Cheradame entitled the "Pan-German Plot Exposed," which I have just finished reading.

It is a book of the utmost significance to my mind, and brings together a lot of evidence which has been drifting into our minds gradually. There is another book written by Naumann entitled "Mitteleuropa," by an authoritative German, which sets forth the plot again. There can be no possible question that this plot, complete as to all details, was conceived many years ago in the minds of the German authorities, and is now in process of fulfillment, and will undoubtedly be carried out, and will place the German autocracy in absolute control not only of Europe, but of America, and the rest of the world, unless by sheer brute military power, her steps can be stayed. The profound danger which attends a premature peace is clearly set forth in this book. No matter how much any of us may hate war, we are bound to choose between the sacrifice of war and the utter sacrifice of the principle of democracy and the rights of man.

It may be that you have already read this book, but if not, please take time to do so, and then I trust that you will add your voice to those of Russell, St. Clair, Ghent and other American Socialists, in an appeal to the Russian Socialists to stand fast in the struggle for universal liberty.

With most sincere regards, I am,

Yours very sincerely,
Clarence A. Royse

TLS, InTI, Debs Collection.

EVD to Clarence A. Royse

May 31, 1917
Terre Haute, Indiana

My dear Clarence Royse: —

Absence from the city has belated my acknowledgment of the book you were kind enough to send me, with its friendly personal inscription, and the personal note that came with it. I shall be glad to give the book careful reading and when we meet again I hope we may have time to talk it over.

I may say in response to your suggestion that I have not one particle of fear that German autocracy will ever destroy what little there is of liberty and democracy in this country. Our own Rockefellers and Morgans and their Roosevelts and Roots and other vassals too numerous to mention constitute the only menace to the liberties of the American people.

Autocracy is autocracy and there are others besides that which bears the German brand, and we do not have to go three thousand miles away from home to fight it. If the German "barbarians" have perpetrated any more brutal outrages upon the innocent than Rockefeller has upon the women and babies of Colorado I have yet to be advised of it. And when it comes to brutal exploitation, England's ruthless slaughter of the Boer farmers and the utter dispossession and spoliation of these industrious and inoffensive people, to say nothing of her unspeakable atrocities in India and Egypt, and Belgium's hellish crimes in the Congo under the degenerate Leopold, and all for cold-blooded robbery and plunder, will match anything that can be justly charged against the "Pan-German Barbarians."

It seems strange to me that it should not appear strange to you that the people here are all wrought up over the suffering children in Belgium when thousands of babies are literally perishing from starvation at their own doors. Let anyone come with me to the East Side of New York and look upon those little living skeletons, thousands of them, the products of our own beautiful democracy and "Christian" civilization, and then tell me why they are so profoundly stirred about the suffering of the little ones in France and Belgium and yet are absolutely unconcerned about the starving children here at home.

According to the U. S. Government's own reports two-thirds of the American people are today below a standard of decent living, underfed, starved, body and soul in this, "the richest country on earth," and to fight this monstrous wrong under our own flag is in my opinion far more patriotic than to cross the Atlantic in the "pomp and circumstance of war" for the alleged purpose of destroying the "PanGerman Autocracy."

The "patriotic" American food pirates and their ilk, all of whom are frantically for conscription and war and not one of whom will take a chance of having his own paunch filled with leaden slugs, constitute the "autocracy" which concerns me far more directly than does the PanGerman. The utter infamy of the latter I do not for a moment deny or attempt to extenuate, nor do I doubt that its fate is sealed, but when it goes down it will be because it has been put down by the German people and not because it has been destroyed by the no less autocratic powers and personalities represented by such servile tools and arch-enemies of the people as Elihu Root.

Thanking you warmly for your kindness and with all loving personal regards I am always,

Yours faithfully,
[Eugene V. Debs]

TLc, InTI, Debs Collection.

☐ *On August 5, 1917, Debs checked into a sanitarium in Boulder, Colorado, for "scientific treatment, diet and nature," which he describes in this letter to his brother. He remained in Boulder for nearly three months.*

EVD to Theodore Debs

August 12, 1917
[Boulder, Colorado]

My dear old Pard:

Your letter of the 9th came this morning. It is all to the good & my heart is full of the sweetness & devotion of it. Each word touches me & I'm filled and thrilled with the fine spirit of it.

Yes, I'm in the right place for once. I'm going to come as near getting well & strong here as I could anywhere on earth. The Doctor allows no one to telephone me or see me without first passing through his hands. Otherwise I'd be swamped. The air is cool & bracing. Have on my winter underwear & slept under heavy blankets. Take 75 drops of Digitallis daily & a cup of special oil at night. That's all the medicine I take. The rest is scientific treatment, diet & nature. Treatment three times daily—every kind of bath, massage, electric accessory imaginable. The diet is meatless,—the doctor prescribes in detail *each meal I eat each day.*

The examination is now completed. My blood is nearly normal— all my organs are perfectly sound except my heart & that's dilated & has a small leak due to strain & exhaustion—& that is what the doctor is concentrating on. He gives me full encouragement & says I'll come out OK but I must have rest & quiet & food & treatment & stick to the program till we get the results. And so I'm following instructions in every detail with the resolute will & determination to win the fight & I'm going to do it, & when I do, old pard, get a steel armor for your beak.

Ranita is dead anxious that I shall spend a month with them before I return—she just begged me to rest with them & promised everything if I would. She's a fine soul, a sweet & loyal girl you can't help but love and I may spend a day or two or more with Ed & Ranita when I leave here. Mrs. Clenenger wants me to go visiting with her to some folks 8 miles from here on Tuesday but I'll have to decline for I've made up my mind to stick to my treatment in every detail & not depart from it if I can possibly help it. If I make an exception I'll make another. All the points around here want me to visit & dine etc etc & I've refused them all. Mrs. C. is a lovely woman & I see her & chat with her everyday. She always sends all of you her love.

I most enjoyed the letter from Ryan Walker—he's a dandy good scout.

Old man, I'm going to get on my pins right this time & when I do & get back we'll set things humming & make up with interest for lost time. Only wish you were here with me.

Love & kisses to you all.

Your old pard to a finish
Gene

ALS, InTI, Debs Collection.

☐ *Though attacked for his opposition to the war and his defense of free speech during wartime and of Congress's right to control war policy, Robert La Follette became a hero to Americans like Debs who were opposed to the war.*

EVD to Robert M. La Follette

October 15, 1917
Terre Haute, Indiana

My dear Senator LaFollette:

Several times I have been at the point of writing or wiring you but hesitated knowing how completely engrossed you were and what little time your enemies left you to yourself. I only want to say to you, and that as briefly as possible, what is in the heart of millions. You have had the central part in the great drama of the past few weeks and you have borne yourself with absolute rectitude, such uncompromising courage, such lofty bearing as to win the admiration and love of the honest people not only of your own country but of the whole civilized world. It is to your glory that the plutocracy of Wall Street is seeking to oust you from its senate and if it succeeds your triumph and vindication will be complete and your political immortality secure. All honor to you for your courage, your manhood and your devotion to the cause of the people in the face of the bitterest and most brutal persecution to which the lawless looters of this nation and their prostitute press ever subjected a faithful public servant.

The people are with you in every hour and every moment of your trial and history will do you justice.

Believe me with all loyal appreciation and unfaltering devotion,

Yours for the people,

Eugene V. Debs

No answer!

TLS, DLC, MSS Division, La Follette Family Collection.

EVD to Robert M. La Follette

November 26, 1917
Terre Haute, Indiana

My dear Senator La Follette: —

Please have your secretary send me, if entirely convenient, half a dozen copies of your speech in the senate on "Free Speech and the Right of Congress to Declare the Objects of the War." I could use a dozen copies to good advantage and am quite willing to remit for them. If the supply is limited I should at least like a single copy for my library.

Permit me to congratulate you heartily upon this supremely patriotic and masterful expression. It is one of the few really great speeches ever made in congress and will take its place among the classic orations of the age and one of the most eloquent, fearless, forceful appeals ever made for human rights and human freedom. The facts you marshalled in deadly array, the historic precedents you cited in support of your convincing, conclusive argument and your masterly, incisive logic made your speech absolutely unanswerable, and it is not at all strange that it has been tabooed and as far as possible suppressed by the prostituted sheets of the Wall street robbers.

The very kind and appreciative letter from you in answer to mine touched me deeply and I thank you from my heart for each word it contains.

Today begins, according to the press dispatches, the investigation by the senate of your alleged "treasonable" utterance at St. Paul which still rings in the hearts of millions. Be proud of this exceptional distinction. It is the only possible tribute the arch-tratiors to the nation could pay you. If you needed to be sustained from without in this hour of trial you would surely find sufficient encouragement and support in the fact that the hearts of the liberty-loving millions are with you.

If the plutocratic profiteers, the most shameless robbers in history, are "patriots" under their own regime then can you well afford to be branded as a "traitor" and be proud of it.

The impudent, insulting investigation of which you are the intended victim is discredited in advance, bearing as it does upon its very face the stamp of robber-class persecution, and its only effect will be to re-act with deadly effect upon its criminal authors and add fresh lustre to your honor and fame.

Please do not take the time to answer this. You need every moment for the hounds that are baying at your heels.

Believe me, dear senator, with every good wish,

Yours faithfully,
Eugene V. Debs

TLS, DLC, MSS Division, La Follette Family Collection.

□ *Following America's entry into the war, thousands of socialists, including many of its leading figures, repudiated the Socialist party's antiwar stance and announced their support of the war and their intention to leave the party. The* Appeal to Reason *changed its name to the* New Appeal *and announced in its December 15, 1917, issue that it supported the war effort as a means of securing a socialist victory in the postwar period. Louis Kopelin was the editor of the paper at the time.*

EVD to Louis Kopelin

December 14, 1917
Terre Haute, Indiana

Dear Comrade Louie: —
I refuse to believe the press dispatch in three lines announcing that the Appeal had become a capitalist war organ. The current issue of

the Appeal just received confirms the report. The news to me is shocking and incredible but I am not altogether unused to such practices. J.A. Wayland would, I think, sit up in his grave if this report came to his ears.

You have been kind enough to send us weekly a dozen Appeals to use in connection with our correspondence and we have been trying to make each copy serve the paper and the cause. Please discontinue these. We will have no use for a so-called socialist paper that becomes a capitalist war organ.

You begin your statement and your attempted justification with an absolute falsehood in the opening paragraph. It is not true that President Wilson has espoused the democratic peace formula and you know it. But I am not going to argue the question.

For obvious reasons it is with profound regret that I bid good bye to you and the Appeal. You will not have to live long to see that the Appeal has committed suicide.

Yours fraternally,
[Eugene V. Debs]

TLc, InTI, Debs Collection.

☐ *The following poem, in Katherine Debs's handwriting but signed by Gene, was found in one of Kate's scrapbooks.*

EVD to Katherine Metzel Debs

January 13, 1918
Terre Haute, Indiana

Kate is my sweetheart and the idol of my heart,
Faithful, loving, kind and true is my darling wife;
Thanks to God that she is mine, may he bless her noble life,
I will worship at her shrine till in death we part.

Eugene V. Debs

Poem (in hand of Katherine Metzel Debs, signed by EVD), EVD Foundation, Debs Home, Katherine M. Debs Scrapbook No. 3.

□ *In 1912 Margaret Higgins Sanger left a career in nursing on New York's Lower East Side to devote her life to birth control. In "The Conviction of William Sanger," published in* Rip-Saw *in November 1915, Debs defended Margaret Sanger's pamphlet on birth control for the working class and denounced the New York City court that had fined her husband $150 or thirty days in jail for distributing "obscene material." In response to Sanger's request for an article for the* Birth Control Review, *Debs wrote "Freedom Is the Goal," which appeared in the magazine's May 1918 issue. In the article Debs argued that as a part of women's struggle for freedom "she shall have sole custody of her body" and "perfect sex-freedom as well as economic, intellectual, and moral freedom." In another article, "Fantine," which Sanger mentions in the letter that follows, Debs dealt with "the fallen women of our day" who were driven to prostitution by the capitalist system and compared them with Hugo's "sublimest of martyrs" in* Les Miserables. *His reminiscence of and praise for Susan B. Anthony, also mentioned in this letter, appeared in* Socialist Woman *in January 1909.*

Margaret Sanger to EVD

February 20, 1918
New York City

Dear Comrade Debs:—
    I have been wanting to write to you for a long time, but heard that you were coming East to be at this National Conference and I waited in the hopes that I might see you then.
    As you did not come, I am now writing you to ask if it would be possible to have an article from you for the May number of the Birth Control Review. I would like, if possible, to make this number a woman's number, using a great many articles that you have written on many women.
    I think the last one I have read of yours was in the New York Call on "Fantine" which was most excellent. I am going to reprint that and also the article of yours on Susan B. Anthony and I wonder if you could tell me any others that you have written of women and where I could get a copy of them. I think that your expressions of woman and your whole interpretation of womanhood is the finest of any of our living men today.
    I am sending you under separate cover the three last issues of the Review and I note upon looking over our files that in some way your name has been missing. Dr. Blossom has left the birth control move-

ment, so we have just been getting ourselves to office work and the routine of getting out a magazine.

I am now trying to combine the magazine with the birth control and feminist movement, for I feel it is not only necessary to have birth control knowledge but also the goal that woman should strive for that they have personal and political freedom.

I hope you are well and will be able to give the time to an article of a thousand or twelve hundred words on any subject that you wish to write about concerning woman or woman's future.

All best wishes to you, I remain

Yours fraternally in the cause,
Margaret Sanger

TLS, InTI, Debs Collection.

□ *Upton Sinclair regularly sent Debs inscribed copies of his many novels. In the following letter Debs thanks Sinclair for* King Coal *and includes high praise for* Upton Sinclair's Magazine, *the first issue of which was dated April 1918.*

EVD to Upton Sinclair

March 5, 1918
Terre Haute, Indiana

Dear Comrade Sinclair: —

Your note is at hand and with it the initial copy of Upton Sinclair's, the contents of which I have examined with special interest. Your introductory message makes strong appeal to thinking people at this critical hour and I hope there may be a sufficient number of these to give you the support you need to make a permanent success of your laudable undertaking.

Upton Sinclair's is clean and attractive in appearance, all that could be expected of paper and type; it is admirably put together and its contents from the first page to the last are of a character and variety to interest and benefit every intelligent reader.

In declaring the mission of your magazine you have sounded the clear note of Social Justice and you have amply and brilliantly sustained your claim in all the pages of your opening number. Very earnestly

do I hope that you and your talented wife may be substantially encouraged and supported in your labors by the wide and sympathetic
response of your many friends and of alert and thinking people generally throughout the country.

Upton Sinclair's has the distinct personality of its gifted and energetic author and will create if it does not find its own field for the
propaganda of industrial freedom and social justice.

Allow me at this late day to thank you for the copy of "King Coal"
which I have read with inexpressible satisfaction. I have not been well
lately or this acknowledgment would have been sooner made.

"King Coal" is a great book—in some respects greater even than
"The Jungle." I marvelled as I turned its pages at your mastery of
the subject to its minutest details. Having served as special organizer
for both the United Mine Workers and the Western Federation of
Miners, and having been warned, threatened and actually driven out
of mining camps for attempting to organize the slaves of the pits, I
am in position to appreciate fully your graphic, fearless {and} startling
exposition of the horrors of slavery as it exists in the mining industry
under private ownership to the utter degradation of the working class
and their families and the shocking disgrace of civilization.

"King Coal" ought to be in every public library. A hundred thousand copies should be spread over the mining regions and a million
copies more among the people.

I have read with particular interest the flattering review of and
comment upon your work by Frank Harris in Pearson's. I have great
regard for Harris' literary judgment and he certainly places a high
estimate upon your work, and I feel assured that his confident pre-
diction of your future will be brilliantly fulfilled.

With socialist greetings to you and Mrs. Sinclair and all wishes for
your success in all things I am,

Yours fraternally,
Eugene V. Debs

TLS, InU, Lilly Library, Sinclair MSS.

□ The "Mooney Case"—that is, the arrest, conviction, and death sentence of
Tom Mooney for murder following a July 22, 1916, bomb explosion at a San
Francisco "Preparedness Parade"—became a national and international cause

célèbre. Debs wrote frequently of the case and raised money for Mooney's defense and appeal, which eventually resulted in the commutation of Mooney's sentence to life imprisonment.

Tom Mooney to EVD

March 23, 1918
San Francisco, California

Dear Comrade, —

Now that the Supreme Court of California has decided that the program of hanging me must be carried out, our fight has been brought to a clear-cut issue. This is only what I expected, from the night of our conviction; and I said then, that our hope was in the organized labor movement, and not in the courts of California. That statment has proven true.

Your splendid efforts in our behalf during these past twenty months, make me feel almost selfish in asking you to do anything further in that regard; but, under these trying circumstances, a man in my predicament perhaps is justified in doing almost anything, as a matter of self-preservation, to say nothing of the great principle involved in this struggle.

Although Weinberg has been taken out of the clutches of the law-and-order gang of the Chamber of Commerce, and although it is very improbable that the prosecution will venture any more "trials," still, by the time this letter reaches you, it is possible that I may have been taken away to San Quentin. Still, I have no fear as to the ultimate outcome of our case. I am absolutely confident that ultimately we shall all be vindicated. That result can only be brought about by the united and determined action of the entire working class in this country, because the forces opposed to us are so powerful, and are still audacious and determined to go as far as they can with the "frame-up."

I wish at this time, to appeal to you to try to interest friends in our behalf, who will contribute to a fund that will enable me to liquidate a debt to my printer, of about $3000. This was incurred for 100,000 copies of "Justice Raped in California," distributed, free of charge, in the city of San Francisco during the recent attempt to recall Fickert. This transaction was a dead-weight expense to me, no returns coming from it; but the work had to be done in our defense, and I undertook it. So far, in spite of all my efforts, I have been unable to meet the obligation. I am sending a copy of this letter to a number of our friends throughout the country. My hope is that, after I am incarcerated in San Quentin, my committee will be able to continue the work of sending out this literature, which has done so much toward bringing our defense to its present wholesome position. If it were not for the publicity that has been secured throughout the entire world, we should all be rotting in a bed of quicklime by this time. Publicity is the weapon that must be used to rouse the workers to the point where they will DEMAND justice for us.

I wish to thank you from the bottom of my heart, for your past support in this splendid, though severe, struggle.

I believe that Rena also will be admitted to bail during the coming week. She joins me in kindest regards and best wishes to you.

Yours,
Tom Mooney

TLS, InTI, Debs Collection.

□ *Thomas Uzzell was a writer and, later, literary critic and lecturer at Columbia University. In the following letter Debs responds to Uzzell's request for his assessment of the status of the Socialist Party of America.*

EVD to Thomas H. Uzzell

April 6, 1918
Terre Haute, Indiana

Dear Mr. Uzzell: —

Your favor of the 3rd. inst. has been received and I take pleasure in giving you my view as to the present political outlook of the Socialist party in the United States. From the reports I receive from day to day from various sections of the country I am convinced not only that the Socialist party as a whole is in a better condition than ever before but that the outlook this year is more promising and that we may confidently expect a decided increase in the socialist vote in the congressional and state elections this fall.

There have been but few defections from the party due to the war and to make up for these there has been a large increase in the party membership, and I am advised by the national secretary of the party that the growth of the party at this time is more rapid than ever before and that the party is in excellent condition to wage an active political campaign.

It is true that the war has interfered with certain activities in the socialist propaganda but it is also true that the war has furnished many object lessons in the way of nationalizing industry to show the people the necessity for as well as the praticability of organizing the industrial life of the nation upon a social and democratic basis, in consequence of which socialism is being discussed as never before and the vote this year will eclipse all previous records.

Very truly yours,
[Eugene V. Debs]

TLc, InTI, Debs Collection.

□ *The Socialist party's stand against the entry of the United States into and participation in World War I was increasingly cited as the cause of defections from the party, which were no doubt accelerated by the massive attacks on the SPA, ranging from the government's suppression of the socialist press and its mailing privileges to violence against individual socialists. In the following letter to the party's national secretary, Adolph Germer, Debs explains the grounds for his belief that the SPA should modify its April 1917 antiwar resolution in light of the momentous changes taking place in Europe.*

EVD to Adolph F. Germer

April 8, 1918
Terre Haute, Indiana

My dear Adolph:—

For some time I have been thinking there should be a special convention of the Socialist party to re-state the attitude of the party toward the war and its policy and purpose when the war is over, in the light of present conditions.

To enter the national campaign this year on the war platform adopted a year ago would be a colossal blunder and make of our campaign a losing one from the start. We cannot go before the country in the present state of affairs on that platform. A year ago when that declaration was adopted, barring certain unfortunate phrasing, it was alright. Today it is flagrantly wrong and it will not do at all. You cannot defend it nor can I or anyone else in its entirety.

The Russian revolution and Germany's treatment of Russia, especially her ruthless invasion and attempted dismemberment of that country and the reduction of its people to a Hohenzollern vassalage has created a tremendous change of sentiment throughout the world which we cannot afford to ignore.

Another matter of which we must take cognizance is the recent conference of the Inter-Allied Labor and Socialist forces held in London for the formulation of the "Labor War Aims" of the labor and socialist movement. You have no doubt read the proceedings of this conference and its report. After going over this report carefully I find myself almost wholly in accord with it. It expresses the conviction and declares the attitude of practically the whole labor and socialist movements of England, France, Italy and Belgium, and I feel that the Socialist party of America should at this time make a similar declaration, defining clearly its present attitude toward the war and the policy it proposes shall be pursued in the making of the peace and in the reconstruction era that is to follow the war. We should have the courage to face the situation exactly as it is and make our declaration as socialists {and} representatives of the Socialist party of America without evasion or equivocation to the world.

If you are in agreement with me I wish you would confer with the members of the national executive committee regarding the matter and see what can be done to have a special convention called to deal with this overshadowing question of the day. I feel that the necessity for action is urgent and imperative.

Please drop me a line and let me have your views.

Yours fraternally,
[Eugene V. Debs]

TLc, InTI, Debs Collection.

□ *Lena Schuhardt had taught in Terre Haute's public schools for seventeen years when, in April 1918, she was dismissed by the school board for failing "to correct unpatriotic ideas expressed by her pupils," for her "opposition to the war," for teaching that "the war is capitalistic and economic" in origin, and for failing to "teach her pupils the proper respect for the Star Spangled Banner."*

EVD to Lena Schuhardt

April 16, 1918
Terre Haute, Indiana

My dear Comrade Schuhardt: —

The morning paper tells the story of your persecution and I drop you this line not so much of sympathy as of congratulation. The silly, trumped-up charges upon which you were dismissed in that farce of a trial deceived no intelligent person in this community. Every one who knows you knows how conscientiously and with what exceptional ability and faithfulness you have done your work, and every one will also know before the matter is over with that the charge of disloyalty is a falsehood and calumny and that you were driven from the service because as a socialist you were persona non grata with the capitalist masters who rule in our schools as they do in their factories and stores.

Your dismissal under such circumstances is to your credit and honor and only those who are responsible for thus attempting to smirch you will ever have cause to blush for it.

You refused to pollute the mind of childhood by glorifying human butchery and national massacre; you refused to degrade yourself by inoculating the youth in your charge with the poison of militarism, and for this we love and honor you and for this you will be remembered when those who hurled the contumelious stone are forgotten. I know you will be patient and I know too that in good time justice will come to you and that the temporary sacrifice {will} bring you the merited compensation.

Mrs. Debs and all of our family join in greetings of affection and assurances of loyal devotion to you, and I am always

Faithfully your comrade,
[Eugene V. Debs]

TLc, InTI, Debs Collection.

□ *In the spring of 1918 various nonsocialist papers reported that Debs had been "whipped into line" regarding the war and was "humbly clambering aboard the band wagon." But in the following letter to his friend Stephen Marion Reynolds—and in what was left of the socialist press—he condemned the report of his support for the war as "capitalist lies."*

EVD to S. M. Reynolds

May 25, 1918
Terre Haute, Indiana

My dear Stephen:—

Your messages are always sweet to me and the one that came in my absence is now in my hands and its loving assurance touches me deeply. But I am not entitled to your felicitations. I have not changed in regard to the war. I have simply been lied about by the capitalist press as I have been many times before. My position has been and will continue to be that of an internationalist. I cannot be pro-war in any war capitalist nations make upon one another. The spirit of the lying press is made manifest in the editorial abuse I am getting for having, as alleged, "changed in the last hour and now come cringing to the band wagon." They need not lay that flattering unction to their deceitful and malicious hearts. I can if necessary stand alone and I certainly would not change my position to be popular or because of threats or intimidations. This is a trying ordeal for us all. We have simply to be true to the light within and all will come well in the end.

We are all loving you and all of you in the same way. There can never be any change. Out on the road many inquire about you and always in the fondest terms. All inquirers are also your lovers. I am just leaving on another speaking tour.

Loving remembrances to Jessica and Marion.

Yours always,
E. V. Debs

TLS, InH, Reynolds Collection.

□ *Debs's speech at Canton, Ohio, on June 16, 1918, in which he set forth ideas and opinions on the war made repeatedly during the preceding four years—the relationship between capitalism and war, the uneven burden of the war on capitalists and workers, the injustice of the convictions and imprisonments being carried out under the wartime Espionage Act—was the basis of his indictment, conviction, and imprisonment for violation of the Espionage Act. A few days after his arrest Debs wrote the following letter to Bolton Hall, a lawyer (who often defended workers' rights) and poet whose work appeared frequently in the radical and socialist press.*

EVD to Bolton Hall

July 6, 1918
Terre Haute, Indiana

Dear Brother Bolton Hall: —

Thank you warmly for your kind and sympathetic message. I am expecting nothing but conviction under a law flagrantly unconstitutional and which was framed especially for the suppression of free speech. I shall make no denial of a word I uttered and it is only for the sake of the party and the cause that I have consented to any defense at all and this only as a means of resisting the attempts now being made to entirely suppress free speech and crush every radical and progressive movement. I am simply one of thousands who have the privilege of doing a bit of extra service for the cause in these days of madness and destruction. Believe me always,

Yours fraternally,
Eugene V. Debs

TLS, NN, Bolton Hall Papers.

□ *Clarence Darrow supported the entry of the United States into World War I but came to view the war as a national disaster and in 1919–20 defended a number of radicals indicted under state sedition laws. When Debs was imprisoned, Darrow worked hard for his release and for the release of other political prisoners.*

Clarence Darrow to EVD

July 20, 1918
[En route to New York]

My dear Debs

I am on my way to England & France & will be gone about two months. I want to send you this line from the coast to say, that I know I do not need to say, that I am sorry for your indictment & that you now as always have my deepest love & sympathy & that if I can ever be of any assistance to you I will give all the aid in my power. I know you always follow the right as you see & no one can do more

With love always
Clarence Darrow

ALS, EVD Foundation, Debs Home.

□ *At his trial for violation of the Espionage Act, held on September 9–12, 1918, in Cleveland, Debs was found guilty by the jury and sentenced to ten years in prison by Judge David C. Westenhaver. The terms of Debs's release during the appeal of his case to the U.S. Supreme Court restricted his movements to Terre Haute and the Northern Federal Court District of Ohio, as he explained in response to a telegram from Otto Branstetter, leader of the Socialist party in Oklahoma and national secretary of the SPA from 1919 to 1924.*

Otto Branstetter to EVD

September 13, 1918
Chicago, Illinois

EUGENE V. DEBS

THOUSANDS OF US SAD BUT PROUD THIS MORNING. YOUR ATTITUDE AN INSPIRATION YOUR CONVICTION A CHALLENGE WHICH WE ACCEPT.

OTTO BRANSTETTER.

Telegram (copy), Collection of Mrs. Philip Taft.

EVD to Otto Branstetter

September 18, 1918
Terre Haute, Indiana

Dear Comrade Branstetter:—

A thousand thanks! your message has inspiration and strength in every line and word of it. I have but done a very small part in a very large work and my one regret is that I cannot do more for the cause.

I had looked forward to the New York meetings with eager anticipation but the order of the court will prevent me from attending them. I know how hard you have worked in the field and I am earnestly hoping that the results may not fall short of your expectations. With all loving greetings to you and the comrades about you I am,

Yours always,
E. V. Debs

TLS, Collection of Mrs. Philip Taft.

☐ *"The Candidate," a character in Upton Sinclair's novel* Jimmy Higgins Goes to War, *strongly resembled Debs, and in the following letter Debs thanks Sinclair for the tribute and for his work on behalf of antiwar political prisoners.*

EVD to Upton Sinclair

September 19, 1918
Terre Haute, Indiana

My dear Upton Sinclair:—
   I have just finished reading the first installment of "Jimmie Higgins" and I am delighted with it. It is the beginning of a great story, a story that will be translated into many languages and be read by eager and interested millions all over the world. I feel that your art will lend itself readily to "Jimmie Higgins" and that you will be at your best in placing this dear little comrade where he belongs in the socialist movement. The opening chapter of your story proves that you know him intimately. So do I and I love him with all my heart, even as you do. He has done far more for me than I shall ever be able to do for him. He is in fact, though but few seem to know it, the actual maker of our movement the wide world over. He more nearly than any other is the actual incarnation of the social revolution and he works unceasingly in and out of season to bring it about. He is scarcely ever seen above the surface. He modestly remains at the bottom where the real work is done and there is no task, however disagreeable, that does not find his heart and his hands ready for it.
   "Jimmie Higgins" is the chap who is always on the job; who does all the needed work that no one else will do; who never grumbles, never finds fault and is never discouraged. All he asks is the privilege of doing his best for the cause where it is most needed. He expects no thanks and feels himself embarrassed if by chance his zealous efforts attract attention. The pure joy it gives him to serve the cause is his only reward. What a fine example of humility, unselfishness and consecration "Jimmie" sets us! I have often in my communion with "Jimmie" envied him and wished I might exchange places with him.
   Almost anyone can be "The Candidate," and almost anyone will do for a speaker but it takes the rarest of qualities to produce a "Jimmie Higgins." These qualities are developed in the "lower class" only. They are denied those who know not the trials and privations, the bitter struggle, the heart-ache and despair of the victims of man's inhumanity to his less fortunate fellow-man.

You are painting a superb portrait of our "Jimmie" and I congratulate you upon the progress and promise of your very laudable undertaking.

There is in my heart much that I should like to say to you about your generous and sympathetic treatment {of} "The Candidate" but for obvious personal reasons I shall for the present have to forbear. I need not say that "The Candidate" feels himself highly honored by you to occupy the center of the stage in company with his beloved "Jimmie" in the opening scene of your drama. It is really "Jimmie" who is the central and commanding figure and deserves all the recognition and applause, "The Candidate" serving only as a background to bring "Jimmie's" noble personality into sharper relief.

Allow me to return my personal thanks for your kindly interest in behalf of comrades who have been sentenced to prison on account of their opposition to war. I have read with special interest your correspondence with the president and members of his cabinet and while I expect, for my own part, no personal consideration at their hands I appreciate none the less the comradely, humane motive which actuated you to make this plea for convicted socialists and others who face prison sentences for refusing to support the war or for asserting their constitutional right of free speech. You have always taken an active part in helping comrades in trouble and in going to the rescue of those in distress, no matter whom they might be, and for this I have always had for you a strong personal attachment.

Allow me in closing to thank you warmly for the place of honor you have given me in the story of dear "Jimmie Higgins" and for the comradely consideration you have always shown me, and with all cordial greetings and good wishes to you and Mrs. Sinclair I am,

Yours always,
Eugene V. Debs

TLS, InU, Lilly Library, Sinclair MSS.

☐ *John Reed graduated from Harvard in 1910 and in 1913 joined the staff of the* Masses, *where he established a reputation as a leading left-wing journalist, thanks to his articles on Pancho Villa, the war on the eastern front in Europe, and the Russian Revolution in 1917. Reed's best-known book,* Ten Days That Shook the World, *was one of the most widely read accounts of the Bolshevik Revolution. In the September 1918 issue of the* Liberator *Reed published an article, "With Gene Debs on the Fourth of July," in which he reported that, despite his arrest and the charge that he was a traitor, Debs remained firm in his opposition to the war. In the following letter Debs thanks Reed for the article and sends greetings to Max Eastman, who covered his trial in Cleveland for the* Liberator, *to Floyd Dell, one of the editors of the* Masses *and the* Liberator, *to Art Young, the artist and cartoonist who illustrated Reed's article, and to Max Eastman's sister Crystal.*

EVD to John Reed

September 21, 1918
Terre Haute, Indiana

My dear John Reed: —
    I have read and have been deeply moved by your fine article in the September Liberator. You write differently than anyone else and your style is most appealing to me. There is a living something that breathes and throbs in all you say.
    Please let me thank you, dear comrade, for the fine and generous spirit in which you have written of me and of my humble service in the cause. I have done so little to deserve so much. It is the bigness of you to which I am indebted for this flattering testimonial which, coming from the heart of John Reed, touches me more deeply than can be told in words. Please extend my thanks to dear Art Young for his fine part in the story. This paltry expression is but a poor return but both of you must know that I love you very much and that I am with you in all things that strengthen our cause and make for the revolution.
    My only regret is that I saw so little of you two royal comrades. I shall hope to see more of you in the future. I had a delightful little visit with Max Eastman in Cleveland. He is certainly one of the gods' annointed.
    Success to the Liberator! It is a flaming evangel of the revolution and deserves the loyal support of every socialist and every radical and progressive.
    My love goes to you all, to you and Art and Max and Floyd Dell and Crystal Eastman and every blessed one of you, and I am
                                                    Yours always,
                                                    Eugene V. Debs

TLS, MH.

□ *The publication of Upton Sinclair's* Profits of Religion *in October 1918 prompted Debs to share with Sinclair his opinion of organized religion in general and of Lyman Abbott, a popular and influential pastor of Brooklyn's Plymouth Congregational Church, in particular. In November 1918 Sinclair published "at the request of Eugene V. Debs" a twenty-page pamphlet, "The Profits of Religion," which reproduced pages 92–109 of the book.*

EVD to Upton Sinclair

October 28, 1918
Terre Haute, Indiana

My dear Sinclair: —

Just a word of suggestion which needs no answer. I am going through your "Profits of Religion" a second time with keen interest in every page. It is one of those books that grows greater with re-reading. You have packed a lot of the most vital stuff into this little volume and a million copies at least should be in the hands of the American people. Let me congratulate you especially upon your courage in unmasking hypocrites in high places and telling the naked truth about the superstitions, frauds and false pretenses which masquerade in the name of religion and which serve now as in the days of Christ to buttress tyranny, fatten insolent parasites, leeches and the whole foul brood of ruling class blood-suckers, {while} keeping their mass of victims exploited to the marrow of their miserable bones, in ignorance and slavery.

You made a very proper example of that arch-hypocrite, that pious, shameless pretender, Lyman Abbott, who prates about "Christian Ethics" while he reeks with the filthy subsidies of his filthy masters.

The suggestion I wish to make is that you put pages 92 to 109 inclusive in a 16 page pamphlet and make a rate on them per 100 and per 1,000 so that this particular expose and eye-opener may be distributed by hundreds of thousands. Every wage slave in America ought to have one of these put into his hands, and if possible into his gray matter to dislodge the superstition placed there by priestcraft which keeps him in bestial subjection to his capitalist master and his mercenaries, the priests and professors and politicians and editorial hirelings.

Yours always,
E. V. Debs

TLS, InU, Lilly Library, Sinclair MSS.

□ *On November 28, 1918, Tom Mooney's death sentence was commuted to life imprisonment, but the general strike hailed by Debs in the letter that follows was opposed by the AFL leadership, notably Samuel Gompers, and failed to materialize. The rumor of a general strike for Mooney's release, combined with the actual general strike in Seattle on February 6–10, 1919, helped prepare the public for the excesses of the Red Scare of 1919–20.*

EVD to Tom Mooney in Care of John Snyder, Editor, *World*

November 30, 1918
Akron, Ohio

TOM MOONEY

"Tear up that commutation and fling the scraps in the brazen face of the corporation hireling that insulted you and the working class by that infamous act. Let Patrick Henry once more speak through you: 'Give me liberty or give me death.' There must be no compromise. You are innocent and by the eternal you shall go free. The working class is aroused as never before in history. They will tear the murderous clutch of criminal capitalism from your throat. All hail the general strike! If they insist upon war let it come. We have nothing to lose but our chains. God loves justice and hates cowards. Stand by your colors and the workers of the world will stand by you to Victory or Death."

Now is the time for the workers of America to prove themselves. Tom Mooney and his Comrades cry aloud to the Proletariat of the world. Arouse ye millions, for whom he risked his life and save that life for the future of his class and for the vindication of right and justice and all things of good report in the civilized world.

EUGENE V. DEBS

Telegram draft, AS, InTI, Debs Collection.

□ *In 1905 Rose Harriet Pastor, a Russian immigrant, married James Graham Phelps Stokes, a New York millionaire with socialist sympathies, and for the next dozen years she and her husband were among socialism's most active and prominent figures. Rose Stokes was also one of the Socialist party's most popular writers and speakers. After attending Debs's trial in Cleveland (where*

she was threatened with contempt of court for leading applause for Debs), she
returned to New York City where she spoke at meetings and rallies on "Debs's
Trial as Witnessed by Rose Pastor Stokes."

EVD to Rose Pastor Stokes

December 5, 1918
Sandusky, Ohio

My dear Comrade Rose;

A thousand thanks for the beautiful letter from your hands which came to me here! Each word from you has cheer and strength and inspiration, and how deeply I am touched and how gratefully I appreciate your continued kindness and devotion I shall not attempt to tell you.

I have heard of your wonderful meetings and your inspiring picture of the trial, including your precious personal tribute, and while deeply, tenderly sensible of it all, I wished some one inspired like yourself had been there to tell of the truly heroic, noble and overshadowing part Rose Pastor Stokes had in that trial.

I'm very, very sorry to hear of the sad end of your faithful little pet but glad indeed that you [one word illegible] the danger—you who mean a world to us who know and love you and a world to our great movement.

I am just leaving for Cleveland—there's no chance to write. You will understand. They still follow me & report my speeches to the Dept. of Justice (!) Let them. We have nothing to fear. The comrades everywhere ask about you—they all love you and well they may.

With all my heart

Yours
E. V. Debs

ALS, CtY.

☐ *Horace Traubel was a literary executor of Walt Whitman, secretary of the Walt Whitman Fellowship, and editor of the* Conservator *from its beginning in 1890 until his death in 1919. The following letter was written soon after*

Traubel suffered a stroke and heart attack from which he never fully recovered and at a time when the Conservator *was in grave financial trouble. Debs's own troubles, as he notes, included the impact of the great influenza epidemic of 1918.*

EVD to Horace Traubel

December 6, 1918
En route in Ohio

Horace Dearest:

Your note and statement have just reached me. My heart aches. It's a damned burning shame. You, dear, beautiful brother, above all others! I'd give the last shred of my garments to be of any real use to you at this trying moment.

For the second time the "Flu" is cancelling my speaking engagements and the secret service agents are doing the rest. You know that under my parole I can only speak within the jurisdiction of the court and here the "Flu" has cancelled my arrangements and sealed my lips. I've had no income for a long time and have had to go deeply into debt to keep up my office and pay living expenses—otherwise you would have had a check from me long ago. I know, dear Brother mine, without a word from your patient and uncomplaining lips, for you're next to my heart and I feel all you suffer and regret only that I can't bear it all. The secret service agents follow me everywhere and the people are so largely intimidated, that my work is made the more difficult and the returns the more meager and fruitless on that account. But we'll not yield, we'll not weaken, we can't—No one knows this better than you.

But you! I'm almost bitter when I think of all you are, all you have been to all, all you have braved and borne, all you have dared and done—and have the great, white, fine soul of you insulted for the want of a few dirty dollars that you wouldn't defile yourself by touching, if the world about you were only half-civilized. But you'll not despair and the Conservator will not succumb. Out of the loves you have fed and of your own great love, help will come and strength and victory. So when I can breathe again I'll gladly share my all with you. Love always and always.

Gene

Love to the Leslie's and Murphy and all the dear ones of your comrades.

Transcript T, DLC, Traubel Papers.

☐ *The Mooney National Labor Congress, attended by delegates from more than a thousand union locals, met in Chicago on January 14–17, 1919, to draw up a plan for the release of Tom Mooney and Warren Billings, who was convicted along with Mooney in the San Francisco "Preparedness Parade" bombing. E. B. Ault was the managing editor of the* Seattle Union Record, *a leading supporter of Mooney and Billings.*

EVD to E. B. Ault

January 15, 1919
Terre Haute, Indiana

E.B. AULT, SECRETARY MOONEY NATIONAL LABOR CONGRESS,

A THOUSAND THANKS TO THE CONVENTION FOR ITS KIND INVITATION. NOTHING WOULD GIVE ME GREATER PLEASURE THAN TO APPEAL TO THE DELEGATES IN BEHALF OF MOONEY AND BILLINGS, BUT I AM IN THE CUSTODY OF FEDERAL COURT OFFICIALS AND NOT PERMITTED TO GO TO CHICAGO. FREE SPEECH PREVAILS IN RUSSIA, BUT IS DEAD IN THE UNITED STATES SINCE WORLD HAS BEEN MADE SAFE FOR DEMOCRACY. THIS MORNING I WIRED DELEGATE WAGENKNECHT A FULL EXPRESSION OF MY VIEWS RESPECTING THE PURPOSE OF THE CONVENTION. THE CONSERVATIVE ELEMENT HAS THE UNQUALIFIED APPROVAL AND SUPPORT OF THE CAPITALIST PRESS, WHICH CAN ONLY MEAN THAT THE CONSERVATIVE ELEMENT IS TRUE TO THE CAPITALIST CLASS AND FALSE TO THE WORKING CLASS. I AM WITH AND FOR THE RADICALS. THE HOUR HAS STRUCK FOR ACTION. LONG-WINDED RESOLUTIONS AND HUMBLE PETITIONS TO CORPORATION TOOLS IN PUBLIC OFFICE AND CORRUPT POLITICIANS ARE WORSE THAN USELESS. MOONEY IS INNOCENT AND THE WORLD KNOWS IT. THIS IS ENOUGH. THE CONVENTION CAN DO NO LESS THAN DEMAND HIS UNCONDITIONAL RELEASE AND ISSUE AN ULTIMATUM TO THAT EFFECT, GIVING DUE NOTICE THAT IF THAT FAILS A GENERAL STRIKE WILL FOLLOW AT A SPECIFIED TIME AND INDUSTRY PARALYZED THROUGHOUT THE LAND. APPEAL HAS BEEN MADE TO THEIR CONSCIENCES IN VAIN, AND NOW LET THE BATTERIES OF LABOR BE OPENED ON THEIR PROFITS. THERE IS NO HALF-WAY GROUND. EVERY EXPEDIENT HAS BEEN TRIED AND FAILED AND NOW THE WORKING CLASS MUST COURAGEOUSLY PROCLAIM ITS PURPOSE AND ASSERT ITS POWER IF THE AMERICAN LABOR MOVEMENT IS NOT TO STAND CONVICTED OF COWARDICE AND TREASON BEFORE THE WORLD. THE CAPITALIST CLASS AND THEIR OFFICIAL HIRELINGS HAVE UTTERLY FORFEITED THEIR RIGHT TO COUNSEL OBEDIENCE TO THE LAW. THEY, THEMSELVES, HAVE TRAMPLED THE

LAW IN THE MIRE IN THEIR COLD-BLOODED DETERMINATION TO MUR-
DER LABOR LEADERS TOO RIGIDLY HONEST TO SELL OUT AND TOO
COURAGEOUS AND SELF-RESPECTING TO BE BROWBEATEN AND INTIM-
IDATED. LET THE ULTIMATUM BE THE UNCONDITIONAL RELEASE OF
OUR FELLOW WORKERS OR A GENERAL STRIKE. IF THE SILK HAT CON-
SPIRATORS AND WOULD-BE LYNCHERS OUT ON THE PACIFIC COAST AND
ELSEWHERE INSIST UPON WAR, LET IT COME. WE HAVE NOTHING TO
LOSE BUT THE GAGS UPON OUR LIPS AND THE CHAINS ON OUR BODIES.
NOW IS THE TIME TO PROVE THE SOLIDARITY OF OUR CLASS. THE
PEOPLE ARE WITH US IN THIS FIGHT AND WILL STAND BY US FROM
COAST TO COAST IN OUR DETERMINATION TO REBUKE CAPITALIST
CRIMINALS AND MAINTAIN OUR RIGHTS AS AMERICAN CITIZENS.

(SGD) EUGENE V. DEBS

TLc, InTI, Debs Collection.

□ *John Haynes Holmes was pastor of the Community Church of New York City
and a leader of countless reform organizations and movements, including the
NAACP and the ACLU. Debs's reference in this letter is to Louis Mayer, a sculp-
tor who did a bust of Debs in Akron, Ohio, in the fall of 1918 following the
trial in Cleveland.*

EVD to John Haynes Holmes

February 28, 1919
Terre Haute, Indiana

My dear Mr. Holmes:—

The very kind and beautiful letter from you has come into my
hands since my return from Ohio and I beg you to believe that it has
touched me deeply and that words are inadequate to express my
appreciation and gratitude.

I feel myself indebted to our dear friend Mayer for many favors,
not the least of which is his generous commendation to his friends
among whom I know you to hold first place. During our sittings at
Akron he spoke often of you and always with love and reverence so
characteristic of the man. He is one of the really fine souls who grows
upon one with contact and becomes nearer and dearer with association.

During my visits to New York during the last few years I heard of you very often through mutual friends and admirers. I also read and was greatly interested in some of your eloquent and appealing addresses and have hoped that it might some time be my pleasure to take you by the hand. I was particularly impressed by your courageous and altogether noble attitude at the beginning of the war, an attitude of moral loftiness and genuine patriotism which you have maintained with unfaltering rectitude and devotion ever since.

Thanking again and again for your very kind and appreciative and inspiring letter and with all good wishes to you I am,

Yours faithfully,
Eugene V. Debs

TLS, DLC, Holmes Papers.

□ *On March 10, 1919, the U.S. Supreme Court, Justice Holmes writing for the majority, upheld Debs's conviction and ten-year sentence for violating the Espionage Act.*

Helen Keller to EVD

March 11, 1919
Forest Hills, New York

Dear Comrade,—

Of course the Supreme Court has sustained the decision of the lower court in your case. To my mind, the decision has added another laurel to your wreath of victories. Once more you are going to prison for upholding the liberties of the people.

I write because my heart cries out, it will not be still. I write because I want you to know that I should be proud if the Supreme Court convicted me of abhorring war, and doing all in my power to oppose it. When I think of the millions who have suffered in all the wicked wars of the past, I am shaken with the anguish of a great impatience. I want to fling myself against all brute powers that destroy the life, and break the spirit of man.

In the persecution of our comrades there is one satisfaction. Every trial of men like you, every sentence against them tears away the veil that hides the face of the enemy. The discussion and agitation that follow the trials define more sharply the positions that must be taken before all men can live together in peace, happiness and security.

We were driven into the war for liberty, democracy and humanity. Behold what is happening all over the world today! Oh where is the swift vengeance of Jehovah that it does not fall upon the hosts of those who are marshalling machine-guns against hungry-stricken peoples? It is the complacency of madness to call such acts "preserving law and order." What oceans of blood and tears are shed in their name! I have come to loathe traditions and institutions that take away the rights of the poor and protect the wicked against judgment.

The wise fools who sit in the high places of justice fail to see that in revolutionary times like the present vital issues are settled, not by statutes, decrees and authorities, but in spite of them. Like the Girondines of France they imagine that force can check the onrush of revolution. Thus they sow the wind, and unto them shall be the harvest of the whirlwind.

You dear comrade! I have long loved you because you are an apostle of brotherhood and freedom. For years I have thought of you as a dauntless explorer going toward the dawn, and, like a humble adventurer, I have followed in the trail of your footsteps. From time to time the greetings that have come back to me from you have made me very happy, and now I reach out my hand and clasp yours through prison bars.

With heartfelt greetings and with a firm faith that the cause for which you are now martyred shall be all the stronger because of your sacrifice and devotion, I am,

Yours for the Revolution,—May it come swiftly, like a shaft sundering the dark.

Helen Keller

Stand up! ye wretched ones who labor.
Stand up! ye galley-slaves of want.
Man's reason thunders from its crater
'Tis the eruption none can daunt
Of the past let us cleanse the tables
Mass enslaved, fling back the call;
Old earth is changing her foundations
We have been nothing, now be all
'Tis the last cause to battle!
Close the ranks, each in place,
The staunch old International
Shall be the Human race.

ALS, InH, Helen Keller Collection.

☐ *Following the U.S. Supreme Court decision, Debs continued to speak at huge rallies in the towns and cities of northern Ohio, the area to which he was restricted by court order. At Youngstown he predicted that he was "about to go to prison for the rest of my life."*

EVD to Theodore Debs

March 28, 1919
Akron, Ohio

My dear old Pard:
    Your letter recd—so glad to have a chipper chirp from you—all the papers have come OK. Meeting at Youngstown last night broke all records. *Thousands* couldn't get in. Marguerite addressed them on the public square. I spoke to the overflow 5 minutes. They were in a frenzy of enthusiasm. Feeling fine as a young buck. So many callers I have no chance to write.
    A thousand loving greetings to you old pard & to Gertrude & Marguerite from

Yours forever
Gene

ALS, InTI, Debs Collection.

☐ *Debs left Terre Haute on April 12, 1919, reported to the federal marshal in Cleveland the following morning, and was taken to the Moundsville, West Virginia, penitentiary to begin serving his ten-year sentence. Theodore Debs's telegram was widely reprinted in the socialist press.*

Theodore Debs to EVD

April 14, 1919
Terre Haute, Indiana

EUGENE V DEBS
    THEY HAVE YOUR BODY BEHIND PRISON WALLS BUT YOUR UNCONQUERABLE SPIRIT, RADIANT AS A SUNBURST, SOARS HUMANITY'S LUMINOUS HEIGHTS A MILLION MILES BEYOND THE FOUL TOUCH OF FILTHY HYPOCRITES AND THEIR PROSTITUTED MERCENARIES. YOUR UNWAVERING FIDELITY TO PRINCIPLE, YOUR UNFALTERING LOVE AND

DEVOTION TO THE CAUSE OF THE CRUSHED AND OPPRESSED WILL BE
AN UNCEASING INSPIRATION. I WAS NEVER SO PROUD OF YOU. MY ARMS
ARE ABOUT YOU, OLD PAL, AND WILL BE THROUGH TIME AND ETERN-
ITY.

YOUR LOVING BROTHER,
THEODORE DEBS

Telegram, InTI, Debs Collection.

☐ *Debs's first prison letter described his trip from Cleveland to Moundsville,
West Virginia, the people who accompanied him on the trip, and his first im-
pressions of Joseph Z. Terrell, the warden of the prison.*

EVD to Theodore Debs

April 16, 1919
Moundsville, West Virginia

My dear Theodore:
  Received your telegram and need not say that it did me more good
than words can tell. Arthur has probably told you that the trip here
was made without special incident. Marguerite Prevey and her sister
and her husband, Fred and Moskovitz —and the rest were all as kind
as they could be to the very last. Karsner, Wagenknecht & Engdahl,
along with Arthur, attended me all the way & did all they could to
make the trip a pleasant one. Marshal Lapp & his deputy Mr. Walsh
treated me with all kindness & consideration.
  Since I had to be imprisoned I congratulate myself upon being
here for it is in all regards the best {prison} I have ever seen. The
Warden, Mr. Terrell, is a gentleman in the true sense of that term
and everyone here without exception respects & loves him. He main-
tains discipline mainly through kindness and the prisoners with rare
exceptions behave themselves accordingly. It is a great institution—
almost 900 prisoners & capacity for at least 600 more. Mr. Terrell
has given me every privilege consistent with the prison rules & I was
never treated more considerately in my life. I have a delightful room
on the ground floor of the hospital bldg & the liberty of the vast
court-yard. In front of me is a spraying fountain & about me the
green lawn & the beautiful flowers. The meals are excellent & everything is scrupulously clean.

Pls. hand enclosed note to Mary & ask her to kindly hand it to Mrs. McGregor when she calls. Pls. don't send me any letters except the really important ones. I do not wish to write or receive an unnecessary one. Mr. Terrell has been more than kind & I do not want to abuse the privileges he allows me.

Don't worry about me in the least. I'm alright. Love to Gertrude & Marguerite.

Your loving brother
Gene

Love to John and Mary

ALS, InTI, Debs Collection.

□ *David Karsner, a New York City journalist who wrote two books on Debs—* Debs: His Authorized Life and Letters *(1919) and* Talks with Debs in Terre Haute *(1922)—served as Debs's chief link with the Socialist party and the general public during the years of Debs's imprisonment. Karsner's articles on Debs in the* New York Call, *a socialist daily, were collected in* Debs Goes to Prison *(1919).*

EVD to David Karsner

April 22, 1919
Moundsville, West Virginia

My dear Comrade David:

A thousand thanks! You can never know how very much I appreciate all your kindness. Your coming here with me was so good of you, and the many fine things you have said and written in your splendid articles will abide with me for all time.

I wish you could have been here long enough to know the Warden, Mr. Terrell, as I have learned to know him. I say this because of a reference to him of a questioning nature in one of your articles. I know you would not intentionally do him the least injustice. He occupies a very trying and difficult position and my being here under the circumstances does not make things any easier for him. He has certainly treated me as well as he possibly can under the rules of the prison which, as you know, he is expected to enforce *impartially*, and there are not a few who would be glad to see him subject me to the severest discipline and set me at the hardest task. Mr. Terrell has had all regard for my health and has in every other way treated me not only humanely but kindly, and I am sure he has the welfare of all the prisoners at heart and does the very best he can by them all. But after all, it's a prison, and I am sure there are many things he would do differently if he were free to carry out his own individual wishes. Please thank all of the *Call* staff for me for their beautiful devotion and support. I can never repay them. My love and gratitude goes to you all.

Kindly send me a copy each of the *Call* of April 13th, 14th, 15th, 16th, 17th, 18th, 19th and 20th. I have given my copies to the Warden's clerks who want the articles for their scrap books.

Believe me always, always

Yours in loving comradeship,
Gene

P.S. Tell the comrades they must not worry about me in the least. I am all right. There is nothing to regret, nothing to fear—there is everything to hope for & to live and work for.

Hundreds of letters, telegrams etc are here. I could not begin to answer them even if it were not for the rules. I appreciate each loving word—each touch of comradely kindness.

ALS, NN, Kars.

□ *Helen Keller's March 11, 1919, letter to Debs was published in the* New York Call, *the* Appeal to Reason, *and other socialist publications in the spring of 1919. In a letter dated April 15, 1919, Theodore Debs asked Keller for permission to circulate the letter and two days later received Keller's telegraphed reply: "YES USE LETTER MY HEART GOES WITH IT."*

EVD to Helen Keller

April 30, 1919
Moundsville, West Virginia

My dear Helen Keller:

You will, I am sure, excuse my seeming remissness. My brother, in my absence, acknowledged the receipt of your beautiful, cheering and inspiring letter, and I meant to write and thank you soon after it came into my hands., but I was kept so busy and in such a state of uncertainty on account of daily expectation of arrest & incarceration that I was unable to give attention to my correspondence. Permit me, my dear comrade, to say to you at this late day that no letter I ever received touched me more deeply or afforded me greater satisfaction. Coming from you this fine, appreciative, characterisic expression compensates in full for a life-time of service.

You have always been to me, since first I knew of your heroic struggle and your incomparable attainment, the most wonderful of women, and your bold, fearless, uncompromising espousal of the cause of the workers won at once my admiration and respect and endeared you to me beyond words. You have used all the power you have won and all the success you have achieved to confer power upon the workers, aye, "the least of these," that they might win the world for the freedom and happiness of all. You have never faltered, never doubted, and never compromised. You are the incarnation of the revolutionary spirit now conquering, freeing, and humanizing the world. You combine all that is fine and brave, sweet and strong, ennobling and inspiring in your contribution to the cause, and I thank you with all my heart, and with love and all good wishes to you, I am always

Yours faithfully
Eugene V. Debs

ALS, American Foundation for the Blind, Keller Collection.

☐ *"Upton Sinclair on the Debs Case" appeared in the* Appeal to Reason *on March 22, 1919. In the following letter to Sinclair, Debs expresses his appreciation.*

EVD to Upton Sinclair

May 4, 1919
Moundsville, West Virginia

My dear Upton Sinclair:

I have just finished reading your stirring appeal in my behalf and in behalf of political prisoners in general, and I want to thank you with a deep sense of the noble spirit which has moved you to put forth your best efforts to secure the liberation of the victims of the espionage act, so-called, which still operates to deprive men and women otherwise good citizens of their constitutional rights. You perceived

the injustice of this from the beginning and protested with such persistency and forcefulness as made itself felt in high official circles, and
when this wrong is finally righted, as it certainly will be, you will be
entitled to a larger measure of credit than any other for opening the
prison doors of your unjustly convicted comrades and fellow men.
And so I thank you for the masterly article and for the more than
kind and generous tribute it contains, only wishing I were more worthy
of such high praises, and with all loving greetings and good wishes,
I am

Yours always
Eugene V. Debs

I have about 900 fellow-prisoners here and there are as fine souls
among them as may be found anywhere. The Warden is a fine man
[illegible words follow].

ALS, InU, Lilly Library, Sinclair MSS.

☐ *In this letter written shortly before his transfer from the Moundsville, West
Virginia, state prison to the federal prison in Atlanta, Debs assures his brother
that he is at peace "as a prison convict at 63."*

EVD to Theodore Debs

[June 4?, 1919]
Moundsville, West Virginia

My dear old Pard:
    Your chipper letter of the 2d gave me several thrills of joy. I only
want to know that all is right at home—*that's all.* The rest does not
trouble me. I know that everything is working to a good end & that
everything is bound to come right. There's never anything the matter
with me. I'm always in tune with the vibrations of the infinite. I'm
getting along the best in the world & my spirits are as vocal as the
springtime. The comrades could not be more loving & loyal, & what
else could I desire or expect? The prison is just now my part and I'm
taking it just as calmly & serenely as if it were staged in some delightful
retreat for my special delectation. At 63 I take what comes with smiles,
be it what it may, especially if it is the enemy of smiles & would banish

smiles from the eyes & souls of men — & *that's victory*, the kind of victory that drives away fear, keeps the heart warm, the spirit young, & fills to the brim the cup of life with the sparkling nectar of love and joy. And *them's my philosophy*, old pard, as a prison convict at 63.

AL, InTI, Debs Collection.

☐ *In June 1919 Debs was transferred to the federal penitentiary in Atlanta. During the two and a half years he spent there, he regularly sent to his brother Theodore notes written on used envelopes, scraps of paper, and in the margins of letters he had received, instructing Theodore to reply to his correspondents. Occasionally, as in this instance, the letter to which Theodore was asked to reply has not been found and the correspondent's name is unknown.*

EVD to Theodore Debs

[1919-1921]
Atlanta, Georgia

Please write him a nice appreciative little letter. He was my cellmate the first two months I was here. He used to make up my bed, wash out my handkerchief, hose etc., & gave me the best of everything. He was kind to me in every way he knew how and I love him and wish him to know that I shall not forget him. He is a thoroughly fine fellow. Tell him I remember having the picture taken here to which he refers but that I have not seen it. I am very glad he is doing well and hope he may do better. Give him my love & best wishes and tell him I shall be more than glad to see him again.

AN, InTI, Debs Collection.

☐ *Following Debs's imprisonment the Socialist Party of America intensified its efforts to secure amnesty for political prisoners, joining various groups such as the Civil Liberties Bureau (later the ACLU) and the AFL. In the following letter Debs shares his ideas on the issue with Otto Branstetter, national party secretary.*

EVD to Otto Branstetter

November 22, [1919-1921]
Atlanta, Georgia

My dear Otto:

Some days ago you were kind enough to invite suggestions from me to the N.E.C. at its next meeting in regard to the campaign of the party for the release of war prisoners, and I now take the liberty to briefly offer my views upon the subject. You understand, of course, that I am opposed to any further petition or request for release so far as I am personally concerned. But this is aside from the general question of amnesty with which the party has to deal as an issue of vital concern to its membership, not only because of those imprisoned but, what is of far more consequence, because of the principles involved which effect not only the fundamental right of free speech but the very right of our party to exist and carry on its propaganda.

Now let me get directly to the point at once. The amnesty campaign is a part of the general fight {we are waging} for our constitutional right to organized life.

Let us then, first of all, place our party in a fighting attitude in regard to it!

No more "Respectfully praying your honorable Body"; no more "humbly petitioning your excellency"; no more catering or Kowtowing to the autocratic power at Washington that has treated every request our friends and comrades have made with insolent contempt.

Let us no longer petition but *demand;* no longer bow to the powers that be but stand erect and fling our challenge into their teeth.

That is my idea of what our attitude and policy should be, and it will awaken the people like a bugle blast and rally thousands to our standards and in our fight for the elementary rights of human beings as well as our constitutional rights as American citizens.

And in pursuance of this policy I beg to recommend to the N.E.C. that it adopt and give to the associated press for publication a short series of *Demands* with a *Capital D.* and that these demands be made in such bold, challenging and defiant terms that they will startle the natives and put the militant spirit into everything on two legs that has a drop of red blood in it.

Meekness and polite petitioning have brought us only contempt and gotten us nowhere. Let us now {stand} straight up with fire in our eyes and face the insolent and brutal power that has robbed us of our rights and fight like men for what is ours and what we propose to have at whatever cost.

This series of demands need not be long but it should bristle like gleaming bayonets.

For example:

We reassert the fundamental principles of liberty embodied in the Declaration of Independence.

We demand the restoration of the Constitution of the United States.

We demand the immediate repeal of all war time laws, especially the unspeakably vile and infamous espionage law, which Russianized America and disgraced its flag.

We demand the unconditional abolition of all war time powers and the restoration of representative government.

We demand the immediate release of all war time prisoners.

We demand the immediate declaration of peace with the nations with which the government has been at war.

We demand the immediate restoration of the fundamental American rights of free speech, free press and free assemblage and we denounce the brutal and lawless interference therewith and hereby declare that we shall resist the same by any means that may be necessary to protect our consitutional rights as American citizens.

Too long have we tamely submitted to the encroachments of Wall Street's autocracy upon our lawful rights and now the time has come to stand up and assert ourselves and we would be cowardly recreants unworthy to be known as men if we failed to do it.

Upon these fundamental issues which involve the constitutional rights dear to us all we make our appeal to the American people in behalf of the Socialist Party, the only political party in America that throws down the gauntlet to the Wall street brigands that rule and loot this nation; the only Party that stands four square for the emancipation of the workers {and} the freedom of the people under real democracy and self-government.

This is but an outline and crudely done but is respectfully submitted to my comrades of the N.E.C. as my view of {what} our party attitudes should be, for such consideration as they may see fit to bestow upon it.

AL, InTI, Debs Collection.

☐ *Mabel Dunlap Curry was the wife of a professor of literature at Indiana State Normal School (now Indiana State University) in Terre Haute. During or soon after Debs's unsuccessful campaign for Congress in 1916, her relationship with Debs changed from that of neighbors who occasionally met socially to a strong bond of affection and love, the intensity of which can best be gauged by reading Debs's letters to Curry during and following his imprisonment.*

EVD to Mabel Dunlap Curry

[1919-1921]
Atlanta, Georgia

Most dearly beloved,   Tuesday 17th
    There are no bounds to patience or endurance or my finish would have been reached long ago. My heart has cried out and I have stilled it with promises until they can deceive no more. And yet we must possess ourselves and learn still further how to wait and cultivate the virtues of the saints, Oh, Juno, do you know, can you know how I long to see you, to be with you, to hear your voice and look into your eyes once more! How I yearn to take you in my arms and tell you what a beautiful, wonderful soul you are and how I love and adore you! Yes, dearest, I know you know, for I can hear your {aching} heart-beats and your cry of loneliness, and I reach out for you as if I can draw you across the intervening spaces and have you with me in happy reunion and loving companionship. No words can ever tell how infinitely precious you are to me, what wondrous vistas you have opened to my vision, and what rare loveliness and beauty have been revealed to me in the pure light of your great white soul. You are all the world to me, most blessed one, soul of my soul, and in the radiance of your beautiful spirit there glow the divinest realities of life. I love you, dearest one, in all tenderness and reverence and with the passionate devotion of my soul.
    May this find you brave as you are sweet and strong as you are true. My love to you, my blessed one, with all my heart!
                                                      Yours now and always
                                                                        Ura

ALS, InU, Lilly Library, Curry Papers.

□ *Hattie Norris was a West Monroe, Louisiana, schoolgirl who was one of Debs's most frequent and devoted correspondents during his imprisonment.*

Hattie Norris to EVD

[1919-1921]
West Monroe, Louisiana

Dearest Comrade —

While taking notes this afternoon I remember an awful mistake I made in my last letter. Please do not think me so igorant as not to know the difference between wholy and holy, for I do. I often make mistakes when I really do know better. I just do not stop to think. I know that I make many mistakes; but now I am trying my biggest to over come them. I am always pleased when some one else shows me my mistakes when I cannot see them myself.

Please, is it alright for me to except a place as teacher in the Union Sunday school When I do not belong to no earthly Church? Every One knows that I do not belong, and yet wants me as teacher.

A thousand good wishes to you.

Hattie

Please excuse pencil, for my pen point is broken and I havent another at present. Also out of type paper. Hard luck isn't it, ha!

ALS, InTI, Debs Collection.

□ *In the following letter Debs thanks the warden and staff of the Moundsville, West Virginia, state prison.*

EVD to J. Z. Terrell

June 27, 1919
Atlanta, Georgia

My dear Mr. Terrell,

It has taken me some little time to get myself adjusted here or you would have heard from me more promptly. The trip here was without incident. Marshal Smith and his deputies treated me very kindly and did all they could to make the trip pleasant for me.

The check you were kind enough to send was duly received and has been placed to my credit. For this and the many other kindnesses I received at your hands I beg you to accept my warmest thanks. The personal effects you sent to my home reached there in good order, as I am advised by Mrs. Debs.

It was with real regret that I parted with you and that fine and manly son of yours on that to me eventful morning. How proud you and Mrs. Terrell must be of that beautiful boy!

My stay with you at the Moundsville prison will always be to me a source of satisfaction and inspiration. This may seem strange to those who are lacking in sympathy and understanding in such a situation, but it is nevertheless true. The Moundsville Prison under your enlightened and humane direction and ministration was to me a study of the deepest interest and I profited immeasurably by my experience there. From the moment of my arrival, when you personally received me, until I bade you good-bye, you treated me with uniform kindness and with all the consideration the rules would allow, as you did every other inmate of the prison, doing the very best you could to help and encourage them all, and for this I shall always hold you in grateful remembrance.

Please thank Mrs. Terrell for me for her kind and gracious attention to Mrs. Debs & Mrs. Curry and give a loving little message from me to sweet little Barbara Lee. Please also remember me kindly to Mrs. Shiltz, to Captain Shiltz, Captain Athey, Mr. Stillwell, Mr. Brown, Dr. Wilson, Dr. Ashworth and dear Doctor Spears who was so very kind to me in so many ways—also to the boys at the Hospital, and not forgetting my good friend "Bill." I formed a strong personal attachment for them all.

I am getting along well here. The work is light and agreeable and the treatment all I could expect. With kindest regards and warmest wishes,

Yours faithfully,
Eugene V. Debs

ALS, NN Kars.

□ *Debs's first letter to his brother Theodore from his Atlanta prison cell describes some of his routine and the rules governing mailing privileges. Gertrude was Theodore's wife; Marguerite, his daughter.*

EVD to Theodore Debs

July 3, 1919
Atlanta, Georgia

My dearest old Pard:

A thousand loving greetings to you and Gertrude and Marguerite—and "Babe"! You know why, under my limited writing privileges, you have not heard from me before. Also you know, too, that you have been in my heart every moment since we embraced in love and farewell at the depot that never-to-be-forgotten night. You are the sweetest, faithfullest darling of a brother a mortal ever had. Kate has been telling me all about how good & sweet & attentive you & Gertrude & Marguerite have been to her, and that has been of inexpressible solace to me. We all may write a special letter on the Fourth of July & it is this letter that I'm now writing to you. Pls. drop a line to Marguerite & tell her why I can't write & that I send my love & tenderest devotion to them all. The ride down here was hot & tiresome but I stood it well. Had but an hour's notice before leaving & everything was kept profoundly secret. *The first five days here I was locked in my cell day & night.* I'm now assigned to clerical work in Clothing Room, very light, and in charge of Mr. Boyle & Mr. Barring, two very fine men. We work from 8 till near four—then 20 minutes in yard—then supper. We are in our cells from 5 PM to 7 AM—Saturday & Sunday P.M. we have out on the grounds from about 1 to 4. *There are 6 of us in our cell*—my 5 companions are the finest kind of fellows & I love them all. One is a German, one a Jew, one an Irishman, & two Americans. They are all fine, bright fellows & they vie with each other in being kind to me. Don't let any one send me *anything* as it can not come to me under the rules. I have not received a package of any kind, nor a socialist paper or magazine since I've been here. Cigars, Fruit, candy, eatables can not come to me, so please notify Germer & the papers not to send me anything as it will not reach me. Tell the comrades I can not write to them. I can write but one letter a week & that to my family. A special letter requires application in writing, special permission, & must be confined to the one subject for which it is written, which must be specified. The application must be approved by the guard before it can be passed on—it may or may not be granted & when written it may or may not be sent. I am treated exactly the same as the common run of prisoners & have no complaint on that score. The prisoner here to whom we sent a little money for tobacco about two years ago has been very kind to me & returned it many-fold. Bread cast upon the waters etc. Enclosed postal card is from Dilon —show it to Getrude & Marguerite & then to Mary & then pass it to Kate. I'm in perfect health. My spirits could not be more serene & dauntless. I calmly await the future. All's well! My love & kisses to you all & forever

Gene

ALS, InTI, Debs Collection.

☐ *In the letter that follows "Big Bill" Haywood combines an optimistic report on the status of the Wobblies and international syndicatism with an insight into the attacks on radicals that were common during the Red Scare of 1919–20.*

William D. Haywood to EVD

November 17, 1919
Chicago, Illinois

Dear Gene:

We have heard many conflicting stories about your physical condition, but so far as your spirits and mentality is concerned, we know that you would be all right wherever you are.

Realizing what a prison life means and the monotonous routine of steamed food, it causes many of your friends to worry. Everyone of us would be glad to know that your health is good, and the thought that you might die in prison causes serious unrest among all of your friends and co-workers.

But Gene, do not worry. Things are moving big on the outside, particularly across the water. In Italy, the Syndicalist movement is taking on the form and principles of Industrial Unionism. The same is true of Spain, while in France Raymond Perricat, in the last issue of the paper received, advocates the endorsement of the preamble of the Industrial Workers of the World.

At a recent convention held at Dusseldorf one million two hundred thousand workers adopted the preamble without change, and endorsed the fundamental principles of the Industrial Workers of the World.

Within the last two months at Hamburg over 30,000 workers have lined up with us.

Geo. Hardy, one of the convicted men of the Chicago group and who has served his time in full, is now in England. He is working under the auspices of the Shop Steward movement, and he is meeting with splendid reception wherever he goes.

In Sweden and Norway the members who were deported from this country are doing equally as well. In Cuba, South America, and Australia the movement is making giant strides, but here in the United States the bitter persecution relentlessly continues.

During the last week halls and offices have again been raided from New York to Los Angeles. Hundreds of members have been arrested, office fixtures and many tons of literature have been destroyed, but even so things are not so bad as the above sentence would indicate. I just received this telegram from New York:

Nov. 16
"All New York halls raided Saturday night. furniture and literature destroyed. Many members brutally beaten, some in hospital. Chumley and John Edwards arrested tried and case dismissed. Raids by the Bomb Squad for the avowed purpose of breaking up organization. Hall Open again and many new members taken in.
Chumley."

To this wire, I replied:

"The old Russianized methods adopted against the members there and elsewhere throughout the country will arouse the working class to the necessity of joining the Industrial Workers of the World as their only means of emancipation. The idea is imperishable."

Be of good cheer, Gene, and kindly remember me to any friends that may be incarcerated with you.
With kindest regards to you, I am
Wm D Haywood

[EVD note to Theodore Debs]
Pls. write Haywood an appreciative note. Tell him his message cheered the boys here & they all send greetings & best wishes. Tell

him not to worry about my health. I'm feeling better now than since I've been here. The cool weather is most bracing to me. I'm gaining steadily in weight—now tip the beam at 167.

TLS (with EVD note to Theodore Debs), InTI, Debs Collection.

☐ *Kate Debs sent this Christmas card message to her husband.*

Katherine Metzel Debs to EVD

December 25, 1919
[Terre Haute, Indiana]

"To that Old Sweetheart of Mine"
    "Greetings and good wishes"
    I think of you lovingly and devotedly each passing hour of the day, at night I lay my hand reverently on your dear pillow and say "good night" and in the morning I step in and say "good morning dear" and kiss your pillow. *Love, Love, how wonderful it is!* And *mine* is true and enduring through all time.

Your devoted wife
K

Christmas card with note (date in hand of EVD), Debs Home, EVD Foundation.

☐ *In the following letter Alex Rahming is probably referring to "The Negro: His Present Status and Outlook," an article that was widely reprinted in the socialist press, in which Debs wrote: "the Negro is my brother and the Socialist who will not speak out fearlessly for the Negro's right to live and work, to develop his manhood, educate his children, and fulfill his destiny on terms of equality with the white man misconceives the movement he pretends to serve or lacks the courage to live up to its principles."*

Alex Rahming to EVD

March 15, 1920
New York City

My dear Comrade Gene:—

"I am indeed thrilled and overjoyed today, not because my position as a worker has improved, but because you, who stands for truth and justice, You who are suffering untold agonies, Yes I am happy, because you, who would gladly give life itself, that humanity may be free, has given your consent to become a Presidential Candidate and may God grant the workers sufficient intelligence to see the light, that the doors that are now locked will fly open, and our Gene will egress to Washington and be crowned lord of all.

I am a Colored man, and although my race has every right to protest, yet we in the social field know, that the present system can only survive by encourageing prejudice based upon religion, race or Nationality however as dumb as many of us are, we will be forced to see the fallacy of supporting a regime, that will keep the masses in illiteracy for their security.

Gene, many months before your imprisonment, you wrote an article in the Call entitled, "the american negro," may I take this opportunity to confess my appreciation of your frankness and to inform you, that in my public talk, the workers of Color, were informed and I hope that they will show their appreciation at the polls, but my Chief Concern is my brothers in the {dark} South who has been feed upon lies but let us hope, that they will awaken, and make this in truth the land of the free. Wishing you continuous health

I am your Comrade,
Alex Rahming

I am going to try and secure a hall for April 13th to protest against your imprisonment, so if possible reply.

ALS, InTI, Debs Collection.

☐ *Lucy Robins, a leader of the AFL amnesty campaign, visited Debs frequently at the Atlanta penitentiary and, as in the following letter, kept him informed about the progress and problems of that campaign. Among the latter was one created by David Karsner, who wrote in the* Call *that, while Debs appreciated Samuel Gompers's efforts on his behalf, Debs had said that "there could never be anything between Gompers and me as long as Gompers remained the kind of labor leader he has chosen to be during all of his presidency."*

Lucy Robins to EVD

April 24, 1920
New York City

My Dear Comrade Debs: —
   I know that I should have written to you before, and believe me I wanted to, but I know that you will forgive me because you fully realize that in my work for a general amnesty it means more work than play. I haven't had an hour to spare since I visited with you. In fact, I only run into New York for a day or two to attend to the most important matters and then run out again.
   I addressed the Cigarmakers Convention, and brought your greetings and message to them. Mr. Gompers presided while I spoke, and after I was through he assured the delegates that he is doing and will do all in his power to help bring about a general amnesty.
   I have helped to organize the Citizens Amnesty Committee which consists of Mrs. Champ Clark, Mrs. La Follete, Basil Manly and others, who left a memorial at the White House for President Wilson.
   I have addressed since I have seen you meetings of Central Bodies, District Councils and Local Unions almost daily and always get good results.
   Local Unions throughout the Country are now receiving letters from Senators & Congressmen of their own districts pledging support to the France Joint Resolutions. Washington is astir on the question of general amnesty. You can rest assured Dear Comrade that we won't leave a stone unturned until a general amnesty is declared.
   Mr. Carsner of the "Call" must have visited you after we did. He surely made a mess of things, with his statement to the Call. We know that all news in the press is painted. Our statement too, was painted to a great extent in the Atlanta Georgia press, but there is a limit even to press exaggeration. Gerber, Solomon, Lee, O'Neil and many many others feel very badly about the statement that Carsner wrote in your name, particularly in reference to the question of an amalgamation of all branches. They feel that you never did give him the

statement as he wrote it. However, I guess we cannot avoid breaks of this kind at any time.

I think you ought to feel proud to know that in many shops the workers are busy making suits, shirts, ties and many other things for you. We know that you don't want it but I am sure that if you would only know the spirit that prompts them to do it you would feel happy indeed.

I am awaiting impatiently for information to know whether you are already on that beautiful farm, which is the dream of Mr. Zerbst, and if so, I am sure you are enjoying the green fields, the budding trees, the well fed stock and the newly born little chicks.

I am very much desirous of getting a letter from you about all these details. I will write to Mr. Zerbst, whom I found very considerate and ask him that if possible to grant a special privilege to you to write me a long letter.

I will try to write to you as often as I can and give you information about the progress we are making.

Accept the loving heart throbs of thousands of your friends. We feel very hopeful that we will have you with us soon. With the best of all good wishes, I am

Sincerely yours,
Lucy Robins

TLS, InTI, Debs Collection.

□ *Walter Cook served as secretary of the Socialist Party of America convention that was held in New York City in May 1920. Seymour Stedman was a long-time friend of Debs from Chicago and one of his attorneys at the Cleveland trial in 1919. Debs was formally notified of his nomination in Warden Frederick Zerbst's office on May 29, 1920.*

Walter M. Cook to EVD

May 13, 1920
New York City

EUGENE V. DEBS,
    THE NATIONAL CONVENTION OF SOCIALIST PARTY HAS BY A UNANI-
MOUS VOTE AND WITH UNPRECEDENTED ENTHUSIASM CHOSEN YOU

TO BE OUR STANDARD BEARER IN THE PRESIDENTIAL CAMPAIGN WITH SEYMOUR STEADMAN AS CANDIDATE FOR VICE-PRESIDENT. A COMMITTEE WILL VISIT YOU AS SOON AS POSSIBLE TO CARRY IN PERSON OUR MESSAGE OF TRUST AND LOVE TO PERSONIFY THE GLORIOUS IDEAL OF OUR PARTY WE PROMISE A CAMPAIGN THAT WILL ENLIGHTEN AND AWAKEN THE WHOLE NATION.

WALTER M COOK, SEC.

Telegram, InTI, Debs Collection.

☐ *The slogan "From Prison Cell to White House," which appeared in the* Appeal to Reason *as early as May 1919, was used regularly by a number of socialist publications.*

Elsie Brown to EVD

May 30, 1920
Pensacola, Florida

Dear Sir:—

No doubt you will be surprised to get a letter from a little girl twelve years old, But I am just one of the ten million children who love your name and put you the head of all the great men. We *class* you as that of Moses trying to lead the children of Israel out of the land of bondage, And we have joined the great host of this great country in their slogan from the prison to the White House. And our daily prayers are that these words will come to pass. How I wish that you were free that you may enjoy this beautiful sabath-day which God has given us. I want you to answer and tell me to what curch you belong. I hope you are a *Baptist* and if you are elected president of the United States do not try to run this great cuntry, alone but always ask Gods help and do his will. I shall be glad to hear from you if you will have time to write to a little girl like me.

Yours truly,
Elsie Brown

My address is:—Elsie Brown, East Pensacola, Pensacola, Fla. R 1, box 55a

Postscrip—read Revelation: 2, 10

ALS, InTI, Debs Collection.

□ *In the following letter Debs describes the ceremony held in Warden Frederick Zerbst's office to formally notify him of the presidential nomination and, in passing, mentions his misgivings about accepting that nomination.*

EVD to Theodore Debs

June 1, 1920
Atlanta, Georgia

My dearest old Pard,

It sometimes seems a thousand years since last I saw you and then again I hold you in my arms and it can not be that we have been apart at all. One thing, however, is beyond seeming and that is that through all the days of separation our hearts have beat as one and no day, no hour has passed that I have not sent you and Gertrude and Marguerite my love and blessing and received yours in return. You have heard, no doubt, of the visit last week of the Notification Committee and of the unique and touching program that was carried out through the courtesy of the Warden. Dr. Stephens will tell you about the proceedings in detail. Isn't she a noble woman and a magnificent comrade! I did not know, though I thought I did, how fine and devoted and courageous and true she really is. She brought me a lovely message from Kate & carried one back to her and she had so much to say about you & Marguerite and Gertrude. She and Wallace love you all very devotedly and are happy indeed in your confidence and companionship. All the comrades on the Committee treated me with the utmost kindness. They were a fine lot of comrades. "Steddy" and "Jimmy" Oneal and Otto Branstetter and Dr. Stephens and "Billy" Feigenbaum and Julius Gerber made up the party. Joe Coldwell of Rhode Island, a fellow-prisoner and leader of the C.L.P. was present, as were also Sam Castleton and Comrade Rhoden the local organizer. "Jimmy" Oneal made a beautiful little address. They all thought of you and paid you every possible tribute of confidence and love. Pictures were taken for the movies and you will likely see the pictures at T.H. When you write Marguerite Prevey tell her I carried out our agreement to the letter & told the committee all she suggested and *more*. Marguerite was too big & noble and understanding to advise me *not* to take the nomination. There will be all kinds of comment & I will be denounced but I'll stake my life I made no mistake. I followed the inner light that God put there to guide through dark places and it has never yet led me astray and never will. So do not worry, but keep chipper and let your heart sing for we're on the road that leads to Camp Victory. Pls. write to Kate O'Hare & tender our congratulations. I was heartily glad to hear of her release. Tell her we're all happy to see her with her dear ones again. You're no doubt pretty busy. Wish I could help. But I'm doing my little here that may not be entirely without its purpose. Kiss dear Gertrude and Marguerite for me and bless them. They are always in my heart. I've often felt sorry about "Babe" —I know how you all loved that faithful friend. Pls. ask Gertrude to remember me with love to Ed & Ranita when she writes. I shall always love those dear souls and remember their kindness & devotion. I'm in excellent fettle—ready for anything at the tap of the bell. When my glims light on you, old scout,—well, you know what happened to Hammerstein. My arms are about you all!

Eternally!
Eugene V. Debs
#9653

Give my love to Phil and Hollingsworth and Wilson and the Hendersons and Carnes. Tell Kate that I'm feeling better every day and that she must not worry in the least. We are on the right track & the future will make up richly for it all. Tell Dr. Stephens I shall never forget her & give her & Wallace my love.

ALS, InTI, Debs Collection.

□ *President Woodrow Wilson and his attorney general, A. Mitchell Palmer, received hundreds of letters and telegrams from individuals and organizations urging them to free Debs. Lucy Robins released the following letter, which was widely reprinted in both the socialist and nonsocialist press.*

EVD to Lucy Robins

July 16, 1920
Atlanta, Georgia

My dear Comrade,

Please say to the comrades in New York that, while I appreciate fully all that has been done in my behalf, I object emphatically to any further appeal being made for me to President Wilson. I wish no special consideration and I wish to fare no better than my comrades. As long as they are held criminals and convicts my place is here. My comrades will therefore understand that they can serve me best by bringing their influence to bear in behalf of all.

Thanking you and through you all the dear comrades and friends who have so loyally remembered us and so faithfully served us, and assuring you that your noble services will always be gratefully remembered.

I remain always

Yours faithfully
Eugene V. Debs

ALS, InTI, Debs Collection.

☐ *Debs's convict number was 9653. From time to time there were rumors of his being ill in prison, and he tries to reassure his brother on that score in the following letter.*

EVD to Theodore Debs?

July 31, 1920
[Atlanta, Georgia]

*Official Report
Physical Condition of Convict No. 9653*

To the Secretary at Large,

The following is an official report as to the physical condition of Convict No. 9653 to date:

Averdupois—Net increase 1 ounce.
Complexion—sun-tanned and swarthy.
Hair—Cut bias: style Pompadour.
Thorax—Ne plus ultra.
Cerebellum—Safe and sane.
Liver and Lights—E pluribus unum
Sweetbreads—well done.
Heart—carroling mellifluously.
Lungs—Leathery and lusty.

Appetite—Prodigious and persistent.
Hands—Feeling their way toward ult. Pudgy.
Feet—Ample and eminent.
Torso—Well barred and secure.

                                                Signed
                                        Uneeda Pill M.D.

Subscribed and sweared to before me this 31st day of July 1920
                                          S. N. Hardy
                                        Notary Private

My commission expires when I do.
P.S. This report is definite, specific and authentic.

ALS, InTI, Debs Collection.

□ *Frank Harris was perhaps best known for his biography of Oscar Wilde and for* My Life and Loves, *both of which were considered too frank (or explicit) for American and European publishers. In 1916 Harris bought* Pearson's *and, despite government harassment during the war and chronic financial troubles, made it a leading literary magazine in the 1920s. He regularly urged the release of Debs and the other political prisoners in his* Pearson's *articles and editorials.*

Frank Harris to EVD

August 17, 1920
New York City

                    PRIVATE AND CONFIDENTIAL

Dear Eugene Debs:
    I haven't heard of or from you for a long time; but you can never doubt my sympathy with your noble stand and unmerited suffering.
    I have written articles time and again in Pearson's pleading for amnesty; in fact every number has some prayer; but this administration is impervious to any appeal either of head or heart.
    Now I think of using a new power.
    I'm going to try to found an organization for Radical propaganda through the "Movies." Some moving motion picture people came to me wanting to buy the right to put my novel "The Bomb" in the

pictures; talks showed me the vast power and influence of the new appeal and I conceived the idea of extending the story and including some dramatic incidents from your life.

Do you approve of the idea?

And if you do will you please tell me one or two of the most dramatic or personally characteristic incidents in your life? I suggest the answer to:

"How or Why I Became a Socialist?" You to supply the answer: — Then —

"My Confirmation in the Faith.": or, "My Baptism of Fire," or both. But first a short letter telling me if you approve the new idea as I feel sure you will.

The other day I pled with Senator Harding to speak for pardon for all of you, but without immediate result; however, it'll come you may be sure and soon. I quoted your words on the trial and told him they could be put in "The Sermon on the Mount" and would be about the best of it which startled the old politician. This is private. I went to Marion to plead for you: I called you "The Beloved Disciple."

Keep up your courage. You must remember Wordsworth's finest lines:

"Thou hast left behind
Powers that will work for thee, air, earth and skies;
There's not a breathing of the common wind
That will forget thee; thou hast great allies;
Thy friends are exultations, agonies,
And love, and man's unconquerable mind."

These words are ever in my memory about you, these and another couplet I will quote in my next letter.

But now I hasten for I want my scheme at work and there's much to be done. One word of encouragement from you will hearten all of us.

Ever your loving friend and comrade in all humanities,
Frank Harris

TLS, InTI, Debs Collection.

☐ *As Debs's vice-presidential running mate, Seymour Stedman provided Debs with periodic reports on the progress of the campaign in which Warren Harding was the Republican party candidate and James Cox the candidate of the Democrats.*

Seymour Stedman to EVD

September 29, 1920
Chicago, Illinois

Dear Brother Debs:

They sent me into Oklahoma for a twelve-day speaking engagement where the temperature rose above a hundred. Thus they prepared me for hell. Then they sent me to the western coast where they have climate, — here they prepared me for heaven. I feel that I am now thoroughly qualified for either place.

All along the route I met countless hundreds who were asking "when will Brother Debs be out," some with tears in their eyes and showing a great deal of emotion. Some would say, "I am glad to shake hands with you, but I would rather shake hands with Debs," and then attempt to qualify it tenderly by saying, "I mean I wish he was out so that I could shake hands with him." I should certainly hesitate before taking the responsibility that you have by reason of the unexampled devotion and affection of the multitudes.

The Party was in bad shape, the movement in very good condition. The meetings and the response was very much above our expectations. The attacks upon the Party by the press and the American Legion and other thousand per cent patriots was vicious but it was astounding to see the rebounding of the movement after the repressive measures due to the war. There is some haziness in the west and there are still a great many who are attempting to change conditions by a boomerang method of tactics, that is, they look at the United States through first looking over at Russian and European propaganda and conditions and hesitate to adopt the tactics which constitute the most direct attack upon capitalism in the United States. The ousting of the New York Socialists again, and the attempt to prevent our political activity should open the eyes of those persons who regard political action as inconsequential to the fact that our growing political strength with its definite and uncompromising purpose arouses our antagonists to a fever heat of opposition.

I note by the papers that you receive a large number of letters and other documents. I have for that reason refrained from writing to you and make this communication very short, therefore.

I am doing the best I can, but fully realize that my abilities are far from reaching the requirements of the situation as a result of your absence from active participation.

The administration is very much perplexed. They don't want to hang on to you, and they don't want to let go. The fall in prices and the closing of industries, unemployment problem, financial bank and industrial depression, which is in its incipiency, may throw us into a fearful industrial mallestrom.

I hope our party may, during the next two years, assemble with a concrete program at every opportunity for an attack upon the capitalist system. The opportunities of the next two to four years will surpass anything we have ever had in the past. If we can use the capacity we have and develop the organization we should have, we will rock this old system off its hinges within the next four to eight years.

I hope you are enjoying the best of health and believe me that many thousands turn their thoughts to you as they feel the inspiration of your devotion.

The last time I met Teddy I left him badly mutilated. I know he was obliged to write you with poltices on his eyes and a twisted beak. That was my work. His vanity will prevent him from confessing the results of a humiliating defeat. You remember Terry McGovern? Well, that's the way I acted toward that brother of yours. I would have sent him to the hospital but I knew he had a lot of letters of yours to answer, so for him you were a life saver.

Sincerely, and with love,

As always,
Seymour

[EVD note to Theodore Debs]

Pls. say to "Steddy" that his letter was especially gratifying & cheering to me, that it reminded me of the old days and that the spirit of youth throbbed once more as I perused its lines and recalled the scenes & experiences of twenty years ago. Tell him I have heard of his wonderful meetings and that his speeches have been reported to me in the highest terms and that I am applauding his splendid efforts and rejoicing with him all along the route, regretting only that I can not be with him to share in the demands of the campaign. Tell him

I am perfectly agreed with him as to the outlook for the future and that we have every reason to put forth our best efforts in behalf of the party and the cause.

Pls. tell him I remember Terry McGovern (he took me to the only prize fight I ever saw — in Chicago — Terry McGovern beat Geo. Dixon, but I nearly fainted) and that when he & I and Teddy meet there will undoubtedly be a busy & interesting time and the shedding of copious installments of fur and entrails. Pls. say that I send love and best greetings to him and Irene and Comrade Soelke.

TLS, InTI, Debs Collection.

☐ *William Henson was one of Debs's fellow prisoners at the Atlanta peniten-tiary. In this and a number of other letters written in 1920 and 1921 Henson expresses his gratitude to Debs for friendship and counsel.*

William Henson to EVD

October 4, 1920
[Atlanta, Georgia]

Mr. Debs, Dear Sir —

I am writing you againg, I can all ways find something to say to you, Mr. Debs. I think you with my whole heart for what you gave me I realy did enjoy it *all*. Sorry that I can't do something for you, But if God spar me I will be of some help to you some day. For I am loing to be with you on the outside, For I am very much interested in your great work indeed, I read your trial in Cleveland, Ohio and Every word you said is very truly, And that is why the government is keeping you in here, For you are a *Man*, a man with a real heart. And that what they don't like.

They get a poor man or a poor woman down just as long as they can, They are making Millions and millions of dollars from poor people, I will be truthfull with [you] I would indeed like to see *you* in the White House and thousands of others would too. The people are just waking up some of them, and it would Please lot of people to see *you* President, Mr. Debs, I read the pace of Mr. John D. Rock-efeller, I did not know what his income was before.

In your great work you win out, I hoping so any way, and you are going to be successfully Too.

Hoping you will get out very soon, But I will Miss you very, very much, But I sincerely wont to see you out, if I don't never get out I want to [see] my Dear Friend in a new world. Mr. Debs, Please any time [you] want me to do anything, just ask me and I will be very glad to [do] anything for you, and I do it with all my Heart, and I Do not want you to give me anything at all, For I am not looking for any thing, For I cant do what I would like to do.

You are my only Friend I have got, And all I want is a chance to show the world that I want to do the Right thing I want to [do] it and I will do it,

Hopeing you are feeling O.K. tonight,

Yours very truly
William Henson,

[EVD note to Theodore Debs]
Read this and weep with compassion over this sweet-souled colored child that never had the ghost of a chance.

ALS, InTI, Debs Collection.

□ *The League of Nations was a central issue in the 1920 presidential campaign. William Tappan was headmaster of the Jefferson School in Baltimore.*

William Tappan to EVD

October 5, 1920
Annapolis, Maryland

My dear Mr. Debs,

Would you be kind enough to write, for the information of many who are interested, what is your attitude toward *the* League of Nations and *a* League of Nations? If you would take a few minutes to state this *in your own handwriting*, it would be greatly appreciated by a large group.

Yours very truly,
Wm. Tappan
1228 Munsey Bldg.
Baltimore Md.

[EVD note to Theodore Debs]

Pls. say that I very much appreciate his [illegible words] and regret that my situation prevents [illegible words] making such a statement as I would wish. Briefly, in the present order of society the "Nation" is the ruling class and not the people, and I am opposed to *a* league or *the* league or *any* league of these ruling class "nations" to further buttress their cruel & oppressive misrule and exploit the world. But I am heartily in favor of a federation of peoples, that shall embrace the whole earth.

ALS, InTI, Debs Collection.

□ *In the November 1920 issue of* Pearson's *magazine Frank Harris wrote that "Eugene Debs and Seymour Stedman . . . are head and shoulders above Harding and Cox as well in depth of thought as in high unselfishness of purpose. Accordingly, I must vote for the Socialists." Harris's references in his October 12, 1920, letter are to George Bernard Shaw and James Larkin, an Irish radical in New York who in 1920 was sentenced to ten years in prison for "criminal syndicalism."*

Frank Harris to EVD

October 12, 1920
New York City

Dear Comrade:—

I am sending you a copy of the November issue of Pearson's. You will see how we are promoting the cause in which you are concerned, and how I have picked you and Stedman as the only worthy candidates for office.

I wish that you would send me an expression of your opinions for the next number of the magazine. I will publish it with a reproduction of a note Shaw has written me. He says: "It serves Larkin right to {go} to America where "liberty is treated as anarchy." I see Stedman tomorrow too and will get some word from him. I mean to put your likeness & that of Stedman on my cover.

Ave atque Vale Affectionately & Fraternally yours
Frank Harris.

TLS, InTI, Debs Collection.

EVD to Frank Harris

October 14, 1920
Atlanta, Georgia

My dear Frank Harris,
   I shall not see your Magazine, to my deep regret, as it may not enter here. You have fought and are now fighting a heroic battle against overwhelming odds, and but for your genius and personality Pearson's could not have lived. You have in fullest measure my admiration, my love and best wishes.

Yours always
Eugene V. Debs

ALS, Leo Miller Collection, New York City.

□ *The Prison Comfort Club was made up largely of socialist women who worked for amnesty, sent "comforts such as food, clothing and books" to prisoners, and helped the dependents of prisoners.*

EVD to Otto Branstetter

October 23, 1920
Atlanta, Georgia

NATIONAL OFFICE, SOCIALIST PARTY,
Otto Branstetter, Executive Secretary
220 South Ashland Boulevard, Chicago, Ill.

Atlanta, Ga., Saturday,
October 23, 1920.

My dear Otto:
   Today the blessed boxes came to the political prisoners here (25 I think) from the Prison Comfort Club, and you should have seen the smiles of joy and gratitude on the faces of the convict recipients. There were roast-beef, ham, pork and egg sandwiches, smoking tobacco, cigars, matches, pecan nut candy, chocolate bars, Malaga grapes, bananas, apples, chewing gum, etc., and best of all, the "dear love of comrades" that came with the boxes to give the contents a delicious spiritual flavor fit for the gods.

We are feasting today, dear comrade, with the proud and happy feeling that we are in the hearts of our beloved friends and comrades on the outside, and if the prison had any terror for us, which it has not, it would not only have been robbed of such terror, but converted into a holy temple by the precious love and devotion of the Prison Comfort Club, made manifest in the generous offerings that were laid upon the altar of liberty today as our sacramental feast. Of course, we are sharing our blessed bounty with our fellow prisoners who have no dear and devoted comrades to remember them in their loneliness and deprivation, and they too now feel the incoming of Socialism even behind the gray walls, and join with us in a shower of blessings upon the loyal and loving members of the Prison Comfort Club.

Each box had in it a card bearing the name of the recipient with the following greeting: "Presented by National Prison Comfort Club. Prepared by Atlanta Prison Comfort Club."

We can almost see the dear comrades preparing the boxes with tender devotion, and we can almost feel the touch of their faithful hands in the delicacies their kindness and generosity have provided for our enjoyment and good cheer.

Please express our affectionate appreciation and our warmest thanks to each member of the Prison Comfort Club, and say to them that their kindness and comfort will never be forgotten.

Yours in the Cause,
(Signed) Eugene V. Debs

TLc, NcD, Socialist Party Papers.

□ *On election day, November 2, 1920, Debs received 913,664 votes, about 3.5 percent of the total number cast and roughly half the share of votes he got in 1912. He was, of course, not surprised by his defeat in 1920, nor, as the following letter indicates, had he lost confidence in "victory in the end."*

EVD to Theodore Debs

November 25, 1920
Atlanta, Georgia

My dearly beloved Theodore,

We are allowed an extra letter today on account of Thanksgiving, and my heart turns to you and dear Gertrude and Marguerite with all the loving greetings of the day and all the good wishes in the world. It would be such a joy to see your dear faces again and press you in my arms once more but as this may not be the written pages will serve to tell you that I feel your loving presence here and that even the shadow of you is to me a source of inexpressible comfort and consolation. The miles do not divide us. I can hear your loving heart-beats and know that by day and by night you are always near me. We have had our trials since we parted in the flesh, but we have also had our compensations, and we have every reason to give thanks today with all our hearts. We are doing in our small way what numberless others have before us in the service of truth and justice, and we were weak and unworthy indeed if we made complaints instead of feeling it a privilege to be chosen to do our part in [one word illegible] the ills and wrongs of our times and bringing better and brighter days to the world. It is enough for us to know that our cause is righteous and that if we are faithful and do our duty it is certain to be crowned with victory in the end. I am very glad you are to attend the coming meeting of the Natl. Executive Board at Chicago. You will be of value to the members and they will be happy to have you with them. They are a fine body of men and you will enjoy their company. What fine and beautiful comrades we have! What rare souls have rallied to us and stood by us through all that has come with a devotion too deep for words and without care or shadow of turning! How rich and grateful we should feel and how highly resolved to be true to them and to our trust to the last breath of life!

Saturday December 4th our revered "Dandy," had he lived, would be one hundred years old. What deep love and reverence the very thought of his noble memory inspires! On that day we shall stand lovingly where "Dandy" and "Daisy" rest and pay to their sweet memory the tributes of our tears—tell dear Gertrude no day passes that my blessing does not go to her and dear Marguerite. We have had many beautiful days together and perhaps we may have again. Sweet Marguerite's picture is always before me and she smiles into my eyes many times during the day. I love and embrace and kiss you all.

Faithfully and eternally yours
Eugene V. Debs
#9653

Have never a care for me. I am better off than all the rest. You can rest assured that I am well and eating and that all is well here.

Please give my love to dear Mary and all the Comrades at home.

ALS, InTI, Debs Collection.

☐ *In the essay "To the Children," published in the Socialist party's* New Day *at Christmastime in 1920, Debs predicted that "under socialism the children of the future will be free and the earth shall be their playground."*

Hattie Norris to EVD

December 25, 1920
West Monroe, Louisiana

My Dearest True Friend:

Yes! it is rather lonely to live among people who dont care for things that intrest you. The only things I have to enjoy is natures gifts and to think of the comming future, but most of all is reading your promising letters. The letter you addressed to us in the, "New Day." has sent my heart thrilling with joy and saddness. Everybody reads it that I show it to, and thinks it wonderful.

The trouble with the most of the people here, is, they dont even know about you being in prison, and when I tell them they always ask for what was you put in prison for. I always answer them: Comrade Eugene V. Debs was cast in the Atlanta Federal Prison because he is too wise for the *Ruling Class* of to-day. I have learned that most people thinks it a disgrace to be in prison making no difference how came you there.

We have gone our last school day this year, and I do hope that the "New Year" shall be so much more brighter and happer that we shall look upon this old one as a past dream. Some people are agreeable in ways, but very ungracious, and most of all ignorant. They goe their way in life buy fearful leaps, and do not consider the dreadful disasters, which might befallen them in the near future.

The whole family sends you best wishes for a very happy "New Year, and a speadly release from that dreadful prison.

Lovenly,
Hattie Norris

ALS, InTI, Debs Collection.

☐ *Benjamin Salmon, a conscientious objector during World War I, was a pris-oner being treated at Walter Reed hospital in Washington, D.C. In November 1920 he began a hunger strike as "a Christmas protest against the imprison-*

ment of Eugene V. Debs and his fellow prisoners." Soon after Debs sent the fol-
lowing telegram, Salmon abandoned his hunger strike.

EVD to Benjamin Salmon

December 31, 1920
Atlanta, Georgia

BELOVED COMRADE:
WE HONOR YOUR HEROIC SPIRIT AND YOUR NOBILITY OF SOUL, BUT
WE CAN NOT CONSENT TO THE SACRIFICE OF YOUR LIFE FOR OUR
FREEDOM, EVEN THOUGH IT COULD BE ACHIEVED AT SUCH AN AP-
PALLING PRICE. PROFOUNDLY GRATEFUL FOR YOUR SELF-SACRIFICING
OFFER, I BEG OF YOU IN THE NAME OF US ALL TO ABANDON YOUR
PURPOSE TO DIE {FOR US} AND RESOLVE TO LIVE AND FIGHT FOR THE
CAUSE WE ALL HOLD DEARER THAN LIFE. PLEASE DO US THE GREATEST
FAVOR POSSIBLE AND MAKE US HAPPY BY TAKING NOURISHMENT AT
ONCE AND SPARING US AND THE CAUSE YOUR PRECIOUS LIFE. WITH
LOVE AND LOYALTY,

YOUR COMRADE
EUGENE V. DEBS

Telegram draft, InTI, Debs Collection.

□ *Efrem Zimbalist was a leading concert violinist and composer who visited*
Debs at the Atlanta prison.

Efrem Zimbalist to EVD

January 10, 1921
Atlanta, Georgia

Dear Mr. Debs
It made me very happy yesterday, to give a little pleasure to so
many unfortunate people, and still more so to have the great pleasure
of meeting you. I wanted to have this opportunity for a long time,

and I hope we will meet again in the near future, under better circumstances.

With all the good wishes

Most sincerely
Efrem Zimbalist

ALS, InTI, Debs Collection.

□ *Founded in February 1919 by Colonel Theodore Roosevelt, Jr., and other staff officers of the American Expeditionary Force, the American Legion soon became the leading veterans' organization in the United States and included among its goals the fostering of "one hundred percent Americanism." In pursuit of that goal the Legion played a leading role in the Red Scare hunt for radicals and subversives and was widely criticized in liberal and socialist publications for the violence of its members' attacks on men and women suspected of less than "one hundred percent Americanism." The Legion flooded the Wilson administration with protests against Debs's release and, following his release, led local opposition to Debs's public appearances and speeches for the remainder of his life. As the following letter makes clear, not all veterans endorsed the Legion's policies and tactics.*

"A Brother Socialist" to EVD

February 1, 1921
St. Louis, Missouri

My Dear Mr. Debs,

I cannot help but write you a few lines and hereby heartily congratulate you that you have so faithfully stood with the working man and are still as brave as you were before you were put behind prison bars for telling the truth and nothing but the truth. I have been a member of the American Legion but after I found out what Socialism is, I dropped my membership with the American Legion and at *once* became a Socialist and will always be a hard worker for the Socialist Party so long as I live. I also notice in the Paper that President Wilson refuses you a Pardon. Do not despair My Dear Mr. Debs You are honored and will never be forgotten and your Worthy Name will go down in History the same as Abraham Lincoln, as a true lover for Freedom and Principal. God Almighty is with you and the *serpent* that sent you to prison has been punished and is now the *most* hated man in the world.

Hats off for Eugene V. Debs and the Socialist Party. I remain,

Yours very truly
A Brother Socialist

ALS, InTI, Debs Collection.

□ *Following President Wilson's final denial of his release on January 31, 1921, Debs responded in a widely reprinted statement that "it was my only fear that I might be indebted for my freedom to Woodrow Wilson . . . the most pitiful figure in history." As the following letter makes clear, not all Americans agreed with Debs in the matter.*

Mamie Burns to EVD

February 4, 1921
La Grange, Georgia

Dear Sir:

Ive read an article in the Journal relative {to} your bitter denunciation of Pres. Wilson & wherein you assert that his only desire is labeled with one word; "denied."

I am so sorry for you, but for Pres. Wilson being denied love of the people, I must differ with you.

I am persuaded that you are bitter & rebellious and giving vent to inward ravings. A great man like you should set an example of *meekness,* & submission rather than fierce antagonism & hatred such as you evidence.

Dear Bro. how is it with your soul? Do you count this life's attainments more value than eternal reward.

God will not let us win victories by harshly denouncing his children. Pres. Wilson has been the most tried, most patient & enduring man I know of in this age, yet he would never (I believe) fling abuse at any one. The way of the transgressor is hard & when overtaken in forwardness man usually rebels instead of repenting & sinning no more. Won't you give your harshness sober reflection & see if you had not rather be close to God in love than popular with the world in hate? This is a burning search light question to consider, but when rightly & satisfactorily answered brings peace & joy that passeth all understanding. I love the staunch courage of Pres. Wilson to *do right* as he see's & feels regardless of worldly opinion and the blessings poured out upon America during last eight years was direct results I believe of divine grace and wisdom, yet the people forgot God and worshipped mammon, bitterly attacking & denouncing the Christian head of the Nation for adverseties they brought on themselves.

Where is any justice in any such? A few years ago I was deeply interested in your socialist party, but serious study of their vindictive attitude towards all things good & unselfish, convinced me that my confidence was sadly misplaced.

I am penning these lines not as a political question but to reach you heart to heart as an individual. The blind leads the blind & both fall in a ditch, there by accomplishing nothing. But if love & unselfishness are the motive, tempered with forbearing patience & Kindness, God *will* aid the man.

Am enclosing some simple leaflets, not too insignificant to be carefully perused even by so great a personage as weak mortals some times think they are.

Anything I can do to make less lonely your hours, will be cheerfully done.

Sincerely
Miss Mamie Burns,
1305 Washington St.
La Grange Ga.

[EVD note to Theodore Debs]

Much as I disagree with this good woman I am bound to respect her honesty and appreciate her sincerity. I tried to keep Christians from slaughtering each other like beasts and for that I am here, and should according to her sit in meekness & submission. But Christ didn't teach that. He went after them with a bull-whip & that's why they spiked him securely to the cross. She says Wilson would not fling abuse at any one. He sat in the White House, and flashed it over the whole country that I, sitting in prison, was an "unrepentant criminal" —But we will not argue, I appreciate her fine spirit & her good intention & send her my kindest regards & best wishes—

She asks about my soul—tell her it is in perfect order, so far as I know, & neither it nor my conscience give me one bit of trouble. Pls. tell her the leaflets did not reach me—taken out by the *Prison censor.*

ALS, InTI, Debs Collection.

☐ *The various groups working for the release of political prisoners, including the Socialist Party of America, the ACLU, and the AFL, stepped up their activities following the inauguration of Warren Harding in March 1921. In the following letter Debs shares his opinion of demonstrations planned for Washington, D.C., and other cities in the spring of 1921.*

EVD to Otto Branstetter

March 28, [1921]
Atlanta, Georgia

My dear Otto,
    The approaching "demonstration" at Washington is going to fare, I fear, exactly as I forecasted it. There is going to be division and dissension that in turn will breed indifference or disgust, and the affair will be nothing compared to what it should be, and its influence for good perhaps negligible or of a questionable nature. I hope I am mistaken, but it looks that way to me now. Of course I would not say a word to discourage anyone but the indications do not seem flattering to me at all. I felt it from the time the administration announced its policy to give prompt attention to our cases, or at least to my case. We should have deferred if only from motives of expediency. You remember that I advised postponement not only of picketing but of the Washington demonstration. You agreed to the former but objected to the latter. I then suggested postponement of the demonstration at the Capitol to May 1st. You objected to that also and insisted that it must take place as scheduled and that it would be a tremendous success. I hope so! But I do not believe it. There may be a good meeting but I fear there will be no enthusiastic outpouring, no impressive parades or overwhelming demonstration.
    I wished temporary postponement, as you remember, with a clear statement to the public saying that we would not attempt to coerce

the new administration before it had a chance to act, but that we proposed to give it ample time to act of its own volition, thus placing ourselves in an attitude of fair play and thereby appealing to the public sense of justice and decency; if however, the administration failed to act within a reasonable time, then we proposed to turn loose the pickets, organize demonstrations and resort to all the means in our power to force the administration to set the war prisoners free.

This was what I believe should have been our policy and I so stated it, in substance, to you when you were here. It is not made quite clear nor complete in the Bulletin Service.

I am being urged to be the speaker of the day at Washington on the 13th, if released. This will be impossible. I fully appreciate the honor intended, but am obliged to decline. I shall not be able, even if released, to speak at Washington on April 13th. There are personal reasons. I shall first require physical attention, and I can make no engagements until thereafter.

With all my heart I wish success, and what little I can do to assure it or help it along will gladly be done.

My love to you, dear Otto and to dear Comrade Winnie and the two sweet daughters I hope soon to see. And my loving remembrances to all the faithful comrades at headquarters.

March 28th

――――――

[EVD note to Theodore Debs]
Please have this typed and a type-written copy sent to Otto. Please make carbon copy and place in my office files.

――――――

Please go over it first and make any changes or corrections that you may think necessary.

AL, InTI, Debs Collection.

☐ *Wednesday, April 13, 1921, was the second anniversary of Debs's imprisonment. During that time Mabel Curry had been working with Theodore Debs as a volunteer in Debs's Terre Haute office.*

Mabel Dunlap Curry to EVD

April 11, 1921
[Terre Haute, Indiana]

My very dear Comrade,

I overlooked the fact that Wed. would be an anniversary! I can say with all the sincerity of my heart that *never* did a mortal pay more bravely nor more uncomplainingly for his ideals than you have done. The last years have been long and tragic for us all but they have proven your stature as a *man* and your integrity as a humanitarian!

Our love and admiration have grown with the passing days, and now your place in our hearts is unique in its security and the reverence in which we hold your ideals.

God bless and keep you dear Gene and bring you back to us very soon! May this little reminder of a sad sad day two years ago find your face turned toward home and your heart filled with hope and good cheer. You will find nothing but devotion here and the warmest hands and hearts ready to receive you. My family sends love and every good wish.

As ever yours
M. Curry.

ALS, InU, Lilly Library, Curry Papers.

□ *In the following letter Debs recalls a recent visit to the Atlanta prison by Lucy Robins on behalf of the AFL amnesty committee, during which Robins took a number of pictures of Debs surrounded by cows at the prison farm. The pictures are part of the Debs Collection at the Cunningham Memorial Library at Indiana State University.*

EVD to Lucy Robins

May 4, 1921
Atlanta, Georgia

My dear Comrade Lucy,

Your very kind letter of the 29th ult. with its interesting enclosures came to me today through the courtesy of Warden Zerbst, a most pleasant reminder of your welcome visit here a few days ago. Please let me thank you with a deep and grateful sense in the name of us all for your continued kindness and devotion. Your visit was a joy to us as always, and we are still being treated to the good things you brought us, as you have always done, in such generous abundance. I knew how you felt when we parted at the prison door and all my sympathy was with you as I saw the tears start in your eyes and heard the faltering note in your farewell words. I know how gladly you would have shared the prison with your comrades instead of taking your leave, could you have had your choice, and thus did you attest once more, with your tears, your fidelity and devotion to our cause — Mr. and Mrs. Zerbst were indeed kind and considerate to us that day and we can never forget it. What a perfect spring day it was and how beautiful the whole world seemed as we went to the great farm and and forgot our cares amidst the calm and peaceable Holsteins,[1] the dear little calves and colts, and other beauties of nature. I wished with all my heart these precious luxuries so abundantly promised by Mother Nature might by enjoyed by my fellow prisoners as well as the children of poverty in the cities to whom they are denied as if they were also here in prison. The little pictures you sent perfectly delighted me. They are all so good and life-like, and the rustic background brings them into happy relief. Please accept my best thanks for the kindness of these precious little tokens of your visit, which are more than appreciated and will be fondly cherished. The action of the Georgia Federation was most gratifying, thanks to your timely visit, and the telegrams sent to which you refer will have their good influence in the general results. You may say to President Gompers that we are entirely satisfied with the plea he and his associates made and the efforts they put forth in our behalf. They did all they could for amnesty, more could not be expected, and their efforts to secure the liberation of the political prisoners, I assure you, are fully appreciated. We thank each and every one who has endeavored to secure our freedom and shall hold them all in grateful remembrance. From the very beginning, dear Comrade Lucy, you have whole-heartedly given yourself to this work, and your unwaving devotion, your untiring efforts, and your personal kindness shall stand to your lasting credit on the book of remembrance. Do not get discouraged! Every effort put forth will bear fruit in the end. We have only to be patient and bide our time. Our cause is eternally just and the longer the struggle the greater the triumph. Believe me, always,

Lovingly and faithfully yours,

E. V. Debs

P.S. Please express my hearty thanks to Comrade Haller and through him to each member of Local 17 I.L.G.W. for their more than generous donation of the use of their office for the benefit of amnesty and say to them that if I ever have the opportunity I will reciprocate their kindness in any service I may be able to render them or their organization. Please also give them my love and comradely greetings, and the same to the members of the United Hebrew Trades, and to the Comrades of the Forward staff, especially Comrades Cahan, Winchevsky, Gillis, Lang and Zimethin.

I hope this may find you in good cheer, stronger spirit and hale of soul, never doubting and never fearing that, however the fates may try or tempt us, we shall keep our heads erect, our faces toward the sunrise, and our hearts beating the stirring march toward Camp Victory.

ALS, InTI, Robins Papers.

☐ *H. Metzger was a schoolmate of Debs at the private Old Seminary School in Terre Haute, which served both elementary and college preparatory students.*

H. Metzger to EVD

July 16, 1921
Joseph, Oregon

Dear Comrade:

Old School Mate though we are far apart but my mind thoughts and Heart turned to you. Probably remember [me] as a Small Raged Boy excepting your urgent invitation to go home with you and have diner from the old Siminary of Terhaute Ind don't remember whether our Teatcher at that time was Silvia Profst or Sifert as my memory is not as good as it was in my younger days. I will be 70 years of age Feb. next is there any way of obtaining a photo of yourself if thare is would like the [one word illegible] the world to have it. I would like to have it just as you appear and look at this time. I will gladly pay the Bill.

And let me now also state the Bill will be and I will close hope this will [find] you in good health will adress this to the Ripsaw and have forwarded to you as I do not no how to direct this.

Respectfully
H. Metzger
Box 162
Joseph Oregon

[EVD note to Mabel Dunlap Curry?]

An echo from the far distant past—the voice of an old schoolmate of 55 years ago. He has the names of the old teachers—Treplo (who later died in the civil war) Seifert and Probst. Theo only remembers the last named. The old "Seminary" stood on the site of the present Normal School. How well I remember it! If there are any of those window portraits left pls. have Theo put one in a tube and mail it. If not have Theo. send him one each of those elections in the little back room. There are four kinds of my picture in as many envelope boxes on the North end of the lower shelf in the back room. Please write to tell him how happy I am to hear of my old schoolmate and tell him I send him my love and greetings and best wishes.

ALS, InTI, Debs Collection.

□ *The World War Veterans was one of several smaller groups that competed with the American Legion for membership at the end of the war. It claimed to represent the common soldier, in contrast to the American Legion, which it viewed as being dominated by the "officer class."*

Andrew C. Cooper, John M. [Levitt], and Carl Parsons to EVD

November 15, 1921
Washington, D.C.

EUGENE V DEBS

THE UNDERSIGNED OFFICERS OF THE WORLD WAR VETERANS {WHO} ARE HERE IN WASHINGTON TO HONOR OUR UNKNOWN COMRADE ON ARMISTICE DAY GREET YOU AS THE BEST KNOWN OF THE BAND OF 140

POLITICAL PRISONERS IN FEDERAL PRISONS FOR OPPOSING THE WAR.
YOU WERE INSPIRED BY THE SAME IDEALS AS WE WHO FOUGHT. WE
DIFFERED ONLY IN THE MEANS OF ACHIEVING THOSE IDEALS. WE RE-
SPECT YOUR VIEWS AND YOUR COURAGE. WE DEMAND FOR YOU THE
SAME FREEDOM OF OPINION WHICH WE ENJOY OURSELVES. BELIEVING
THAT WE HAVE APPEALED TO THE PRESIDENT TO GRANT A GENERAL
AMNESTY TO ALL SUCH PRISONERS. OUR APPEAL TO THE PRESIDENT
HAS BEEN ENDORSED IN A MEMORIAL BY HOLDERS OF THE CONGRES-
SIONAL MEDAL OF HONOR. WE ASSURE YOU THAT THE HEARTS OF THE
MEN WHO FOUGHT FOR AMERICAN DEMOCRATIC IDEALS ARE WITH
YOU. YOUR RELEASE AND THAT OF OTHER PRISONERS WILL MARK THE
RECOGNITION OF THOSE PRINCIPLES ON WHICH OUR COUNTRY'S IN-
STITUTIONS REST.

ANDREW G COOPER
NATIONAL CHAIRMAN
JOHN M LEVITT
EASTERN DIVISION CHAIRMAN
CARL PARSONS
MINNESOTA STATE CHAIRMAN

Telegram, InTI, Debs Collection.

☐ *President Harding issued a proclamation on November 15, 1921, formally
ending the war with Germany. In the following letter Debs mentions the proclamation and shares with his brother his opinion of the American Legion and
the wartime draft system.*

EVD to Theodore Debs

[November 15, 1921]
[Atlanta, Georgia]

The packet went forward this morning and also the letter. May
they both be with you on time. The morning paper contains the
Proclamation. Three years after *the war is ended the war is ended* and
the people are supposed to know that *the war is over.* It will be startling
news to them and we may well be alarmed about the possible effect
upon their nerves. The same report also declares that the procla-

mations in regard to Austria and Hungary will be issued in a few days. The treaties of peace with Haiti, San Domingo and West Virginia, I suppose, are still to be heard from. In connection with the proclamation there appears a statement by Daughterty in which he says for about the thirty-ninth time in the last seven months, if my count is correct, that he may have some changes to make in the "phraseology" before submitting his recommendations. Oh you "phraseology!" Also Taft, Wall street et al! He is the greatest phrasologizer in captivity. The wee bit of real news is the Call on the President by the representatives of the rank and file of the soldiers who did the actual fighting and had honor medals to show for it (as distinguished from the jackanaper and man milliners in gold lace and silk stockings—the strutting Prussianized officers who never smelled smoke—for whose pomp and glory, and incidentally to kidnap women, to tar and feather an objectional speaker, and serve as strike-breakers, the American Legion was organized and financed by the Wall Street brigands and profiteers) to demand in behalf of the American soldiers the liberation of the war prisoners, and they put their demand upon the ground that as one of them I opposed the war for the same reasons that they went into war. These men spoke for the soldiers who did the fighting, just as the American Legion spoke for the officers, the tools of Wall street, who remained safely in the rear and came back to strut about in military flammery and exploit their "patriotism." I know that a majority of the rank and file soldiers are my friends and when I get out I am going to put it to the test and demonstrate it to Wall street and its fawning hirelings. One of every 50 soldiers that went to France volunteered. 49 out of every 50 were drafted, taken by the neck and forced to go there, while more than two thirds of all who were drafted applied for exemption as a last hope of escape, and this is the great American army that fought for the "liberation" of the world. They have yet to fight for their own liberation from slavery.

AL, InTI, Debs Collection.

□ *Debs retained a special bond of affection for his friends from the old days in the BLF and ARU.*

EVD to Theodore Debs?

December 15, 1921
Atlanta, Georgia

Leaf from a sprig of holly handed me with his love and regret that it was all he had to give, by a fellow-prisoner from Galveston, Texas; who was a member of the American Railway Union, and local leader in the railway strike of 1894. He was sent to jail for six months for cutting a Pullman car from a train in obedience to the A.R.U. Boycott.

We are still pals! We were in the strike together 27 years ago and we are now in the penitentiary together.

A sprig of God's holly from a human heart—a precious holiday gift indeed!

AL, InTI, Debs Collection.

□ *On December 21, 1921, the* Socialist World *reported that 35,000 signatures of Terre Haute citizens had been gotten for "a special Christmas petition which is being taken to President Harding." The petition was signed by the leading business and professional people of Terre Haute and by Terre Haute mayor Charles R. Hunter. In the following letter Debs notes the petition drive and his prospects for release from prison.*

EVD to Theodore Debs

December 19, 1921
Atlanta, Georgia

My darling Theodore—

The great government of which you are but a subject and I a more or less honored guest, has been magnanimous, and by its gracious favor one extra letter has been allowed, and it goes to you and dear Gertrude and sweet Marguerite with all the greetings of the season and all the love of my heart. It is highly possible that I may join you before the Yuletide sun has set, but I am not counting on it. Kate has given me full particulars in a letter just received of the Terre Haute amnesty petition, the good people who org'ned and helped to launch it, and the "patriots" who in the Christian spirit of their tribe gave impetus to the enterprise by attempting in their characteristic manner to suppress it. I appreciate it all, but if "mercy" is shown it will not be of the kind that is not "strained," but because Wall street has concluded that for purposes and ends of its own we traitors should now be treated with clemency (sic) and granted a pardon. It is too bad we can not express our gratitude and appreciation in repentance but I can assure them that we shall make up for it in some other way.

My beautiful old Pard, I shall never (this is a prison pen I'm writing with as well as in, and you'll allow accordingly) be able to tell you how grateful I shall {always} be to you and dear Gertrude and Marguerite for your loyal, steadfast, unflickering devotion from the very beginning and all through the struggle to the present moment. You have been everything to me and you have done everything for me, and the thought of you enriches my spirit and fills my heart with sweetness. You have not counted the cost and you have spared nothing. You never faltered a moment, and never lisped a complaining word. God bless and keep you! I have your blessed souls in my heart forever. And I want to thank you especially and love you with added love for your goodness and kindness to dear Mabel. Her letters are full of you. Not one tender, loving word or act has been lost on her. The true nobility of her soul responds to yours in all that is beautiful and divine, and in sweetest sympathy and understanding. How perfectly devoted, how marvellously courageous and self-sacrificing, and how utterly consecrated she has been to our cause! I can never repay her in the smallest measure. My love with all my heart to you and Gertrude and Marguerite! Yours, old pard, world without end

Eugene V. Debs
#9653

May the Christmas hours bring you peace and hope and joy. My heart will be with you and I shall share in all the happiness that comes to you. God bless you all & keep you as you are!

The miles may lie between but our hearts can never be divided. May joy and cheer come with the New Year!

ALS, InTI, Debs Collection.

☐ *Debs was released from prison on Christmas Day 1921. On December 26 he reached Washington, D.C., where he visited with President Harding and Attorney General Daugherty. After a large demonstration in Indianapolis, Debs returned to Terre Haute on December 28, where a crowd estimated at 25,000 and including the mayor of Terre Haute and prominent labor and socialist leaders from around the country greeted him at the train station.*

EVD to Katherine M. Debs

December 25, 1921
Atlanta, Georgia

KATHERINE M DEBS

    MY DARLING KATE GREETINGS OF LOVE TO YOU AND DEAR SWEET MOTHER THE DAY HAS COME AND OUR BLESSED COMMUNION IS NEAR A NECESSARY TRIP TO WASHINGTON AND THEN HOME TO YOU MY BELOVED WITH AN OVERFLOWING HEART I EMBRACE YOU AND GOD BLESS YOU

EUGENE V DEBS

Telegram, Eugene V. Debs Foundation, Debs Home, Katherine Debs Scrapbook No. 3.

□ *James Edward Dyche replaced Frederick Zerbst as warden of the Atlanta prison in June 1921 and, like Zerbst, befriended Debs and worked in many ways to make his confinement as painless as the rules would allow. In the following letter Debs thanks Dyche and other members of the prison staff.*

EVD to J. E. Dyche

January 16, 1922
Terre Haute, Indiana

My dear Mr. Dyche: —
    Please pardon me for my delay in dropping you this line of greeting from home and appreciation to you and your family. I had intended doing so immediately on my return but you can hardly imagine how busy we have been early and late, day and night. The letters have been coming in a perfect deluge, thousands of them from all directions, and the visitors and telephone calls have pretty severely tested our sanity. I am sure you will understand and make allowance for seeming remissness. I wish to thank you for the perfectly fair manner

in which you treated me, you and your blessed family, in which Mrs. Debs and my brother and his family join heartily. I can never forget dear Mrs. Dyche and the dear, tender, motherly spirit of her in a trying hour. The thought of her beautiful solicitude will always be to me a grateful memory. Theodore and I will always cherish the happiest recollections of the farewell visit at your hospitable home. The picture of the breakfast table will remain vividly with us through the coming years. It was all so genuinely hospitable and kind and heart-warming, and I can assure you that it went deeply into the heart of one just released from prison and found a permanent abiding place there. Each member of your dear family shared in the beautiful spirit of that memorable morning.

Please let me say to you confidentially that I made a personal plea to Mr. Daugherty for Mr. McDonald, your splendid secretary and I wish you would kindly impart this {to} the latter and ask him to treat it as personal. Mr. Daugherty made full notes of what I had to say in Mr. McDonald's behalf and I hope it may have some little effect, and I think it will. Please give my very kindest regards to Mr. McDonald for he was always very kind to me and I am glad to be his friend.

I will ask you also to please give Mr. Fletcher and his family the cordial greetings and good wishes of Mrs. Debs and myself. Mr. Fletcher treated me with all kindness and I can only remember him in a very pleasant way.

But what touches me more deeply and what I appreciate more than all else that was done for me personally is the observation I made that you and Mr. Fletcher put yourselves in human touch with the prisoners there, the most helpless and friendless among them. Of such kindness is the very essence of religion and what you do for these erring or unfortunate brothers of ours you do tenfold for me. If the world but knew the infinite power of human love and the touch of a kindly hand! There is much more I would wish to say but you are a very busy man and happily I am now the same, and we will give our attention to those who most need it. You need not take the time out of your busy hours to answer this. Just give the benefit of it to some poor fellow there in your own characteristic way.

Mrs. Debs and Theodore and his wife and daughter and all of our family join in all loving greetings and best wishes to you and dear Mrs. Dyche and her noble sister, and your fine boys, and all of your hospitable household.

Yours faithfully,
Eugene V. Debs

TLS, Eugene V. Debs Foundation, Debs Home.

□ *Debs wrote the following letter in response to David Karsner's proposal that he write a book on Debs's prison experiences. Debs himself wrote a series of ten articles dealing with his prison experiences and his ideas on prison reform which ran from June to August 1922 in papers served by the Bell Literary Syndicate. These articles were later collected in a book,* Walls and Bars, *published in 1927.*

EVD to David Karsner

January 18, [1922]
Terre Haute, Indiana

My dear David: —
    Your letter came a moment ago. I am dropping everything to say yes to your proposition. You have done me a thousand loving and helpful kindnesses and there is nothing I can do I would not do gladly for you. I have already arranged partially for a series of prison articles that are to be launched with the intention of turning the prisons of this country inside out and letting the people see them and their vicious influence and debauching results, just as they are. The purpose of these articles will be to make prisons less brutal to their victims and to make them as decent as such barbarian institutions can be made. These articles will probably be syndicated and appear simultaneously in a number of the biggest papers in the country. But please treat this with absolute confidence for nothing of a definite nature has yet been agreed upon and no mention of it must be made to anyone. I give you the information to enable you to understand my situation in connection with your proposition.
    But the matter contained in these articles and the purpose of their writing will be entirely different, as I understand it, from the book you and your proposed publishers have in mind. The articles I propose writing are intended at their completion to be put into a book but these two undertakings will not only not interfere with each other but can, I think, be made mutually complementary and helpful. Please do not enter into any definite arrangement with the publishers until after a definite understanding has been reached in the negotiations in regard to the articles. There are several propositions here from big papers and syndicates of publishers. I shall get through with the matter as soon as possible but there will be delay for they give me no chance to get down to my work and I am not well as I should be. I am undergoing a course of drugless treatment and trying to be quiet until I get normal again but the callers keep coming and the mail continues to be very large.

We shall be able to see further about the matter a little later on and to make sure that everything is right we would better have a personal interview before reaching a definite conclusion. Your articles are beautiful and touching and heart-warming. You are a flowing fountain of loving kindness and you have been to me and mine everything in the world. We are all sending you our love and blessing and I am always

Yours faithfully,
E. V. Debs

Please tell Ervin that I intend to write an article for the Call as soon as I can get to it. I would have done so before now if they would only let me get to work. Please give our love to "Jimmy" Oneal and all the good comrades about you except Ryan Walker. I will settle with that gross libeller personally.

Please give our special thanks with love to Ethel Nelson We know how faithful she [has] been and all blessings on her devoted head.

ALS, InTI, Debs Collection.

☐ *Louis Untermeyer, a New York manufacturer and businessman, achieved fame and distinction as a poet and literary critic. A socialist, Untermeyer wrote for the* Liberator, *the* Nation, *and the* New York Call, *and in 1919 published* Modern American Poetry, *an anthology that enjoyed huge success and was reprinted many times.*

EVD to Louis Untermeyer

February 6, 1922
Terre Haute, Indiana

My dear Louis Untermeyer:—
    I have long been deeply mindful of all I owe you for your loyal devotion and the poetic inspiration that so thrilled and sustained me during my prison days and it has been in my heart to say this to you and to thank you and send you my love ever since my return but there has been scarcely a spare moment allowed me by the good friends and comrades who have literally overwhelmed me with their kind and joyous attentions. The beautiful poem you inscribed to me touched me more deeply than I can tell you, and the book of inspiring

modern poems with your more than kind inscription which is now in my hands is a treasure indeed that I shall cherish through all my days.

You will pardon, I am sure, this very inadequate expression of my appreciation and gratitude. Some good day when I can take you by the hand I shall try to tell you in person what appears so formal and almost meaningless on the written page. You are a real poet of the world of freedom and fraternity now in the making and your name will have a permanent place and a radiant one in the struggle to achieve it. My wife and brother and all of our family join in love and all best wishes to you and yours with all our hearts.

Yours faithfully,
Eugene V. Debs

TLS, InU, Lilly Library.

☐ *As editor of the* American Monthly *George S. Viereck wrote frequently of Debs during his imprisonment and in the February 1922 issue criticized "Mr. Harding's tardiness in freeing his rival candidate [which] takes the savor out of his action."*

EVD to George Sylvester Viereck

February 14, 1922
Terre Haute, Indiana

My dear Mr. Viereck:—

If you knew how very busy I have been kept since my return, and how many visitors and messages of all kinds that have been coming in a steady stream all these days you would not think me remiss for not sooner acknowledging your latest kindness and the many others that preceded it and returning my warmest thanks for your sympathetic interest and your loyal devotion during my prison experience. I have been ill too and I have not yet recovered. I was persecuted and threatened daily for two years preceding my confinement and although my spirit remained undaunted my physical health has been undermined and it will take a considerable period of quiet and rest to restore my strength.

Your kind note of the 31st. ult. and your splendid editorial in the current issue of your "American" have been read with real satisfaction and full appreciation. Please let me say that each kind word you have spoken in my behalf and each helpful service you have rendered me is remembered gratefully and will be to the last of my days. This brief and inadequate expression contains but little of what my heart holds for you. I think a man who has had the prison in his life has an appreciation all his own of the friends who were loyal and true while the enemies were seeking to dishonor and destroy him.

My wife joins me in greetings of affection and all best wishes to you and all of your household.

Yours faithfully,
Eugene V. Debs

TLS, NNU Tam, Feinstone Collection.

☐ *Following his release from prison Debs was immediately besieged by advocates of countless causes, none of them more persistent than those radicals and former Socialist party members who sought Debs's support for the Soviet government abroad and for one of the various Communist factions at home. In the following letter Debs responds to Otto Branstetter's request for a statement declaring his continued support of and loyalty to the Socialist Party of America, a declaration Debs finally made in October 1922 in the* New York Call.

EVD to Otto Branstetter

March 25, 1922
Terre Haute, Indiana

Dear Otto: —

Your letter of the 23rd. to Theodore has been passed to me and carefully read. You cannot seem to understand that I am sick and worn and that I have not had the ghost of a chance to rest since I got out of the penitentiary. The visitors come every day and most of them have grievances and troubles to tell me about or want something done. I have just had two hours with a communist. Another is waiting for me. I am just about able to be on my feet. To make good a promise I have been sitting or rather standing every spare moment for a bust during the past month when I was not actually in bed. Our house is all torn up under repairs that have been neglected for years. The house was literally falling to pieces. My wife has been ill for weeks, lately with an attack of the flu and on the verge of utter nervous prostration. Last night all night, after I got through with my day's work at nearly eleven o'clock I sat up or walked about because my heart would not allow me to lie down, all due to utter exhaustion of my nerves and my physical system generally. I am thirty pounds underweight. Under these circumstances I am trying with the help of Comrade Karsner who is here to write a series of promised prison articles, to keep up with my correspondence which consists mainly of troubles that are brought to me and of requests of one kind and another, to see all the people who come, and at the same time to keep perfectly quiet and retired and see no one and avoid all excitement under strict orders of the doctor who has told me that I was committing suicide. But this probably does not mean anything to you for I doubt if you can understand it. You may be sure that it is not to my liking to write to you this way. I have made it a life-long rule to keep my troubles to myself. But your persistency must be my excuse. You and those you speak for insist that I must declare myself and of course declare myself your way. It seems to me you would not care much what became of me so I did what you wanted me to do. Now of course I know {what} you are pressing me to do and I should not blame you for it. But I am not going to do it. At least I am not going to do it in my present physical condition. I have given all but my life and I would like to keep that for a little while yet. Perhaps I may and perhaps not. As between keeping the breath in my body and "declaring" myself the latter does not appeal to me. Nor would it to you. You simply know nothing about my situation. Twice since beginning this letter I have been interrupted by visitors. A letter has just come from Maynard Shipley saying that he and his wife had quit the party because they could no longer stand it. They said it was run by politicians who would trade anything in it for votes. Another letter from a comrade mortally offended because a very long letter written by him was answered too briefly and the charge is made that we "killed his enthusiasm, a very wicked thing" by not giving proper and detailed attention to his long and to us very uninteresting letter. So many comrades would have us believe that the particular matter they have to offer us is the most important of all and should have first consideration. When I entered prison there was a united party. When I came out it had been torn to pieces. I had nothing to do with it. But promptly on my release I am expected to get into the factional fight, utterly disgusting in some of its phases and side with everybody against everybody else.

Of course I would not have waited so long to take a definite position had it not been for the state of my health. I did not know to what extent I had been sapped of my physical strength until the reaction set in, and I have been given no chance, nor will be given any here to rest and be quiet. The comrades will not permit it. I suppose they think now that the capitalists are through with me for awhile it is their turn. If it is at all possible I am going to get away from here as soon as I am through with certain things that have to be done and go to some retreat in the mountains where I may have a chance to get into condition to do something. It is quite sure that in my present state I am outraging myself every day and putting off and perhaps making forever impossible my rehabilitation. It will take two or three months at least under favorable circumstances, perhaps six months or even a year to recover my health and strength. I do not know. I do know what nervous prostration is and if the devil had it I would pity him.

Now you know as well as I do what would result from my "declaring" myself as you and those you speak for want me to do. You know that would not be the end but the beginning and that forthwith I would be in the factional dogfight and in the low state of my vitality I would be consumed in it. I have never engaged in that sort of thing, having always considered it beneath me, and I shall not do so now. If you are right in saying that the great majority of the party insist upon it then I shall quit the party. I am still a member and that ought to signify that I have not turned against the party as has been intimated, and just why it is incumbent on me, to "declare definitely" my position and where I stand in the present chaotic and disgraceful condition with which I had nothing to do, in bringing about, especially at a time when I am fighting for my life that I may be of some real use to the cause, is not clear to me. It is true that I agreed to do this as soon as I was able to do it and back it up and sustain myself and I expected that time to come before now but it has not come. I pledged myself, as you know, to hear certain representatives of other factions before taking a definite stand, but I have not yet been well enough to do so and that is the reason and the only reason it has not been done, and surely that should be reason enough. Now if I live I am going to keep that promise as I keep every promise I make and yet I would break it and violate my plighted word if I yielded to your insistent demand that I issue a statement declaring just where I stand without further delay. As a matter of fact I do not know where I stand in reference to certain very vital phases of the present situation. There is a good deal that I do not know that I would like to know but have had no means of knowing.

You recite the outrages perpetrated by the communists upon the Socialist party but unfortunately the outrages were not confined to one side. I have never approved but have opposed and condemned the disruptive and destructive tactics that certain elements have resorted to in their insane attempts to destroy each other.

You publicly charged Wagenknecht with being a thief. You were called upon to produce the proof or retract the charge. So far as I know you have done neither. I am assured that the charge is an infamous slander and it certainly is unless you have evidence to sustain it {and if not you} should retract the charge. I am sending you the suit I wore when I quit the prison which you expressed the wish to have and with it I am sending my prison cap.

I am as ever with kindest wishes,

Yours fraternally,
E. V. Debs

TLS, IN.

☐ *This letter was written from Lindlahr Sanitarium, a nature-cure facility in the Chicago suburb of Elmhurst, where Debs spent most of the summer and fall of 1992. On July 22 Debs sent a cablegram to Lenin (which was reprinted in both the socialist and nonsocialist press) protesting "with all civilized people in the name of common humanity against the execution of any of the Social-Revolutionaries or the unjust denial for their liberties."*

EVD to David Karsner

July 30, 1922
Chicago, Illinois

My dear David,

The first page of the Call has just been received with your very kind letter. Please accept my best thanks and tender the same to Comrades Ervin, Oneal and Walker for the prompt and very satisfactory manner in which you handled the matter of the cable to Moscow. I need hardly say that I very much appreciate the splendid service you have rendered me and the generous consideration shown me in presenting the matter to your readers.

Branstetter writes me that agents of the Associated Press and the United Press called on him for full copies of the message from Berlin and to Moscow and I referred him to the Call. I had no idea the plute press would have any interest in the matter.

Now if you have not sent the bill of charges to Theo. as I requested him to have you do, please let me know the amount and I will remit.

Thanking you all many times and with love as always I am

Yours forever

E. V. Debs

Have a vigorous protest from a Communist Editor about the cable to Moscow. I shall answer him. If we believe {in and inflict} a capitalist punishment and commit murder in the cause of justice, as the capitalists do, we are not a damned bit better than they whose system we condemn as criminal and whose ethics we renounce as barbarous and inhuman.

The social revolutionaries are charged with attempting the assassination of Lenin. If they were not only charged with but actually guilty of attempting to assassinate me instead of Lenin my attitude would be the same. I would punish them with liberty.

Writing a funeral address for an old friend who has just died at T.H. and must get it off right away.

Please land lustily on Ryan Walker and charge to my account.

Later — This moment recd. Call page of 28th. with your interesting and to me very flattering column and comment. You're a flowing fountain of love & kindness

Thanks and Love!

ALS, NN Kars.

☐ *During his stay at the Lindlahr Sanitarium Debs sometimes complained that too many visitors were delaying his recovery, but he clearly welcomed visits by Sinclair Lewis, whose* Main Street *(1920) and* Babbitt *(1922) transformed him into a major literary figure, and Carl Sandburg, who at the time was an editorial writer on the* Chicago Daily News.

EVD to David Karsner

August 22, [1922]
Chicago, Illinois

My dear David,

Your letter is beautiful and your article is fine and both give me inexpressible satisfaction. Thank you, dear David, with all my heart. I'd love to say a good deal more but have not a chance. The mail increases day by day and I can't take care of it.

Sinclair Lewis is here and will be here for ten days. He's great and fine and I can't tell you how I love him. Last night for the first time I had to break one [of] the Sanitarium rules. I was with Carl Sandburg and Sinclair Lewis at the Sandburg house till midnight, and then that beautiful brace of great white souls brought me home. It was a wonderful occasion—an event in our lives. Mrs. Sandburg and her Mother and the three dear children did the hospitable and we were in paradise after our own hearts. You were of course with us. Lewis and Sandburg love you just as I do. Sinclair Lewis will stay here until he is fed up in a way to satisfy him. He has the all-seeing eye and the all understanding soul & nothing escapes him.

Carl gave me his poems inscribed by himself and Lewis in a way to make me blush red with humility. Carl came with his guitar Saturday eve & gave the patients here a most cheering entertainment in folk-lore etc. It was a complete conquest & they all love him. Lewis will also entertain them and the patients here feel big with importance. No "Main streeters" here.

Love dear David always
Gene

ALS, NN Kars.

□ *William Z. Foster, who rose to national prominence as leader of the historic and unsuccessful steel strike of 1919, ran for president as the candidate of the Communist Party of America and was that party's national chairman from 1930 to 1957. Foster had recently been chased out of Colorado and Wyoming by state authorities who were, according to Foster, "taking revenge" on him for his role in the great steel strike.*

Theodore Debs to William Z. Foster

August 26, 1922
Terre Haute, Indiana

Dear Comrade Foster:

My brother has read of your brutal and shameless persecution with feelings of deepest indignation and resentment and wishes me to write to you as follows: "If I were not confined to a sanitarium under treatment I would at once be with you and tender my services in any way in my power. The miserable wretches in Colorado and Wyoming, especially the capitalist hireling who masquerades as governor of the former state, who so brutally manhandled you in the name of law and order, have sown dragons' teeth from which will spring in due time the warriors of the revolution who will sweep the corrupt system of which they are the servile lackeys from the face of the earth.

You are to be congratulated, after all, upon the infamous outrages perpetrated upon you in the name of capitalist law and justice, for in these outrages, committed by their liveried hirelings, is revealed the fear of their thieving and brutal masters, and this is the highest compliment they could possibly pay you. They know you cannot be bought, bribed or bullied, and so they set their dogs at your heels to drive you off their reservation.

I need not sympathize with you nor bid you be strong for you have the strength to stand and withstand, and you need no sympathy, and all I have to say is that when I have recovered my strength sufficiently to take up my work again, I shall be with you shoulder to shoulder in your stand for the working class and industrial freedom, and meanwhile I am

Yours fraternally,"
Eugene V. Debs

Please let me concur heartily in the above sentiments of my brother and to also subscribe myself, with great respect and all good wishes.

Yours fraternally,
Theodore Debs

TLS (typed signature with signed note from Theodore Debs), IN.

☐ *In the letter that follows, Debs gives David Karsner his opinion of Sinclair Lewis's and Carl Sandburg's literary strengths.*

EVD to David Karsner

September 9, [1922]
Elmhurst, Illinois

Dear, sweet David,

When I hear from you it is always in loving kindness. The village postmaster has just handed me the latest book from your hands bearing the love in which it was sent in its flattering inscription, and I thank you utterly with the wish that I could think of at least some little thing in return for the big and beautiful things without number you have been doing for me these many years. I am keen on "The Trail of the White Mule" in zestful anticipation of an early conquest but as to his being "stabled in Terre Haute" — well, if there's a cranny anywhere without his stall I don't know where it could be found unless it would be in Ryan Walker's festive imagination. Anyway, I shall read the book, and coming from you, it will of course be with profit and joy.

Sorry to say that Sinclair Lewis was called East before your book and letter came. I had a beautiful farewell letter from him saying he would see me soon after I got back to Terre Haute. Carl Sandburg is forwarding to him your book and letter. He is a great-souled genius and one of the choicest spirits I have ever known. He is just a big, beautiful boy, free as air and natural as sunshine, and Theodore and I both loved him at sight. Lewis and Sandburg are fit companions, genial, fun-loving, whole-hearted and generous, as well as princes of the pen and masters of {the} literary art. Lewis and Sandburg as distinctively American novelist and poet with the cosmic understanding and the universal appeal have already acquitted themselves with enviable distinction and achieved enduring fame, but they are still in their adolescence and have but laid the foundation of the temple that will bear in fadeless letters their deathless names.

We had some wonderful sessions here and you should have been at each roll-call. We settled all the great questions of the day with ease and dispatch, and in the plans we laid the sidereal universe will rank as a small concern. We sped in our flight "from star to star as far as the universe spreads its flaming walls," and infinitely beyond in our dreams and aspirations, and {we} decided to remain here until they are all triumphantly realized. God smiled, I know, for he put us up to it and he knew that we knew that he would stand loyally by and see us safely into the radiant realisms of our rosiest dreams. Yes, dear David, you missed it for we were loaded with riches and soared among the stars—while it lasted—and that was long enough to keep our spirits attuned to the infinite and our torches flaming forever.

With my love in my heart, dear little brother o' mine

Yours always
E. V. Debs

ALS, NN Kars.

□ *In the following letter Debs addresses Lucy Robins's complaint that his prison articles had not given proper credit to the role played by Robins, Samuel Gompers, and the AFL in securing his release and that of other political prisoners.*

EVD to Lucy Robins

September 9, [1922]
Elmhurst, Illinois

My dear Lucy,

Your letter has come and I have given it careful reading and consideration. I can not answer as you are kind enough to understand, but I can at least say that nothing could have been farther from my intention at any time than to do you or Mr. Gompers injustice, or to give hurt to your feelings. I am quite ready to believe that the visit of Sam and yourself could have been much better written, but if you know under what circumstances the articles were prepared and that I was so ill at times, and tired and worn, that I could scarcely hold up my head, I am sure you would make full allowance for all shortcomings. The visit of Gompers and his earnest efforts in behalf of amnesty for all politicals I appreciated in good faith, setting aside all else about which we had differed, and I have had occasion more than once since to repeat my expression of appreciation to those who disliked Gompers and protested against any credit being given to him. Of course there are narrow minds we have to deal with and we expect to be criticized and condemned by some, no matter how consistently we do our work or how faithfully we serve the cause.

As to yourself, Lucy, I have only to say again that all the unhappy incidents connected with your work are blotted from memory, and I think only of your patient, persistent efforts in behalf of the political prisoners, of the pleas you so impressively made in my behalf before trade union conservatives, conferences with public officials, and on all possible occasions of the anxiety you suffered, the trials you had to undergo and the privations you endured—all this I remember, including each of your welcome visits to the prison with your arms filled with loving and substantial evidence of your kindness and your steadfast devotion—your messages of good cheer, your intercessions with the Warden, your gladness in making my lot a little more comfortable and your sadness and tears as you took your departure leaving us behind—yes, dear child, I remember and shall remember it all, not forgetting the touching and all too generous personal tributes in your book, and with renewed thanks and appreciation and love to you and to all your faithful associates in the good work, I am as ever

Yours sincerely
E. V. Debs

ALS, InTI, Robins Papers.

□ *With the following letter Debs enclosed a copy of the* Searchlight, *a Ku Klux Klan paper published in Atlanta, whose headline announced "Klan Declares War on the Radical Forces in America."*

EVD to David Karsner

October 11, [1922]
[Elmhurst, Illinois]

My dear David,

Have you received one of these jokers from the *Jawgia* goblins? You will see by the one enclosed just at hand that the Ku Klux Kayotes and Krackers down in Lynchland have stopped barbecuing "Niggahs" long enough to discover that the foundations of the government are being dug up by the roots. Gread Gawd! Who could have konjured up such a Kalamity, and why, oh, why are we kursed with such a kruel katastrophe! Let us rejoice that the knights of the White mule and illiteracy have boldly seized the tumbrel and sounded forth the alarm, and that the Kleagles and Kligrapps and Klans and other Klams are now sallying forth with their trusty lynching lariats in hand to Americanize the Bolsheviki and save our Kristian civilization from being Bolshevized.

Sic Semper Moonshiner Lynchem and Roastem!

Beware!

[drawing of skull and crossbones]

Pull ye radicals, pull for the shore The white Mule has brayed and he will bray no more!

AL, NN Kars.

□ *Born in Terre Haute in 1871, Theodore Dreiser knew the worst of that town's poverty, which he recalled briefly in a 1916 book,* Hoosier Holiday. *The publication of* Sister Carrie *in 1900 launched his career as a major novelist; by World War I his works included* Jennie Gerhardt, The Financier, The Titan, *and* The "Genius." *Dreiser's older brother, Paul (who had changed the spelling of his name to Dresser), was a famous songwriter ("On the Banks of the Wabash") in whose honor a Terre Haute organization sought to erect a memorial. The following exchange of letters deals chiefly with the proposed Dresser memorial.*

EVD to Theodore Dreiser

October 14, 1922
Elmhurst, Illinois

My dear Mr. Dreiser,

Please allow me to add my name to the petition being addressed to you by the Paul Dresser Memorial Association to grant your consent to the removal of the remains of your famous brother to Terre Haute as the fitting place for their final repose. The people of Terre Haute he loved and who loved him would feel highly honored to have the "Banks of the Wabash" he immortalized chosen for his last resting place.

I hear from you or rather of you, aside from your splendid literary works, through our mutual friend David Karsner with whom you are an immense favorite, and I hope that some good day it may be my privilege to take you by the hand.

Believe me with all cordial regards and best wishes

Your friend and admirer
Eugene V. Debs

ALS, PU, Dreiser Papers.

Theodore Dreiser to EVD

October 17, 1922
New York City

Dear Eugene Debs:

First let me say that I am one of the many who voted for Debs—
on occasion & who was gloomy because of the powers that could
prosecute & lock him up. I admired your stand & I do now and I
hope all good things for you. More I could not say to any man.

As to the matter of the ashes or bones of my late good brother. I
am now placed in an odd position. The logical place for a monument
is Terre Haute—and on the banks of the Wabash there. Paul liked
Terre Haute. He liked to go back there. In the first days of your
fame he knew of you & spoke of you to me. Several years ago a man
by the name of Charles T. Jewett, of 492 W. Center St. wrote me &
wanted me to obtain {the} permission of the various members of the
family for the transfer of the body there—in case a place & monument
for it could be arranged. I consulted all those living & advised him
that there was no objection. Then I heard nothing except this—that
it was probable that the body would be removed to Indianapolis. I
undertook some publicity for the idea—outside the state but this
seemed to meet with little favor from those in Terre Haute, so I
dropped that. Not a word since.

Recently came a letter from the Indiana Society of Chicago, saying
that it wanted to place a monument over the grave in Chicago. (St.
Boniface R.C. Cemetary—North Side) It wanted the family consent.
I explained about the Terre Haute idea & stated that there had been
no objection there & would be none but that it might be best to see
if the Terre Haute idea had fallen through. At the same time that
your letter reached me yesterday (here) came one from Edward. W.
Halloway, Secy of the Chicago Indiana Society. He states that now
the Indiana Society desires to co-operate with D. N. Foster, President
of the Soldiers Home at Lafayette. That Governor McCray favors
having the monument & body there—or, so I gather. That places me
in an odd position. Personally I favored & do now, Terre Haute, as
do the other members of his family. But if a quarrel is to develop
which will mean no monument for a long time, I would rather see
the Lafayette project go through. Actually, in the crisis I would like
your sincere advice. I do not know Indiana very well & you do. What
do you suggest. I am writing Mr. Halloway about your letter & state

that personally I favor Terre Haute—as would Paul. He was born there & always liked it. But also I hope that no delaying quarrel arises. Perhaps you have influence with Gov. McCray—or the Chicago Indiana Society. Why not write them direct? As to the consent of the family—I can get the written consent of those living I am sure. My compliments, my thanks & my sincere good wishes for yourself & your happiness.

Theodore Dreiser.

ALS, Eugene V. Debs Foundation, Debs Home.

EVD to Theodore Dreiser

October 20, 1922
Elmhurst, Illinois

My dear Theodore Dreiser,

Your good letter of the 17th inst was a most gratifying surprise to me and was read with full appreciation. I did not know that you or your brother had such a kindly interest in me or in fact any interest whatever, and I had often regretted that although we were born on the same spot we drifted out into the big world and far apart without ever once coming into personal contact. It was therefore with real delight that {I learned} you and your brother both entertained for me the same friendly feeling and held me in the same high regard I did you.

I have very carefully read your letter and can appreciate your feeling in the quandary in which you find yourself in regard to the final disposition of your distinguished brother's bodily remains. It is another case of "Homer dead" and a high and well-deserved compliment to your brother to be now the object of such rivalry in the claim for his monumental dust, but I can understand perfectly your own delicacy and embarrassment in being called upon to become a partisan in the controversy.

You have been good enough to suggest that I write to Governor McCray and express my views in the matter and I should like nothing better than to comply with your wish but for the circumstance that not long ago the Governor made a speech before the American Legion in which he said, calling me by name, that he profoundly regretted that the state of Indiana was disgraced by being the home of the one arch-traitor in America. Of course this does not disturb me, but you will realize that the Governor is not interested in my views in this or any other matter.

You have also been partial enough, and I feel deeply touched by the confidence it implies, to ask my advice in your situation and I shall give it with the perfect frankness you have a right to expect from me and with due regard to the conflicting claims with which you are confronted. It seems to me, beyond any question of doubt, that Terre Haute, the city of his birth and boyhood, the place he loved and to which he fondly returned as often as he had the occasion, and among the people "On the Banks of the Wabash" he loved and who loved him — it seems to me, dear friend, that that is pre-eminently the logical and fitting final resting place for {your brother's} remains, and I feel equally confident that the future will vindicate your judgment should you decide in favor of his native city which so ardently and lovingly claims the high privilege of doing him and his family that honor.

If there is any way in which I can possibly serve you in the matter I am at your command with pleasure in any way in my power.

Thanking you sincerely for your kind and generous consideration and with all cordial greetings and best wishes I am

Faithfully your friend
Eugene V. Debs

ALS, PU, Dreiser Papers.

□ *Debs returned to Terre Haute from the Lindlahr Sanitarium at the end of November 1922. In the following exchange of letters Sandburg and Debs recall Debs's visit to Sandburg's home in Elmhurst, Illinois.*

Carl Sandburg to EVD

November 28, 1922
Chicago, Illinois

Dear Gene:

You will always be close to us. The only way we can decently remember you and what you left with us here will be a certain way of living it, maybe dying it.

And some day I hope to get the strong truth of those hands of yours into into [*sic*] a poem. It's only a hope but I'll try for it and learn something.

My signature goes for the whole bunch under our roof. As you went away out the front gate one of them said, "He's a big rough flower."

With you it isn't really a good-by because you are still here.

Carl Sandburg

TLS, EVD Foundation, Debs Home.

EVD to Carl Sandburg

December 9, 1922
Terre Haute, Indiana

My dear Carl:

You will always be close to me too. Close as a young brother. You can hardly know how your loving message warmed my heart. Each line and word touched a responsive chord. If you ever get "those hands of mine in a poem"—and I know you will for it is in your heart—it will be wondrous big and beautiful for it will be the radiant reflection of your big and beautiful self.

No, dear Carl, I did not leave your blessed cottage home out there in the little jungle you are trying to save from civilization for my heart is still there. I enjoyed every moment under your happy and hospitable roof. Dear Mrs. Sandburg and her sweet-souled mother and the three darling little gods of your heavenly household, how vividly and smilingly and whole-heartedly you are all before me this morning, and what a beautiful and inviting picture you present to my glad eyes! We shall meet again and meanwhile my wife and brother and his wife and daughter, all of us join as one in love and blessing to all of you, and I am, while the stars shine,

Yours loyally,
Eugene V. Debs

TLS, IU, Sandburg Papers.

□ *Francis T. Hayes served as secretary of the City Club of Cleveland from 1916 to 1923 and was credited with making the club a nationally respected public forum. The invitation to Debs in the following letter badly split the club and led to the resignation of forty-seven of its members. Debs's reply notes the controversy created by the invitation.*

Francis T. Hayes to EVD

January 10, 1923
Cleveland, Ohio

My dear Mr. Debs:
    On behalf of The City Club of Cleveland may I invite you to address a luncheon meeting of the club in the near future?
    I believe you are familiar with the type of organization The City Club is and the character of meeting planned.
    Our meetings are held at noon on Saturday, and the dates of January 20th, February 10th, March 10th, 17th and 24th are now open on our calendar for this meeting.
    Will you let me know as soon as possible whether you can accept our invitation and what date will be preferable to you?

Very sincerely
Francis T. Hayes
Secretary

TLS, InTI, Debs Collection.

EVD to Francis T. Hayes

February 12, 1923
Terre Haute, Indiana

My dear Hayes:
    Since advising you of my acceptance of the invitation to address the City Club of Cleveland extended by you in behalf of the Club I have had occasion to learn of the disagreement of opinion among the members as to the propriety of sponsoring me as a guest and speaker and of the dissension incident to the discussion of the question, re-

sulting in the protest and resignation of a number of members, and feeling disinclined, as I certainly do, to aggravate such variance of opinion among the membership or to obtrude myself where there is any question of my being welcome or as to the right of being heard in a forum avowedly open to free speech, I beg to withdraw my acceptance and to respectfully decline the invitation of the Club.

In arriving at this conclusion I beg to assure you, and through you the members of the Club, that I have not the slightest feeling of resentment toward those who objected to me on account of my opinions as I have long since become accustomed to such opposition and it has taught me to not only freely accord to every one the right to speak according to his light, but in the spirit of true tolerance to encourage him in doing so, more especially the misguided brother who would forfeit his own right to be heard by denying me mine.

Please convey to the Club and to each of its members without regard to his opinion or attitude my sincere thanks for the kind invitation extended and for the flattering consideration bestowed upon me in connection therewith, and with all cordial regards and good wishes I remain,

Yours faithfully,
[Eugene V. Debs]

TLc, InTI, Debs Collection.

☐ *Algernon Lee was educational director of the Rand School in New York City, to which Debs donated a large collection of his books, files of the various magazines and periodicals for which he had written, and scrapbooks filled with press clippings tracing his career.*

EVD to Algernon Lee

February 16, 1923
Terre Haute, Indiana

My dear Comrade Lee:

The collection of books etc. went to you by express yesterday. There were five cases. Please see that that number is delivered to you. You will find the express receipt enclosed. The packing had to be hurriedly done and therefore not as carefully as could have been desired. It will take you some little time to get the books and papers in order but you will no doubt have the comrades there to help you in their leisure hours. You will find some papers that are old and I think of some value. Please see that the Locomotive Firemen's Magazines are placed in their proper order and taken care of as I think they will be in demand for future reference and I believe it is the only complete file up to the time I severed my connection with it in existence. I have just received a letter from W.S. Carter, Ex-President of the Brotherhood of Locomotive Firemen and Enginemen, and now at the head of its research department, who succeeded me as editor, making certain inquiries regarding the early history of the organization and informing me that his magazine files were incomplete. I have advised him that my files had been turned over to the Rand School where they would be accessible for reference purposes. I hope the collection I sent you will be of some use to the School. I hated to part with some of the things that have been with me so long and with which I grew up but they were of no use here while at the School they may be of service to others.

Affectionately your comrade,
E. V. Debs

TLS, NNU Tam, Debs Collection.

☐ *Some of Debs's earliest writings and speeches following his return from Lindlahr Sanitarium were devoted to an appeal for aid to the victims of terrible famine in Russia. The following letter of thanks came from Olga Kameneva, a sister of Leon Trotsky, and M. Kalinin, who held many positions of power in the Soviet Union, including service on the editorial staff of* Pravda *and as chairman of the Presidium of the Supreme Soviet of the USSR.*

Olga Kameneva and M. Kalinin to EVD

March 30, 1923
Moscow, Kremlin, USSR

Dear Comrade,
    The Central Commission for fighting the After-Effects of the Famine congratulates you on your liberation from imprisonment, and your return to active work, one of the sides of which — your energetic

and indefatigable efforts to assist the starving children of Soviet Russia—the Commission particularly appreciates.

We hope that you will, with your customary vigor, extend this campaign for relief.

We think it would be most advisable for you personally to visit Russia and become acquainted with the position in the former famine areas on the spot.

By the decision of the Commission of March 3rd we are instructed to invite you to come to Russia.

In case you acquiesce, you may receive a visa to enter the RSFSR from Com. Krestinsky in Berlin.

Anticipating your early arrival, We are, with comradely greetings,

M. Kalinin
Chairman of Commission.

Olga Kameneva
Member of Commission and
Chief of Foreign Section.

TLS, InTI, Debs Collection.

□ *Debs's efforts on behalf of Russian famine relief, according to the Russian publication* Izvestia Tasika, *led to the conversion of a former summer resort, Novikov, to a "Children's City . . . name[d] after Eugene V. Debs, the great American labor leader and friend of the people."*

K. Mairova et al. to EVD

March 31, 1923
Kasan, USSR

To Comrade Debs in America—

We, the children of the Children's Homes bearing your name, thank you as well as the children of American workers for the support we are receiving now through the International Workers' Relief. Owing to your care, we children in the Children's Colony are under comparatively better conditions as far as food, etc., is concerned.

The children's colony in which we live is a joint organization of eight children's homes and two babies' homes. We have at our disposal a park, a bath house and spacious buildings. In one work, the external conditions of our life would be favorable if it were not for the great scarcity in clothing (clothing, underwear, shoes) as well as school utensils (paper, crayons, pencils, pens, books, etc.) which greatly hampers our educational work.

Finally, we beg that you, yourself, should visit us and see how we live and under what conditions our child life goes on. We will be greatly thankful to you and will never forget your care of us.

Presidium of the Children's meeting:

K. Mairova

L. Antonova

L. Porshutkina

N. Solovieva

E. Zedrick

And Tartar signatures.

A true copy of the original: International Workers Relief, Kazan Rogolla

We, the children of the house Number Seventeen in the Children's Colony "Eugene V. Debs" are sending from Kazan to far America our brotherly greetings to the American workers and our child's thanks for the help which you rendered to us, the children of the proletariat in Russia. We send also our child's thanks to the Comrade DEBS after whom our children's colony is named, and we express our most sincere wish to see our Comrade Debs here in Kasan in order to show him where and how we live.

With all our heart we invite Comrade Debs to come to us, to our Children's Colony.

The Children's Soviet

Signatures

International Workers' Relief Kazan

A true copy of the original Hans Rogalla Manager of the Branch Kazan of the I.W.R.

TLc (with translation), InTI, Debs Collection.

☐ *M. Tomsky was a member of the Central Committee of the Communist party and of the Politburo. A. Andreyev joined the Bolshevik movement in 1914, participated in the 1917 revolution, and for more than thirty years held key positions in the Soviet government, both during and after Stalin's time.*

M. Tomsky and A. Andreyev to EVD

April 5, 1923
Moscow, USSR

EUGENE DEBS
    HAVING LEARNED OF YOUR WISH TO VISIT SOVIET RUSSIA WE SEND YOU HEARTY INVITATIONS STOP ROSSIAN WORKERS KNOW YOU WILL AS AN OLD MILITANT IN AMERICAN LABOUR MOVEMENT.
                TOMSKY PRESIDENT ALL RUSSIAN CENTRAL COUNCIL
                                            TRADE UNIONS
        ANDREYEV PRESIDENT CENTRAL COUNCIL RAILWAY UNION

Telegram, InTI, Debs Collection.

EVD to M. Tomsky and A. Andreyev

April 14, 1923
Terre Haute, Indiana

My dear Comrades:
    The cablegram from you under date of the 5th. inst. was received here in my absence and I beg now to acknowledge its receipt and to thank you warmly and through you the organizations you represent for the cordial invitation you extend to me to visit Soviet Russia, a pleasure I have been promising myself for some time but have been unable to realize on account of my health and affairs here at home, long neglected on account of my imprisonment, which will require my attention for some time to come. But I hope at a later time when the circumstances are more favorable to accept the very kind invitation you extend and to visit our comrades in Russia and bear witness to the brave struggle they are making and the noble efforts they are putting forth to establish a true working-class Republic within their own borders and at the same time set an illuminating and inspiring example of proletarian achievement to the whole world. I have been

with you, dear comrades, with all my heart since the beginning of your epoch-making Revolution and I shall be with you, I trust, when you finally celebrate its triumphant and glorious consummation. Please let me thank you heartily for your kind and appreciative words and accept for yourselves the assurance of my fraternal affection and esteem and convey the same to all the comrades and fellow-workers you so loyally represent.

Please do me the kindness also to present my sincere regards and warmest wishes to Comrades Lenin, Trotzsky and other comrades who are standing so staunchly for the Soviet Republic against a hostile capitalist world, and believe me always,

Yours faithfully,
[Eugene V. Debs]

TLc, InTI, Debs Collection.

□ *Arthur Henderson, a leader of the British Labour party from its founding in 1906 until his death in 1935, was awarded the Nobel Peace Prize in 1934. The following letter from Debs was in response to Henderson's request for a short article for the May Day issue of* Labour Magazine.

EVD to Arthur Henderson

April 16, 1923
Chicago, Illinois

My dear Comrade:

Your cablegram has just been placed in my hands by National Secretary Branstetter and I am taking pleasure in enclosing a brief May Day greeting as requested which I hope will reach you in time. We are in the midst of a campaign of re-organization here and meeting with the most gratifying results. We shall soon have a more powerful Socialist Party than we ever had before in these states. We are more than gratified to note the splendid progress you are making in England in overcoming your opposition and in the great work you are doing to place labor in power and to make the working class the rulers of Great Britain.

With all cordial greetings to yourself and comrades in which we all join, I remain

Yours fraternally
[Eugene V. Debs]

[enclosure]

GREETINGS FROM AMERICA

Your cablegram and I reached Chicago at about the same time and it is with real pleasure that I comply with your request. We have just concluded a most interesting municipal campaign here in which the vote cast for Socialism was more than doubled. The war hysteria has now subsided to a considerable extent although we still have some fifty political prisoners serving sentences of twenty years and more for holding opinions adverse to the late international slaughter, a fact that disgraces the plutocratic United States Government before the world.

It is with special satisfaction that I advise our British comrades that the Socialist Party which was all but destroyed during the war is now rapidly reorganizing upon a more secure foundation and I feel justified in predicting that within a twelvemonth the party will be stronger and more efficiently organized in every way than ever before.

We have noted with deep interest and full appreciation the splendid progress made by the Socialist movement in Great Britain, especially since the recent election and the surprising increase in the Socialist representation in the House of Commons. From now on Socialism is the one commanding issue before the people and whatever may be the result of the immediate contentions between Socialists and their adversaries it is certain that the final victory will be achieved in the not remote future and that England will soon be transformed into a Socialist commonwealth.

In behalf of the Socialists of America I beg to send cordial May Day greetings to our British comrades with the ardent hope that the splendid efforts they are now putting forth in behalf of the working class may soon be crowned with complete victory.

Yours faithfully,
Eugene V. Debs

TLc, InTI, Debs Collection.

□ *On September 4, 1923, Debs began a month-long western speaking tour that took him to Montana, Washington, Oregon, California, Utah, and Idaho. His description in letters to his brother of the meetings in Everett and Tacoma, Washington, made it clear that he was greatly encouraged by the crowds that turned*

out to hear him and enraged by the efforts of American Legion posts and local
chambers of commerce to prohibit or disrupt his meetings. As he notes, he met
Luther Burbank in Santa Rosa, California.

EVD to Theodore Debs

[September 11, 1923]
Everett, Washington

My sweet old Pard,   Tuesday 11th
    The meeting here last night was wonderful — the theater crowded
to the doors, and I never addressed a more beautiful, sympathetic
and enthusiastic audience, and this in Everett where they massacred
a number of union men who came here by boat from Seattle six years
ago and drove the rest from the city and swore there should never
be another socialist meeting in Everett. But ah, there's been a wonderful change & now the people understand in part at least and are
with us, and they dare not lay their dirty, cowardly hands on us. They
(the A.L. & C. of C.) were going to stop the meeting here — but they
didn't. Then they said if I said anything "radical" they would stop
me and disperse the meeting but by God, they changed their minds.
I cut loose and gave them hell from start to finish & ripped their
rotten system wide open but they knew better than to monkey with
me or try any rough stuff on that meeting, and it is well they did for
if they had tried to pull anything off their hides would be on exhibition
this morning. I'm feeling very *hostile* & if you were within landing
distance I'd treat you to the most artistic whaling ever administered
to a mortal pelt.
    I hope you and Gertrude are well and chipper as chipmunks. It's
a beautiful morning — cool and bracing and I'm feeling like a young
panther at a cake-walk.
    With a heart full of love to you & Gertrude.
                                                    Your old pard forever
                                                                    Gene

    This {tour} is like a tidal wave sneeking over the Northwest &
they are lining up in the party in a way to warm the cockles of your
heart.

ALS, InTI, Debs Collection.

EVD to Theodore Debs

September 13, [1923]
Tacoma, Washington

My dear old Pard,

If I'm not mistaken this is the anniversary of Dandy and Daisy's wedding day. God bless their sweet and precious memory! It will bloom perennial in our hearts forever. We will have a great meeting here to-night and leave on the midnight train for Portland. The damn fools at Long Beach Cal (A.L. & C of C.) cancelled the meeting there as you know & now Long Beach people want a date more than ever & half a dozen other points want the date. We have given it to Santa Rosa where Burbank is & I'll get to see him. The Long Beach "patriots" telegraphed it all over the country that they had cancelled my date to hurt me & only helped me. All the T.H. papers published the dispatch. They eagerly seize upon that sort of stuff about me as eagerly as buzzards light upon carrion {but} the nasty little sheets have never a decent thing said about me, & it's just right for I wouldn't have any favor at their dirty hands. The only trouble we are having is that the houses are too small to hold the enormous crowds for which our thanks are due in no small measure to the A.L. & the C. of C. the Wall st. twins & I tell them so. I'm going to tear the hides off the plutes in California & their outrageous despotism if I go to jail for it. The keepers of Tom Mooney, the lickspittle judges & rotten courts & politicians. I'm going to burn them alive & tell them they have made California stink to the skies, & that some day the whirlwind they are sowing will sweep them into red hell where they belong. We'll have tremendous meetings at L.A. & S.F. & I'll give them the straight gospel smoking hot—feeling fine as the Prairieton Prince & hope you & Gertrude are chipper as humming birds.

Love & kisses & a "short-arm" swish in the beak. A la Hammerstein! Wow!!

Gene

ALS, InTI, Debs Collection.

☐ *When Debs was released from prison in 1921, he devoted his $5.00 "freedom payment" to the defense fund for Nicola Sacco and Bartolomeo Vanzetti, Italian immigrants and anarchists who were convicted in July 1921 of a payroll robbery and murder in Massachusetts. The Sacco-Vanzetti case became an international cause célèbre during the 1920s. Many Americans, including Debs who wrote and spoke numerous times on their behalf, believed the two men, who*

were executed in 1927, were victims of persecution for their declared philosoph-
ical anarchism and their alien status.

Bartolomeo Vanzetti to EVD

September 29, 1923
Charlestown, Massachusetts

Dear Comrade E. Debs: —

It is long time, since your unforgettable visit to me, that I am
wishing to write to you.

I have told to one of the noblest women of this nation that I am
ashamed to have been unable to speak to you; and she answered "Do
not whorry of it, E. Debs understan it." And, as prove, she told me
a similar case in the life of her mother, who has understood and
appreciated the silence of a friend.

I realize that you have understood me — but, nevertheless I wished,
I wish to express to you my gratitude, my respect and my love.

As you know, I belong to the extreme anarchistic school — but
maybe you ignore the admiration and affection that we, Italian anarchists, have for you — or, rather, that you won from us.

You and Lucy Parson are the two American for whose personal
acquaintance I have longed for many years. Now I have the pleasure
to know both of you.

Once, when living in Farrel P. I have heard that you would have
come to speak in Charlestown, O. All the Italian anarchists of the
neighbourhood were there, waiting for you. But a telegram came,
and told your impossibility to reach the city. So I have had to wait
many years before to see you. And I must confess that when I saw
you I went near to cry.

You and I belong to different schools of socialism — but you are
my teacher.

I do not vote, but I would trust unto you the sacrest and dearest
things of the life.

Because you have superated this age, arose above the narrow limits
of parties and of sects, and masterly preach by exemples.

I am firmly convinced that the results of the human convivence:
miseries, darkness and death, or health, light, happiness and life, are
more determined by the qualities and the deeds of the individuals
than by parties' and sets' programs and creeds. And I am positive
that if a minority would follow your {practical} example the reality
of the to-morrow would be above the dreams of many dreamers.

I expect to be bring in Court next Monday; also, have some letters to be wrote; and wish to write an article before to-morrow night: for these reasons I must close this letter, praying you to exscuse my poor English and to accept my sincere sentiments.

Your, with great heart,
Bartolomeo V[anzetti]

ALS, InTI, Debs Collection.

□ *Debs's western tour in September 1923 was followed by a trip through Michigan, Ohio, Pennsylvania, and New York in October. The largest crowd of the western and eastern tours was at Cooper Union in New York City on October 28. Sandburg's* Rootabaga Pigeons *was a children's book published in 1923. His work as a poet was highly praised by Carl Van Doren in the* Century *magazine in September 1923.*

EVD to Carl Sandburg

November 6, 1923
Terre Haute, Indiana

My dear Carl:

Returning from the East after a series of most remarkable meetings including the final one at Cooper Union, New York, I find your beautiful volume "Rootabaga Pigeons" awaiting me for which I hasten to return my warmest thanks. It is a beautiful book, issued in a unique style befitting its contents and I shall have this to add to my collection of literary treasures and to serve as a precious and beloved companion to me always. No one but you could have produced this wonderful volume. It required your peculiar genius and your marvellous imagination to conceive and execute this strikingly original and appealing production.

I have read with deep interest and full appreciation the article about you in the Century. You are growing amazingly and I can see you stepping from peak to peak with your soul aflame and your head among the stars. May the uttermost extent of your incomparable dreams all be triumphantly realized!

I have never for a day since leaving you and your beautiful wife and little household gods failed to think of you and return my thanks and blessings for the rest and comfort and inspiration that I found there. We are all devotees, you may be sure, of the House of Sandburg, and we are all joining, Mrs. Debs and Theodore and his wife and all of our family in love and salutation and a million good wishes. Count me always

Your loving friend and comrade,
Eugene V. Debs

TLS, InU, Lilly Library, Sandburg Papers.

☐ *In the following letter Debs suggests to David Karsner various sources for a biography of himself that would be "completer" than Karsner's 1919 book* Debs: His Authorized Life and Letters. *The proposed biography was never finished.*

EVD to David Karsner

November 10, 1923
Terre Haute, Indiana

My dear David:

I have been very busy and not very well or your good letter of the 5th. would have been more promptly answered. It is gratifying to me to know that my suggestion as to your writing a completer "Life" has met with your hearty approval. I agree with all you say in regard to the documents, letters etc., and only lack time now to select the ones of which you would wish to make use. I am just getting ready to leave for the West and it is impossible for me to get these things together in the little time I have here between engagements. I have a great mass of letters, clippings, documents, manuscripts, etc. (all mixed up, and {it has} continued to grow ever since I went to prison) which I have not yet found time to get into any sort of shape for use. I shall do this as soon as possible but cannot promise to do anything until I get through with the season's speaking engagements. How soon this may be I cannot at present say. But I shall keep your request in mind and when the time comes I shall of course be glad to place anything and everything you need in your work that is in my hands at your service. Let me suggest that if you have not yet seen the department assigned to my collection in the Rand School that you do so at your convenience. I sent them a lot of old books, records, pictures, personal scrapbooks, etc. for which I no longer had room here. These included the Locomotive Fireman's Magazines from the first number issued in 1877 with which I was connected until 1894. In the scrapbooks you will find a lot of personal matter from which you may care to quote as your leisure will allow in a sort of a preparatory way. These records in one form or another contain most of my life of any public interest in the form of raw material. You will find in the large bound newspaper volumes in the collection the pages taken from the current press over a good many years containing the record of events in which I have been interested. Among these you will find the files of the Railway Times, organ of the American Railway Union, probably the only copy in existence, and in these there is material for the very eventful period to me covering the years between 1893 and 1897, the beginning and end of the A.R.U. and the beginning of the Social Democracy, now the Socialist Party.

I was more than delighted to have the brief visit with you. My heart was glad every moment and on my return Theodore and Katherine and Gertrude were all happy to hear from you and to receive the message of your loving remembrance.

Love and life to you increasingly!

Yours always,
E. V. Debs

TLS, NN Kars.

□ *In a letter to William Foster dated July 23, 1924, Debs defended the Socialist party's and his own endorsement of Robert M. La Follette for president, expressed his "poor opinion of the Communist Party," and noted that "having no Vatican in Moscow to guide me I must follow the light I have." The following letter is Foster's response.*

William Z. Foster to EVD

July 30, 1924
Chicago, Illinois

Dear Comrade Debs:—

In your letter of July 23rd to me you evade the main issue. You fail to tell the reason why Debs, the "revolutionary" Socialist, endorses LaFollette, the anti-Socialist. I can appreciate your difficulty in this matter. You content yourself simply with making a series of attacks against the Workers Party, as though that were to blame. These I cannot permit to pass unchallenged.

You speak of the "sorry and discrediting" figure which the Workers Party will cut in the coming election campaign, as compared with the role of the Socialist Party. Let us see. Faced by the great petty bourgeois movement headed by LaFollette, which is engulfing whole sections of the labor movement, the Workers Party has dared to stand true to its revolutionary mission and to denounce this false leader and his class collaboration program. It ventures to defend the slogans of the class struggle and to make the election fight upon a revolutionary basis. As against this uncompromising attitude, the Socialist Party has abandoned even the last remnants of its lip-service to revolutionary principles and is unreservedly supporting the ridiculous and reactionary trust-busting program of LaFollette; it has betrayed the farmer-labor movement and, adopting the C.P.P.A. plan, it will either accept openly or wink at the endorsement of "friends" of labor on the two old party tickets in the approved Gompers manner. You may blind yourself to the significance of this pitiful surrender to LaFollette and Gompers, but the revolutionary elements in the working class will not. Without difficulty they will discern that in the present situation it is not the W.P. but the S.P. which is cutting a "sorry and discrediting" figure. The recent letter of Landfersiek, former National Secretary of the S.P., condemning LaFollette and endorsing the Workers party candidates, voices the true sentiments of the few proletarian elements still remaining in the S.P.

In one respect your letter is correct — I have an exceedingly poor opinion of the Socialist party. I have learned something of the treachery of its sister parties in Europe, of how they have betrayed the revolution time and again. Abundant experience shows that the American Socialist Party is cut from the same cloth. The Hillquits and Bergers are only Scheidemanns and Noskes lacking opportunity. Consequently, I, for one, expected little else from the Socialist Party in Cleveland than the complete surrender that it made to LaFollette. It was to be expected, however, that you, at least, would sound a revolutionary note of opposition against the opportunistic debacle. In the past couple of years you have winked at the oppostion of the S.P. to the amalgamation of the trade unions, its calumniation of Soviet Russia, its refusal to form a united front on the political field, and its enforcement of many reactionary policies which run counter to the principles you have so often enunciated from the platform. This failure to fight for these principles in the S.P. was bad enough, but now when you not only acquiesce in the surrender to LaFollette, but actually defend it, you by that action definitely leave the camp of the revolutionaries and go over to the opportunists and petty bourgeois reformists.

But you contend that we Communists have no right to condemn your endorsement of LaFollette, because you say we proposed to endorse him ourselves. This is an unpardonable misstatement. Never at any time did the Workers Party propose to endorse LaFollette or his program. On the contrary, the W.P. has long been keenly awake to the menace of LaFollette-ism and has been fighting it on all fronts. This is proved by a hundred articles and statements in our party press. For the Workers Party a leading tactical consideration has been how best to fight LaFolletteism. The Workers Party realized the influence LaFollette had on the farmer-labor ranks. In order to prevent the absorption of the farmer-labor movement by LaFollette and to prevent the isolation of the Workers Party from the Farmer-Labor Party forces, the Workers Party considered the adoption of the following policy, which, however, was not supported by the Communist International: If the St. Paul Farmer-Labor Party Convention nominated LaFollette over the opposition of the Workers Party, we would not split away from it on that issue, but would accept, under protest, an alliance of the Farmer-Labor Party and a third party in support of LaFollette's candidacy and would endeavor to organize the Farmer-Labor Party during the campaign as a class party in oppostion to the LaFollette third party. Under any circumstances, the Workers Party would have carried on a campaign of strong opposition against LaFollette and his program.

It was later proposed to accept him as a candidate at the St. Paul Convention of the Farmer-Labor Party, but only upon the condition that he subscribe to the radical program of the Farmer-Labor Party, run as that party's candidate, and accept its control over his electoral campaign and campaign funds. In other words, LaFollette would have had to cut loose from all his capitalist party connections, accept a real proletarian program, and head a genuine farmer-labor ticket. Even then the Workers Party would have accepted him only under protest. It would have continued its ceaseless criticism of his petty bourgeois notions and its propagation of revolutionary principles among the masses in the Farmer-Labor party. It is absurd to campare this revolutionary policy with the S.P. surrender to LaFollette. Hillquit, without a word of protest in the convention, humbly swallowed LaFollette's program of petty bourgeois reform, his anti-labor party attitude, his "reward your friends and punish your enemies" political policy, and his insulting and dictatorial control. And now you endorse this proceeding. As for the W.P., when it saw that because of the surrender of reactionary trade union leaders and pseudo-revolutionaries to LaFollette it would be impossible to organize sufficient masses in the new Farmer-Labor party to make a successful united front fight against

LaFollette, it raised its own banner and will make the fight in the open field.

In times past you have stated repeatedly from the platform that you admire Lenin as the greatest figure produced in the world war. Yet, in your letter, you sneer, in orthodox yellow-Socialist fashion, at our affiliation with the institution that incorporates the very soul of Leninism, the Third International. Tastes in Internationals vary. You, although claiming to be a left-wing revolutionary, calmly content yourself to accept the leadership of the Second International, the organization of Scheidemann, Noske, and other butchers and betrayers of the revolution. As for us, we repudiate such traitors and all association with them. We deem it not only absolutely vital to the revolutionary movement in this country, but also an honor to be associated internationally with the men who carried through the Russian revolution and with those who are making the revolutionary fight in all other countries. We make no apology for accepting the guidance of the Third International. On the contrary, we glory in it. Our party is proud to be a section of the revolutionary world organization, the Communist International.

Fraternally yours,
Wm Z Foster

TLS, InTI, Debs Collection.

□ *Debs had returned to the Lindlahr Sanitarium in Elmhurst, Illinois, for treatment when he sent the following poem to Carl Sandburg.*

EVD to Carl Sandburg

September 4, 1924
Elmhurst, Illinois

Prison Ode

~

Beyond these walls
Sweet Freedon calls;
In accents clear and brave she speaks,
And lo! my spirit scales the peaks.

~

Beyond these bars
I see the stars;
God's glittering heralds beckon me;
My soul is winged: behold, I'm free!
Eugene V. Debs

Elmhurst, Sept. 4 — 1924
To Carl, with love and loyalty
Gene

Beatitude

———— ~ ————

Blessed are they who
expect nothing, for they
shall not be disappointed.
Eugene V. Debs

To Carl,
With boundless love and admiration—

Gene

Elmhurst, September 4th 1924

A poems, IU, Sandburg Papers.

☐ *Lilian Sandburg was Carl's wife and the sister of the famous photographer Edward Steichen. The pictures discussed by Debs in the following letter were taken during his visit to the Sandburg home in September 1924.*

EVD to Lilian Steichen Sandburg

October 1, 1924
Terre Haute, Indiana

My dear Mrs. Sandburg:

How shall I thank you for your very kind and generous rememberance in sending me the many copies of the pictures taken by you of Carl and your sweet children and myself on the occasion of my visit at your home last summer! I am delighted, I need hardly say, with the excellent and most interesting little pictures which will certainly have their proper place in the casket of my precious little treasures. You may certainly flatter yourself that you are an artist as a photographer for in your posings {as} in all else you prove your high efficiency as a picture-taker as is shown conclusively in the evidence I hold in my hands. Each of the prints you send is an excellent reproduction of the life which had its being in your garden and in the jungles surrounding it when it was my good fortune to be your guest and to be decorated with beautiful roses pressed upon me by the loving hands of your little household gods. Each of the pictures is good and better than good and has its distinct interest and merit. I feel myself highly honored in them all and as I look upon them one by one my heart turns to you in grateful homage for having thus honored me.

Carl shows his usual discriminating taste in expressing preference for the very happy little picture of Helda and myself on the bench. I think you were never more fortunate in snapping your subjects at precisely the right moment. That particular picture is a gem. It could not possibly be better, and it flatters me enormously. Helda's eager, searching and amusing expression and pose is a subject for the best of the movies, and I am sure that Carl never saw anything of its kind to excel it. It is so utterly and so beautifully characteristic of the sweet, innocent child full to overflowing with the spirit and animation of childhood. It requires only a glance to see that she and I are lovers and that we are in delighted and blissful communion with each other. How my emotions are quickened and thrill within me as I recall this happy scene and look once more, as I often shall in the future, into the sweet face, the quizzical eyes of that lovely child!

The pictures of Carl and myself and Margaret and indeed of all three of the little dears are excellent and most precious and interesting to me, as they are also to Katherine and to my brother who have had the pleasure of seeing them.

I shall always remember each happy and comforting moment spent beneath your hospitable roof. The very thought of you and Carl and your trinity of sweet daughters gives me joy.

If my humble companionship helped Carl, as you suggest, in the very least in his work on Lincoln, I shall be forever the subject of enviable distinction.

Thanking you with all my heart and with all loving greetings and the best of good wishes to you and Carl and your three lovely little girls, in which Katherine, Theodore, Gertrude and Marguerite join, I am always,

                                                    Yours faithfully,
                                                    Eugene V. Debs

TLS, IU, Sandburg Papers.

□ *During the 1924 presidential campaign the Republican National Committee circulated a document charging that Robert La Follette was supported by "the most incendiary and revolutionary elements in American politics" and that the "foremost in the group is Eugene V. Debs."*

EVD to Republican National Committee

October 11, 1924
Chicago, Illinois

Gentlemen:

A copy of your campaign screed "Socialists, Anarchists and I.W.W's Flock to the La Follette Standard" has come into my hands and I think I ought to return thanks for the compliment paid me in that document, the only compliment your committee is capable of paying an honest man. I should feel myself disgraced indeed to receive any testimonial of approval from the thieving, hypocritical and utterly conscienceless gang you represent. It is true that I was robbed of my citizenship by the political perverts you are seeking to keep in the offices they have befouled, but I still have my manhood and self-respect. I went to prison for a principle, but as you do not know what that is you are excusable for attempting to libel me while yourselves functioning as the servile lackeys of Wall street, the profiteering pirates and highbinders who are looting this nation and debauching its institutions; whose putrescent filthiness was revealed in but the minutest part in the recent uncovering of the stench-pots in Washington, while their diminutive political manikan sat silent and supine in the executive chair once occupied by Lincoln, whose grave clothes have been stolen and whose memory is outraged and insulted by the grafting gang now in control of the Republican party.

If you time-serving adepts in crooked politics were not stone-blind in the practice of your political shell game on your one hundred percent American dupes and morons you would see the hand-writing burning luridly on the wall of your ignominious political fate.

Yours for Socialism,
[Eugene V. Debs]

TLc, InTI, Debs Collection.

☐ *In a note to Debs on October 18, 1924, Sandburg wrote: "If you hadn't stayed so long you wouldn't have left such a big lonesome spot. We can nearly see a ghost in the doorways where you came and went."*

EVD to Carl Sandburg

October 21, 1924
Terre Haute, Indiana

My dear Carl:

If there was a lonesome spot in your doorway when I left there there was also one in my heart and I can feel it yet. I shall never forget those jeweled moments and those golden hours. I note what you say about the book that is coming and I shall be happy indeed to see it. It is going to be a very big book. As much of its illustrious subject as can be put into a book will be packed in its pages along with as much of the famous {author} as the book will hold. Yes, I will take care of myself and so must you for we shall be needed, both of us, for the big job ahead. My love to you all!

Yours always,
Eugene V. Debs

TLS, IU, Sandburg Papers.

☐ *In the following letter Debs tries to comfort David Karsner, who had left the* New York Call *to join the* New York Tribune *but was dissatisfied in his new job. In the process Debs reveals some of his own views of life and the sadness he felt as he observed the changes that had taken place in "my beloved little community of Terre Haute."*

EVD to David Karsner

December 6, 1924
Terre Haute, Indiana

My dear "Davy": —

I have finished reading your letter of the 1st. with the feeling that the game of life had its galling inning at the moment it was written. I am grieved but not at all surprised. At your age, in your years of boyhood no such shadows should fall upon the heart as I feel are troubling yours. I think I can sense the situation at a glance. Knowing how delicately you are wired, how keenly sensitive you are to a surrounding that jars on your moral and spiritual nerves, I feel convinced that the atmosphere of a big capitalist daily, permeated in every fibre with commercialism, is not at all compatible or rather reconcilable with your temperament or conducive to your happiness. But it may be that just this experience is a part and a necessary part of the ampler and completer education and equipment you must have to do the greater work awaiting you and to fulfill your higher destiny. That you will learn things in such a position you never could or would learn in one perfectly congenial to you and your taste goes without saying, and it is one of the every day facts of life that we profit most in every essential way by adverse and disagreeable experiences than by the more pleasing and happy ones.

Yes, dear David, you are right in your philosophizing about apartment cages with a synagogue at one end and a graveyard at the other to look out upon for good cheer and serene meditation. Every damned thing about you is mechanical and artificial, hard and cold and automatic, so that all you have to do is to press a button or touch a lever to have things dance attendance upon you and to finally consign you to a self-acting coffin in which you are rolled {away} into the great mystery. I often fondly yearn to see once more and to once more live in the enchanting little village on the {river} bank, shaded by the great sycamores, in which I was born, but which has now been swallowed up and utterly buried in a wilderness of concrete and steel, a commercial metropolis as cold and callous as the arctics and in which my beloved little community of Terre Haute, where all were neighbors and all friends, and where there was green grass instead of gray concrete and sturdy oaks and beautiful maples instead of hideous steel prison walls, {is now but a memory.} Our good friend Ingersoll used to say: "Oaks and elms are infinitely more beautiful and eloquent than spires and chimneys."

My heart is touched as you recall the intensely dramatic and pathetic scene as I left the prison. No pen, however inspired, could ever do it justice, and least of all my own. When I have tried to set down what my heart overflowed with I found myself mute and silent and my hand palsied. What would I not give were it in my power to paint in words or on canvas that vivid, unparallelled, bewildering and overwhelming demonstration of almost three thousand so-called convicts, human souls in cruel iron fetters, in the presence of which the warden and deputy warden stood paralyzed and speechless and I, standing between them, trembling with emotions that almost choked me while my heart stood still and the tears ran down my cheeks! Ah, dear David, that vivid, eternally memorable and heart-wringing scene, those pallid faces in all shades and representing all races and all ages, and all bearing the tragic stamp of "man's inhumanity to man," will never be written in any book unless it be in God's own book of record and remembrance.

But in my very humble way I am going to do my best and I am going to wage war in every way I know how on the god-damned prison institution everywhere, as I pledged myself on leaving Atlanta I would do, while there is a breath of life in my body.

Cheer up, David, it is a great and glorious battle after all and the greater the odds, adversities, griefs and sorrows, the more valiantly will we fight, the more unconquerable in spirit will we become, and the fuller and richer, the nobler and diviner will life be to us.

Theodore and Gertrude and Kate and I all join, and Marguerite would be with us heartily were she not far away, in love and all happy greetings and fond wishes to you and your dear Esther and sweet Walta.

Yours always and
Eugene V. Debs

TLS, NN Kars.

□ *Harry Weinberger was a New York City attorney who specialized in civil liberties cases and, in 1919, was counsel for Emma Goldman and Alexander Berkman in their unsuccessful fight against deportation to Russia. In 1923 Goldman published a series of articles, based on her experiences in Russia and generally critical of the Communist regime there. Her book* My Disillusionment in Russia *appeared the same year.*

Harry Weinberger to EVD

May 25, 1925
New York City

My dear Gene:

I received a letter from Emma Goldman and she asked me to write to you giving you her affectionate greetings and to say that she has retained a warm spot in her heart for you, even though you have failed to understand the motive which made her go into the "Morning

World" with her first articles, and she thinks you are a grand old soul and she likes you immensely, and she sends me a reply to the Business Trade Union Delegation Report and a copy of Time and Tide Magazine and her article on Women of the Russian Revolution, which I am sending you under separate cover.

Personal regards also from

Very truly yours,
Harry Weinberger

TLS, InTI, Debs Collection.

EVD to Harry Weinberger

June 1925
[Terre Haure, Indiana]

My dear Harry Weinberger:

Please allow me to thank you most warmly for your very kind letter of the 25th just received and for the enclosed pamphlet and copy of Time and Tide which I am glad indeed to have and to which I shall give careful reading at my earliest leisure.

The articles by Emma Goldman on "Women of the Russian Revolution" will be of especial interest to me, as is everything of a printed nature that bears her name.

I have not infrequently found my self in disagreement with Emma Goldman but I have never for one instant doubted her rectitude or courage, nor have I been unmindful of her very decided ability as both speaker and writer.

I have been heartily with her in all the brutal, shameless persecution to which she has been subjected by our cruel and cowardly capitalist government which will one day be pilloried in history for having climaxed its outrages upon her by driving her from the country under the most disgraceful circumstances.

It is gratifying to me indeed to know that Emma Goldman entertains such a friendly feeling toward me. This certainly honors me and I can say in all frankness that I have the same affectionate personal feeling for her and otherwise hold her in the highest esteem as a woman battling bravely against great odds to serve humanity and to bring freedom to the world.

No one who really knows Emma Goldman can fail to appreciate her as one of the commanding personalities in the struggle of our day to emancipate labor and to humanize the race.

When you write her please do me the kindness to say to her that I feel the outrage perpetrated upon her by the United States government even more keenly and resent it more bitterly than if I had been the victim of it, and that although I may disagree with her about some matters I can and do honor her for her fidelity to her convictions, and that I send her my loving greetings and warmest wishes and hope some day to see her again.

Thanking you again and again for your kindness I am as ever,

Your faithfully,
EUGENE V. DEBS

TLc, MiU, Labadie Collection.

□ *Bertha Hale White was the office manager at the Socialist party headquarters in Chicago and assistant executive secretary of the party from 1919 to 1924, when she was elected executive secretary, the first woman to hold that position. In the following letter Debs harshly criticizes the strategy, tactics, and daily operation of the party, which he viewed as being "as near a corpse as a thing can be."*

EVD to Bertha Hale White

June 3, 1925
Terre Haute, Indiana

Dear Comrade Bertha:

There are some important party matters I must write to you about and I wish you would please let Comrade Kirkpatrick and also Comrade Birch and Lilith Wilson read this letter if they are there, and then let me know what you think of its contents.

In what I have to say I am going to be perfectly frank as I have always tried to be in party matters. The Convention and Demonstration at Cleveland were flat, humiliating failures compared to what they should have been, and will have anything but an encouraging influence upon those that are to follow. There were several reasons for the failure of the Demonstration. The intense summer heat of the day and the fact that people sought the outdoors and found their enjoyment in the local automobile races which were the exciting public event of the day and attracted some fifty to a hundred thousand people were probably the main deterrents to a successful indoor meeting. The 50c admission rate did the rest. Had there been a 25c rate as I have always insisted, with 50c and up for reserved seats, boxes and special positions the crowd would have been very much larger and the results better in every way.

But the Convention was the weakest feature of all and there is no use blinking the fact that it was a dismal affair and the communists and their organ have good grounds for their ridicule of the affair. In a great city, an immense industrial center, where we once had a local of nearly two thousand members and where the Socialists cast nearly 30,000 votes for Mayor, we were able after months of beating the bushes and advertising and spending hundreds of dollars to get just enough Socialists together from half a dozen different states to make a fair-size local or branch meeting. And that is all. That convention demonstrated as clearly as anything could that the Socialist party is as near a corpse as a thing can be and still show signs of life. There is a reason for this that I propose to discuss in this letter with the frankness due to you and the rest of my associates in the National Office. Either there is something dead wrong with the Socialist Party or there is something dead wrong with the management of its affairs. We shall see.

There are in this country hundreds of labor organizations of all kinds and they all have funds in their treasury, pay their way and get along without begging like paupers to keep alive. There are numbers of Jewish labor and socialist societies of various kinds which conduct stores, schools and other enterprises and have plenty of money to meet all their demands. The Socialist party is the only organization in the entire lot that is a perpetual mendicant and beggar, that is always dead broke, pressed for debts it cannot pay, squeezing the last cent and bleeding to the last drop the few loyal souls it has to draw upon, and the more money it gets the poorer it becomes and the worse it is off. Why is this?

In the last seven years, since I was first arrested at Cleveland on account of the war, several hundred thousand dollars have poured into the National Office, mainly on my account, and not a dollar has remained there. For myself and my brother who have given ourselves wholly to the service of the party during all that time with all the means at our command, we have not received enough to pay our living expenses. During this time I have refused all kinds of lecture and speaking engagements that would have made me independent, refusing steadfastly anything for myself and giving everything to the party. I do not say this to claim anything for myself at this time or to make any complaint for I am not of the complaining kind, but simply that we may have the facts of the situation before us in dealing with the questions at issue.

Now let me say to you, dear comrade, that I have reached some very definite conclusions in this matter and one of them is that this state of affairs is due wholly to mismanagement, and in saying this I want it understood that I accept my full share of the responsibility for that mismanagement.

We have been living beyond our means and beyond our income and we are doing so at this very hour and that is the fundamental cause of our pitiful plight and our gloomy outlook for the future.

When in 1880, after the Brotherhood of Locomotive Firemen had been bankrupted and was overwhelmed with debt and threatened with dissolution, I was made grand secretary and treasurer, the very first thing I did was to cut off every dollar of expense that could possibly be cut off, reduce every item to the most rigid economy and confine the expenditures from the very hour of my appointment within the income. The income was very small, but the outgo, the expenditure, was still smaller, leaving a little margin that soon began to grow. Within a year every dollar of the debt had been paid and the organization was on its feet and grew steadily in numbers, in power and financially, and never again did it want for a dollar for anything it needed in carrying on its work. I did not stop in swell hotels at that time and invite the poverty-stricken party members to banquets at $2.00 per plate.

When at the banquet in Cleveland Comrade Birch Wilson announced pathetically in his speech that the party was bankrupt, the National Office not having funds enough to meet its payroll, I felt not only humiliated but disgraced. There we sat in one of the highest-priced hotels in Cleveland, consuming an extravagant banquet, and confessing that we were paupers and beggars and could not even pay the help in the National Office of our party. In that financial condition we had no business whatever in that kind of a hotel nor at that kind of a banquet. I have been going to Cleveland for years and I always stopped at a hotel and had a decent, comfortable room at a dollar and a half a day less than I paid at the hotel chosen by our people. But this hotel and its kind are not good enough, it appears, since we have become absolutely penniless and have to put in most of our time begging for enough to keep us alive. I am objecting right now against this extravagance as long as we are self-confessed bankrupts and cannot pay for our keep. I shall never again speak at a banquet at two dollars a plate.

Why must we, a pauper and beggar party, give our banquets at plutocratic hotels and charge plutocratic rates to our poverty-stricken comrades? There is no sense in it but a whole lot of indecency which offends me and my sense of what is proper. Why can we not give our banquets in an ordinary hall instead of a swell hotel, and have it served by some ordinary caterer at not more than a dollar a plate? There would be far more in attendance, it would be far more consistent and satisfactory, and the financial and other results would be far different from our present method of making the affair so expensive to our comrades for sheer and senseless extravagance that they have nothing left when it comes to contributing funds to the party.

In the present state of our party every cent should be carefully guarded. I see no use in members of the N.E.C. voting by telegraph on matters that come before them and I refuse to do it. There is nothing so important that cannot wait a day or two and go by mail. I do not use the long distance telephone for I cannot afford it, and I use the telegraph only in cases of extreme necessity for the same reason, and the National Office in its present state can get along without these items of expense. It is true they are small but they are indicative of a policy that has kept the party in a beggarly financial condition.

Now my conclusion is that the Socialist party has got to get within its income at once or give up and quit as a failure for it will certainly end in that at the rate we are now going.

I object to any organizer being put into the field until the National Office has been put on a basis of expenditure within its income. If it cannot meet its payroll it has got to cut its payroll; not only this it has got to cut its rent roll. I understand the rent is now $250.00 per month. Now it is perfectly senseless to have that rent to pay when we have nothing to pay it with, and that has been the trouble all this time and will be the trouble more and more until the party is finally completely wrecked.

When I was told that the national debt was something over five thousand dollars and I agreed to personally set about to raise the money to pay that debt, and it was raised, I supposed a new leaf would be turned and there would be a decided change for the better but instead of this we are, if possible, worse off than before. The more money we raise the poorer we get because we spend it faster than it comes in, a very simple matter in mathematics.

As I now feel I shall not sign another note for a bank loan for the National Office. It is no use. It is like pouring water through a seive.

I do not in the least blame Comrade Whitlock for refusing to put any more money into the national office. Whitlock is a shrewd business man and he can see at a glance that with our way of doing business we are getting nowhere with the money he is giving us, and he has wisely concluded to give no more, and I shall certainly not ask him to. I have been used all these years as a kind of bait to draw funds to the National Office and I have concluded to quit serving in that role. I would not so humiliate myself on my own account and I shall do so no longer for the party for it is quite clear that it does the party no good.

Now as I have said we have got to get within our income and if the National Office cannot and will not do that then I have made up my mind to resign from the N.E.C. for I can see nothing but disaster and ignominy ahead and I do not propose to lead the party to that kind of an end. I shall fill all the engagements made for me in good faith, but I shall do so in my own name and not as a national party official.

If the National Office cannot conduct its business on a basis of spending less instead of more than comes in, then it is simply a dead weight upon the party, and I am almost persuaded that the best thing that could happen to the party to give it a chance to grow would be to entirely abolish the National Office for the next six months. It absorbs everything our poverty-stricken locals can raise and I do not see that it is giving them anything like an equivalent in return. No wonder they and others refuse any longer to be bled to the last penny to keep up a party so managed as to be in a state of perpetual bankruptcy. It was this very thing that I had to face in New York and that is the deep-seated conviction on the part of many that our party is mismanaged and weak and almost hopeless because we don't know what to do with the money that is contributed to its support.

Now it is clear that we can't pay the rent of our present quarters. Therefore we have got to get out and that without delay and we have got to limit our rent and other expenses to what we can pay and no more, if we have got to shrink to the size of one room and one desk. That is how we will get our start and if that policy had been pursued in the past we would not today be in our pitiable plight, and I am feeling it today more keenly than I have ever felt it before, and this because I know beyond doubt what can be done if the party is given a chance, and the crushing load that has rested upon its emaciated body is removed and it is no longer halted and paralyzed by chronic bankruptcy and lack of means. I know that a little store room could be secured on Halsted or some other street for half and less the rent now being paid, that would serve our purpose just as well. If there is a mass of junk in the National Office for which there is no room, then it must be gotten rid of for it is eating itself up right along in excess rent. Our shrivelled little party cannot support a headquarters such as we now have and such as is a dead load under which it cannot stagger out of its impotency and poverty.

In presenting these matters I have had to be plain and candid, but I am sure you must know there is nothing of a personal nature intended to reflect upon you or anyone in the National Office. It is not persons but a policy I am criticizing and objecting to, a policy if persisted in that will lead inevitably to disaster and ignominy. I know you have borne a terrible burden and I know that all of your associates have done their very best and I have never found any fault with them and do not now. Your individual services have been all and much more than could have been expected but the policy has been wrong and this has got to be righted and at once if the party is to be saved and made what it ought to be.

With love and warmest wishes as ever,

Yours fraternally,
(Signed) EUGENE V. DEBS

Dear Bertha:

There is a point I omitted in my letter to you this morning through oversight that I wish to emphasize now. And that is that as long as we are moneyless, insolvent, bankrupt, all efforts to organize will be paralyzed from the very source from which they should receive their help and inspiration. No one wants to join a bankrupt party or have anything to do with an insolvent concern. In other words no one wants to have any identity with a failure and it is as such that the Socialist party appears to the thousands today who ought to join it but won't. If it had a full treasury and was known to be prosperous instead of a moneyless mendicant become a chronic beggar, these thousands would flock to it from every quarter. There is nothing that money runs away from and stays away from as persistently as it does from where there is no money. A bankrupt concern, especially a so-called revolutionary party, is like a smallpox patient in quarantine. The whole world steers clear of the moneyless man or the moneyless concern and it is useless to try to organize unless and until the National Office first organizes itself out of debt and becomes solvent by keeping within its income. It would be a tragedy in my life and an everlasting rebuke if that money I got from the New York Jewish comrades for the party went the way of the rest with nothing to show for it in the end, and that is the way it will go if the present policy is not radically changed.

With love as ever,
(Signed) EUGENE V. DEBS

P.S. When Comrade Wilson in his speech at the banquet laid the state of the Socialist Party bare by declaring it flat broke, in effect, and even unable to meet its payroll, that blow did more to flatten out what was left of the party, to discourage all efforts to rebuild it, and to paralyze all efforts at organizing than any blow the capitalists or their government could have dealt it. Comrade Wilson was perfectly right in coming out with the truth, feeling, no doubt, that it had to be told and not a little humiliated, I can well imagine, in the telling, but the deplorable state of the party thus laid bare revealed a corpse instead of a living thing, and who wants to have anything to do with revivifying a corpse?

TLc, WiH, Hillquit Papers.

☐ *One of Debs's enduring heroes was John P. Altgeld, the governor of Illinois who was savagely attacked during his lifetime for his pardon of the men who were convicted of the Haymarket Massacre. In the following letter Debs thanks Clarence Darrow for an inscribed copy of Waldo Browne's* Altgeld of Illinois, *published in 1924. George Schilling served as secretary of the Illinois Bureau of Labor Statistics under Governor Altgeld.*

EVD to Clarence Darrow

June 4, 1925
Terre Haute, Indiana

My dear Clarence Darrow:
    You and our fine old mutual friend, George Schilling, true to your record of many years' standing, have been extemely kind and thoughtful in sending me the copy of "Altgeld in Illinois" by Waldo R. Browne, so flatteringly inscribed, which I found awaiting me on my return from Ohio. I had already read with intense interest and appreciation, not unmixed with sad reflection and painful memories, this very excellent, high-hearted and courageous biography of the shamefully maligned and pre-eminently great Altgeld, but this par-

ticular volume coming from your hands, bearing your more than beautiful and generous tribute inscribed in its pages, gives it a value Rockefeller does not possess and makes it a treasure indeed of priceless worth for which I beg you, dear friends, each of you, to accept my warmest thanks with the assurance of my lasting gratitude and devotion.

When I think of how great, how supremely great Altgeld was in heart and brain, in soul and conscience, and how petty, mean and contemptible Bryan was and is, and that Altgeld was rewarded with contumely, malice, hatred and almost oblivion, in fact was literally murdered by that inexpressibly despicable thing called Patriotic Americanism, and that Bryan was popularized almost to idolatry and glorified by press and pulpit as an apostle of truth and an evangel of religion, this shallow-minded mouther of empty phrases, this pious, canting mountebank, this prophet of the stone age, my blood runs hot in my veins with indignation and resentment at the utterly cruel and perverse ways of the world in which we live and the age-old rule of crowning frauds, hypocrites, time-servers and scoundrels, and murdering prophets, pathfinders and all other true leaders of the people and saviors of the race.

But there are nevertheless forces at work underlying all that is false and vicious and damnable in our present ignorant, superstitious and brutal social life, and in time, though ages may pass, the truth will triumph and right will prevail in the world.

In that day history will be revised with a searching eye and with a pen "dipped in the lead of rock forever" and in that day John P. Altgeld the hero and martyr, the apostle and savior of his age will be known and loved of all men and his memory honored and revered throughout the world.

Thanking you again and again from the depths of my heart, and with love and greetings and best wishes to you both I am

Yours to the last turning of the road,
Eugene V. Debs

TLS, IHi.

□ *Debs was under more or less constant pressure to lend his name in support of a variety of liberal, leftist organizations. In 1922 he had agreed to serve as vice-president of the Labor Defense Council, an organization founded by Will-iam Z. Foster and soon dedicated to promoting Communist causes. Debs's role as vice-president of the council was hailed by the Communists as proof that Debs was one of them and "a socialist in name only," an allegation Debs vehement-ly denied.*

EVD to Roger N. Baldwin

June 15, 1925
Terre Haute, Indiana

My dear Roger Baldwin:

The communication signed jointly by you as Director and John Haynes Holmes as Acting Chairman of the Civil Liberties Union, under date of the 13th. inst., inviting me to membership on the National Committee of the Union has been received. The request honors me and compliance therewith, hereby made, is a pleasurable duty. Please accept my thanks for yourself and for Chairman Holmes for your kind consideration in the matter.

I am also in receipt of a copy of your letter to the Labor Defense Council under date of the 12th. inst. and thank you for your thought-fulness in sending it. I received urgent calls from the Council by letter and by wire to approve their announced conference but I wrote Secretary Maurer advising him that I could not give my approval in the face of your objections, suggesting that the Civil Liberities Union should have been consulted and also that the conference be postponed until an understanding could be had so there would be no dissension or complication in carrying on the work. As ever,

Yours faithfully,
E. V. Debs

TLS, NjP, Mudd Library, ACLU Archives.

□ *As secretary-treasurer of the Workers (Communist) party, Charles Ruthen-berg wrote to Debs on July 6, 1925, urging him to join the party in "a united front" in support of striking Chinese textile workers.*

EVD to Charles E. Ruthenberg

July 13, 1925
Terre Haute, Indiana

Dear Comrade Ruthenberg:

Your communication under date of the 6th. inst. forwarded from Chicago, came into my hands this morning and has had careful reading.

Answering I have to say that we have now pending before the National Executive Committee of the Socialist party a statement similar in substance and purport to the one submitted by you, declaring the attitude of the party toward the Chinese situation, and until this is disposed of I can give you no definite decision as to my position. I may say however that considering the relations existing between the two parties and the spirit which characterizes such relations, I should deem it futile, to put it mildly, to attempt to pledge them to united and harmonious action upon this or any other matter.

Yours fraternally,
[Eugene V. Debs]

TLc, InTI, Debs Collection.

□ *Not uncommonly Debs's speaking tours galvanized intense opposition from local "one hundred percent Americanism" groups and organizations. In the following Debs describes one such episode.*

EVD to Theodore Debs

[October 17, 1925]
Scranton, Pennsylvania

Dear old Pard:

Here is where they were going to mob me—sent me telegraphic warning not to come—the papers & press dispatches all carried the report that the meeting would not be permitted & that I would be arrested etc etc—the Am. Legion, Ku Klux, Junior Order of Mechanics, Chamber of Commerce and all the rest of the nervous joined in the Anti-Debs demonstration & swore by all the gods that I shouldn't speak. Then they decided if I spoke they would have a committee put a lot of questions to me as to my Americanism. The Mayor was a Dandy & said I should be protected & had his cops on hand. Well by god, just as I predicted when the showdown came the damned cowards failed to show up & this morning the rest of the Community are calling them damned asses & laughing at their jackasserie. We had a grand meeting—the audience went wild & we organized a big local & sold all our literature & this morning I'm not only a patriot but a hero. The audience nearly mobbed me with enthusiasm & I could hardly get out of the hall.

Pls. send Bennett Gruber Cedar Ave at Birch St. Scranton Pa 1 Hollings—1 D.C. & 1 Red Ap. Folder and the same as above to Edward A. Wieck 213 West Lincoln St. Belleville Ills.

Speak at {Brownstown} to-morrow with two comrades here from England & then leave for home—Will reach home Tuesday morning finer than a fox. It has been a great trip all around & the party is coming grandly to the front.

Love & a swish
Gene

ALS, InTI, Debs Collection.

□ *The following letters to Rose Pastor Stokes were written at the time of Stokes's widely publicized divorce from J. G. Phelps Stokes and her decision to join the Workers (Communist) party.*

EVD to Rose Pastor Stokes

October 19, 1925
Pittsburgh, Pennsylvania

My dear Rose Pastor Stokes,

The days that have passed since last we met have not dimmed the radiance of your fine soul, and I drop you this line of loving greeting to you this morning that you may know I remember gratefully your loyal devotion in the days that were dark and trying, and that I hold you, as all do who have the privilege of knowing you, as a lofty, courageous, noble-hearted woman and a consecrated soul in the service of humanity.

Believe me, dear, brave, comrade, always

Yours faithfully
Eugene V. Debs

ALS, CtY.

EVD to Rose Pastor Stokes

October 27, 1925
Terre Haute, Indiana

My dear Comrade and Friend:

The little message from you just received in response to my note touches me very deeply. We are perhaps none of us as strong and courageous as we sometimes appear but when the trying and testing experiences come, as they will and do, we at least have each other to comfort and sustain us in our crucial hours and to keep alive the faith that after all life is well worth the living and that somehow the things that perplex us, the struggle we have with the fates, must work out right in the end.

You may be sure, dear Comrade Rose, that those who love and understand you are near you now as perhaps never before and that if for the moment the road seems dark and weary and the clouds hang low, the sun must surely shine again to light the new and better way, and what now seems as cruel adversity will but strengthen you for greater service to the cause that is your life, and add fresh lustre to your radiant soul.

It does not matter how widely our view-points may be at variance in these days of readjustment and realignment the time will come when we will again stand beneath the same banner as we have in the past and meanwhile, whatever betide, I beg you to believe me always

Faithfully your friend and comrade,
Eugene V. Debs

P.S. Please take no trouble to answer this.

TLS, CtY.

□ *By 1925 most Americans, including thousands of former socialists, had written off the Socialist party as a relic of American third-party movements. But their numbers did not include Debs, who describes in the following letter his plan to launch a new socialist weekly, the* American Appeal, *as a means of restoring the party's strength.*

EVD to Upton Sinclair

October 24, 1925
Terre Haute, Indiana

My dear Sinclair:

Returning from the eastern states after a strenuous speaking campaign I find your letter of the 5th. inst. with copies of yours to Kirkpatrick of the 29th. ult and the 5th. inst. awaiting me, and I have just finished careful reading of the same. I hope you have not grown impatient over my long delay. It is simply impossible in my present situation to give personal attention to my correspondence and I either have to give up all attempts to keep up with it or quit the road, one or the other. It is physically impossible for me to meet all the demands of both. I have not had the ghost of a chance to look over the manuscript of your novel, nor of the scores and scores of other articles, documents etc. etc. that come in a steady stream from all directions.

Since my return, thoroughly tired, I have been busily engaged in clearing up the accumulation here but it cannot be done in a very satisfactory way for I {am} soon off again and shall be during the next two or three months, holding meetings and filling speaking engagements as the most necessary work at this time to keep the party alive.

I am unable to advise as to your novel for the reason that I have no chance to go over it or to familiarize myself with the conditions under which you wish it published. From present indications there will be no funds upon which we can draw to pay for articles, although I should be ashamed to think of accepting your work without at least half decent compensation for it. I should have no objection to what your communist might say against the socialists or the Socialist party or what kind of a plea he might make for communism or for the soviet government. I believe in free speech to the uttermost and I can think of no circumstances under which I would feel inclined to muzzle a character in your novel.

You have doubtless been informed ere this that Murray King, of Minneapolis, has been appointed as Managing Editor. I have great faith in his judgment in such matters and since it is impossible for me to give the matter personal attention I shall have to refer it to him and Comrade Kirkpatrick jointly, relying upon them to come to an understanding with you that will be mutually satisfactory. Comrade Kirkpatrick is not now on the paper but I shall certainly favor his selection for important editorial service when the paper gets started.

I have a number of speaking engagements in December but expect to get to Chicago in time to have my part in launching the paper and getting it under way. I would like to give the paper my entire time from the beginning but the condition of the party, critical as it is, and urgent as its demands are, makes this impossible at least for the present, and so we are having to do the best we can under the circumstances with the hope that within another six months or a year the party will once more be functioning normally in its various departments.

I am asking Comrade Kirkpatrick and King to decide in the matter of your novel as soon as Comrade King arrives at Chicago, and I sincerely hope the decision may be favorable and satisfactory.

Yours fraternally,
E. V. Debs

☐ *In* Mammonart, *published in 1925, Upton Sinclair argues that all art is propaganda, whether political, social, economic, or religious, and cites the world's major writers to support his thesis.*

EVD to Upton Sinclair

October 31, 1925
Terre Haute, Indiana

My dear Sinclair:
I have just finished a second reading of "Mammonart" one of the very few books I have ever found time to read a second time. It is a wonderful book and must be an eye-opening one to many of the artists, writers and others who serve the leisure class in everything they do but indignantly resent the idea that there is any propaganda in their work. What libraries of books you must have gone through

to have produced such a work and I marvel how you did it along with your numberless other intellectual activities. I would like very much an inscribed copy of "Mammonart," simply your name in it in your own hand for my little collection of the immortals.

Check enclosed

Yours always,
E. V. Debs

TLS, InU, Lilly Library, Sinclair MSS.

□ *Debs's seventieth birthday, on November 5, 1925, was celebrated at a number of banquets that month and the next. In the following exchange of letters he mentions the banquet at St. Louis which, according to the* Post-Dispatch, *was attended by more than five hundred "comrades."*

Morris Hillquit to EVD

[November 5, 1925]
[New York City]

EUGENE V. DEBS,
    HEARTY GOOD WISHES ON YOUR SEVENTIETH BIRTHDAY. FEW MEN HAVE MADE BETTER USE OF THEIR LIVES THAN YOU; FEW MEN HAVE FOUGHT MORE VALIANTLY FOR THE COMMON GOOD; FEW MEN ARE LOVED AS DEEPLY AS YOU; NONE HAS EARNED THE LOVE OF HIS FELLOWS AS MUCH AS YOU. MAY YOUR ENOBLING EXAMPLE INSPIRE OUR LIVES AND SUSTAIN OUR STRUGGLES MANY MORE YEARS.

MORRIS HILLQUIT

Telegram (copy), WHi, Hillquit Papers.

EVD to Morris Hillquit

November 13, 1925
Terre Haute, Indiana

My dear Morris:
    The beautiful and touching telegram from you came to me while seated among our comrades at the banquet at St. Louis and was read amidst applause that would have compensated you in some measure

at least for your loving birthday remembrance. It was perfectly fine in you to remember me, busy as I know you to be, with such a loving, appreciative and heart-warming message, and I only wish I but half deserved it. But anyway I am glad you think as you do and shall try my best to give you no cause hereafter to think otherwise. How I wish you and Mrs. Hillquit could have been with us!

With loving greetings to you both,

Always yours faithfully,
E. V. Debs

TLS, WHi, Hillquit Papers.

□ *Karl Kautsky, editor of a leading German socialist journal,* Die Neue Zeitung, *in Stuttgart, was the author of a score of books on Marx, socialism, and social democracy.*

EVD to Karl Kautsky

December 4, 1925
Terre Haute, Indiana

My dear Comrade Kautsky:

It was well worth while to have a birthday just to receive so fine and cheering and complimentary {a} message as the one from you and dear Mrs. Kautsky which I now hold in my hands and which fills my heart and dims my eyes. Each kind, comradely word you have written touches me, and coming from no other source could such a generous expression of greeting and congratulation give me greater satisfaction.

It was from you, dear comrade, that I learned some of my earliest and most precious lessons in socialism, and I have always felt myself in debt, gratefully and with a deep sense of appreciation, to your gifted pen for having opened my eyes to the light which guided me into the socialist movement. I was in jail, one of the innumerable victims of capitalism, sitting in darkness as it were, when your pamphlets first came into my hands and your influence first made itself felt in my life, and I have since wondered often how any one, however feeble and benighted mentally, could read your crystal-clear Marxian expositions and interpretations without becoming and remaining a socialist.

It is a great joy therefore and an honor I esteem beyond words, in which my beloved wife Katherine shares gladly, to receive from Karl and Luise Kautsky such a flattering testimonial of regard on the occasion of the anniversary of my natal day. I only regret that I am as sadly deficient in my German as you are proficient in your English or I should with pride and pleasure return the compliment of making this acknowledgment in your native tongue.

It so happens that these lines in regard to your flattering recognition of my birthday are written on the one hundred and fifth anniversary of the birth of my revered father who in life, to its latest breath, with my brave and beautiful mother, stood staunch and true in the service of the socialist movement.

I note with special interest what you say about the movement in America and feel confident that you are right in what you say of the situation and the outlook, and that in time your words will prove to have been, as they have so often in the past, prophetic.

And now thanking you both with a full heart and wishing length of years and increasing fulfillment of your highest hopes and aspirations, in which Katherine and my brother Theodore and his wife and all of our household join heartily, I am always

Faithfully your friend and comrade,

Eugene V. Debs

TLS, International Institute of Social History, Kautsky Papers.

☐ *The following letter was written in response to Emanuel Haldeman-Julius's article "What Has Become of the Pre-War Radicals," which appeared in the January 1926* Haldeman-Julius Weekly. *In the article Haldeman-Julius criticizes Upton Sinclair and Clarence Darrow, among others, for supporting World War I and attacks Woodrow Wilson as "an arch-hypocrite." He praises Debs who, he says, "went to prison to his glory."*

EVD to Emanuel Haldeman-Julius

January 4, 1926
Terre Haute, Indiana

My dear Haldeman-Julius:
    First of all, though a trifle belated, a Happy and Prosperous New Year to you and Lady Marcet and the junior gods of the household!

And next I want to thank you for the fine things you have said about
me in the current issue of your Weekly in your answer to the question
as to what had become of the pre-war radicals. I appreciate all this
fully and I have certainly not forgotten and can never forget what
you did to secure my release from prison. With most of what you
had to say about the pre-war radicals I am in hearty accord but there
are some things which I cannot understand and with which I am not
at all in agreement.

Your characterization of Wilson suits me exactly. History will pillory him as the arch-betrayer of the American people. It is now known
beyond a doubt that he was for the war, that is, for putting this country
into the war from the very beginning and that his "neutrality" was
a sham and false pretense. He allowed himself to be elected president
for "keeping us out of war" when his mind was fully made up to put
us into the war and he did commit that monstrous crime within six
months after his election. He would have dumped us into the diabolical
slaughter sooner had he dared to do so.

During this time he continually voiced with tongue and pen the
semi-socialistic and idealistic platitudes which won for him the confidence of the masses. Coming from his lips these glib mouthings were
the veriest flapdoodle. At heart he was an aristocrat and autocrat and
he tolerated no equals in the sphere in which he was the central
luminary and all others had to be satellites to reflect his majesty and
glory. He had no real friends but only sycophants, lackeys and un-
derlings. He promptly fell out and insulted those of his official associates who presumed to approach him on a basis of equality. He
gave expression to the true Wilson when he was still President of
Princeton College and in a baccalaureate address to the students
denounced and condemned labor unions and the labor movement in
general for "making unprofitable servants for their masters." Then,
following this lead, he applied to Andrew Carnegie to place him on
his pension roll of retired pedagogues. That was the real Wilson and
he did not change after he was elected president, his first act being
to insult and deny his campaign manager who had sacrificed everything to elect him and did more than {any} other to make him
president and who later, in a series of articles written before his death,
in which he felt that he must tell the truth to the American people,
he told the sordid story of Wilson's base ingratitude and his utter
lack of personal honor or political self-respect.

So far we are in perfect agreement. I now take up the points of
divergence upon which I am inclined to think we are wide apart.

You refuse to forgive Sinclair for having at the beginning of the war been misled into giving his sanction and support to that criminal slaughter. You repeatedly say in effect that all the atonement he has since made counts for nothing. He made a mistake and according to you he is apt to make another and he has therefore forfeited the confidence of the people for all time. This seems to me a very strange statement coming from you and I cannot at all understand it for I am not inclined to believe you are putting Sinclair in the pillory as a discredited leader from any personal bias, although that seems to be the only ground upon which it can be accounted for. Sinclair made a mistake, I readily admit, but he has since frankly confessed his error and done everything in his power to make amends for it, and should he now be forever damned for doing what thousands of other men good as you and I are, were also guilty of but {who} have made no {such} expiation as stands to Sinclair's credit? You have made mistakes and so have I, plenty of them, and I expect to make a good many more, but I should certainly not consider myself fairly treated if my friends condemned me and forever denied me their confidence on that account.

But this is not all. You have set Sinclair down as a false adviser and a discredited leader. While at the same time you hold up Clarence Darrow as a true leader of the people and avail yourself of every opportunity to glorify his leadership. I do not object to this but I wish to point out the glaring inconsistency, to say nothing of the injustice of your position. You will not misunderstand me, I know, in regard to Darrow. I love him and with good reason. For many years he has been my friend, loyal and steadfast, and I have been his, and no one rejoices more than I to hear his merit, his splendid qualities of character, his crowning virtues appraised at their true value.

But Clarence Darrow was a super-patriot during the war. He plunged in headlong from the very beginning as one of Wilson's leading champions in saving civilization and making the world safe for democracy. He even went to England as Wilson's personal representative to give eloquent and convincing assurance of Wilson's greatness and glory and of the patriotism that inspired the American people to make common cause with "God save the King" and God damn and slaughter the common cattle.

You did not condemn and do not now condemn Darrow for that and neither do I. You do not exile him as a false leader who has made a mistake and will therefore make another and is therefore unworthy to ever again be trusted by the people.

I do not understand this in Darrow; it has puzzled me and perplexed me, I confess, not a little, but I would never have dreamed of damning him for it for an instant, to say nothing of forever.

Now if you can tolerate a mistake in Darrow and continue to trust him with leadership, why not Sinclair? Darrow's mistake was far greater than Sinclair's, in my opinion, for he was far more active in whooping it for Wilson and the war than Sinclair was, and he has never pretended for a moment that he was mistaken or that he had the slightest inclination to make atonement.

Quite the contrary. He still regards Wilson, whom you denounce as an arch-hypocrite and betrayer, as almost a Messiah. In his speech in his debate at Denver a few days ago he justified his patriotic attitude during the war and then threw in this choice compliment, according to the report in the Rocky Mountain News: "I revere the name of Woodrow Wilson above almost any other name on earth." How does that strike you? For the life of me I cannot understand it, and I do not think you can understand it any more than I can. No such sublime faith and supreme adulation for the Woodrow Messiah can be charged to Sinclair.

In the same speech Darrow said there was one thing worse than war and that was the tyranny of centralized power. And yet at the last national election when Darrow's friends confidently expected he would give his support to LaFollette who had fought that power all his life he coolly championed the cause of Davis, the darling of that centralized power, the tool of Wall street, than which there is no more tyrannical, criminal and corrupt power on the face of the earth. How do you account for that? I simply can't and don't try to. Nor do I permit it to interfere with my love for the man, nor my confidence in his integrity, nor my faith in his leadership in other directions.

I have often wondered about some of Darrow's attitudes and actions but they were his own and I have not felt called upon to judge him by my standard and to condemn him accordingly.

No one has ever been able to classify Clarence Darrow and I am quite sure he would not be able to classify himself. He is simply not of the classifiable kind. He is neither {a} republican, nor a democrat, nor a progressive, nor anything else in politics. I know for a fact that he hates politics and politicians and yet somehow he is always lined up with them and is {as} active in their campaigns as any of the rest of them. He has often been called an anarchist and as such he has no use for politics or politicians; he does not believe anything worth while can be accomplished by either and he has said this often enough to dispel all doubt upon that point. And yet, somehow, and to me it is simply inexplicable, in every political campaign he is found in the democratic camp, lined up with the rottenest politicians, office-seekers and spoils-hunters, whooping it up quite as zealously and patriotically as if he were one of their most loyal leaders. He has never supported a socialist ticket or a socialist candidate for office and although he has all the years of his active life denounced and condemned the capitalist system and exposed the rottenness of its misrule he regularly, when a political campaign comes on, gives his unqualified approval and support to that system by giving his splendid talents and his great influence to the utterly rotten democratic party, so-called which supports that putrescent economic, political and social system.

And now let me ask you, my dear Haldeman-Julius, how you can condemn Sinclair for his inconstancy and false leadership without at the same time condemning Darrow. For my part I want neither condemned. I recognize in them both men of great qualities of mind and heart and soul; men who have achieved great and lasting good in the service they have rendered to struggling humanity, and neither of whom should be branded as unfit for further counsel or leadership because there are some things about him we don't understand or he does some things we cannot approve.

You have toleration enough to bear with Darrow who crowns Wilson as a Messiah while you yourself hold him to be the basest of betrayers, a spirit of forebearance entirely commendable, but I venture to suggest that this same spirit be shown to others who certainly have offended to no greater extent.

I did not mean to write at such length but when I read your article I felt moved to write you frankly in regard to it and this must be my apology, if any be necessary, for inflicting a very busy man with such a long communication.

With the greetings of the season and all good wishes to you for the future I am as ever,

Yours sincerely,
[Eugene V. Debs]

TLc, InTI, Debs Collection.

☐ *B. Charney Vladeck was the editor of the* Jewish Daily Forward, *a Yiddish-language paper published in New York City, where Debs was immensely popular among Jewish immigrants. Altogether some twenty thousand dollars was raised and given to Debs on behalf of the Daily Forward Association.*

B. Charney Vladeck to EVD

January 5, 1926
New York City

PERSONAL

Dear Comrade Gene:

The enclosed check is the second installment of the Debs Testimonial Fund which we have been raising in connection with your 70th birthday.

At the last meeting of our Board of Directors, at the initiative of Comrade Schlesinger, we again discussed the relation of the fund to you and we have decided unanimously to convey to you the following:

A great number of the comrades and sympathizers who are contributing to this fund are under the impression, rightly or wrongly, that this fund is for your personal use and is not to be turned over to the Party. Although we have repeatedly stated that it is up to you to do with this money whatever you please, we feel that some of the contributions wouldn't be as generous if not for the assumption on the part of the contributors that this money will be used by you for your personal needs so that you have no worry about things of the world and are in a position to devote all your energy and ability to the cause to which you dedicated your whole life. For this reason we wish to ask you to accept this check for yourself as well as all other checks that may be forthcoming.

As to the pledge we have made to the Socialist Party, our Board of Directors are willing to include our pledge in our budget for 1926 and to pay it from the treasury of the Forward which means that every cent raised by the Forward for the Debs Testimonial Fund should go directly to you, without you turning it over to any other but your personal use, — the Forward reimbursing the party from its own funds.

This action of our Board of Directors is to come up before the next meeting of the Forward Association for approval but I have no doubt that the comrades of the Association will take the same view. If they should not, I shall write to you again.

With very best regards and wishes for a Happy New Year, I am,
Very truly yours,
JEWISH DAILY FORWARD
B. C. Vladeck
General Manager

TLS, InTI, Debs Collection.

☐ *W. S. Van Valkenburgh was a journalist and close friend of Emma Gold-man, whose writings on the Soviet regime Debs discusses in the following letter. The death in Debs's family was that of Katherine Debs's half sister, who was killed in a car accident in Terre Haute on December 30, 1925.*

EVD to W. S. Van Valkenburgh

January 15, 1926
Terre Haute, Indiana

My dear Comrade Van Valkenburgh:
    Your communication of the 6th. inst. with copies {of} correspon-dence between Emma Goldman, the London Herald and others, came during my absence from the city. Since my return there have been illness and death in our family and my office work has in consequence been subjected to enforced neglect, and this will account for my belated acknowledgment of your kindness.
    In answer to your inquiry I should be glad to have any further articles or letters you may receive from Miss Goldman and are disposed to let me have.
    I took this correspondence home with me that I might give it careful reading, which I have done, and I now beg to write you briefly in answer. First of all let me say that I have always had the highest personal regard for Emma Goldman whose high ability no one who knows her can fail to recognize, and I have always had perfect faith in her integrity as a leader in the revolutionary movement of the working class. I am not an anarchist but I have sufficient sense of decency and breadth of vision to recognize all those who are consci-entiously serving the proletarian cause according to their light, and giving them credit accordingly.

During all her years of service in this country, Emma Goldman stood staunchly always on the side of the struggling workers in every battle and for this she was hated, feared and persecuted by the exploiting capitalists, their prostituted newspaper scribblers, their tools in public office, and all the rest of their minions and mercenaries.

I blush to think of the brutal and shameless manner in which this great soul, {this} self-sacrificing woman was treated by the United States government. Her farcical trial and her cruel deportation will leave an indelible blot on the pages of American history. I protested to the limited extent of my power but I was myself in the toils at the time with but little chance to wage any effective opposition to the cowardly performance of the Hessians, the self-styled "one hundred percent Americans."

And since Miss Goldman's deportation it appears by this correspondence as well as by other reports which have filtered through, that she has been treated even more brutally where she should have been received with open arms and treated with the most generous consideration.

I was quite surprised when the first reports came from Russia about the experience of Emma Goldman and Alexander Berkman under the Soviet government. I never for a moment suspected that they would be other than welcome guests of that government and of the Russian comrades in general. That they would be harshly treated and indeed persecuted and forced to leave the Russian borders was a distinct shock to me.

I never personally met Berkman more than once and that was for a few moments only in the Warden's office when we were both inmates of the federal penitentiary at Atlanta. But while I saw little of Berkman personally I knew the man and his record and I always had and have now the highest regard for him for he has always been a brave fighter for the working class, and how any proletarian government could persecute such a man as Berkman and such a woman as Emma Goldman passes my understanding.

Nor am I able to understand why the London Herald should have refused to give space to her story. No matter what Miss Goldman's statement may set forth it is certain that it is reliable and can be depended upon for she is a truthful woman and would never set down anything that is false even to vindicate herself.

Certainly the radicals and socialists, as well as the communists and anarchists, should know the truth about affairs in Russia as well as elsewhere, and if the statement made by Miss Goldman is true, and

I do not doubt it, then there is certainly something that is radically wrong with the policy of Soviet Russia in dealing with those who are not in accord with its program.

I have heartily favored Soviet Russia from the hour it was born and have supported it with my pen and from the platform to the full extent of my power, but I have been utterly opposed to the cruel Soviet policy which has proscribed the expression of opinion and made a crime of all honest opposition. I have protested against this in various ways and shall continue to do so as long as this pernicious policy is pursued, which is not only outrageously cruel to its victims but reflects most discreditably upon the government guilty of such atrocities, and all the less excuse is there for such a repressive and subversive policy under a proletarian government.

I realize of course the absolute necessity of protecting the government and its institutions against counter-revolution in all its forms but there is a sharp line which may be readily recognized between a counter-revolutionist and an honest dissenter or opponent. There are today thousands of men and women in Russian prisons or exile, undergoing the most fiendish torture, who were brave fighters in the revolution which overthrew the Czar, many of whom knew the inside of the prisons for their opposition to the Czar and their loyal devotion to the people. All this is so well known that the wonder to me is that this cruel and reprehensible policy of the Soviet government have not long since been abandoned, not only in common decency and humanity, but for the sake and to the credit and advantage of the government itself.

Perhaps one of the reasons is the unfair suppression of truthful reports of conditions, as in the case of Miss Goldman, who at least in England, where freedom of opinion and expression is supposed to be most advanced, might have expected fair hearing in the interest of truth and understanding, and for the benefit of all concerned.

When you have occasion to write to Miss Goldman or to Alexander Berkman, please remember me to them with cordial greetings and all good wishes as personal friends and as comrades in the common cause.

Thanking you for your kindness which is very much appreciated I remain

Yours faithfully,
[E. V. Debs]

TLc, InTI, Debs Collection.

☐ *Claude Bowers's* Hamilton and Jefferson *had recently been published when Debs wrote the following letter, in which he repeats his oft-stated view that socialists should seek to "Americanize" their movement and that histories should focus more on ordinary people and their lives.*

EVD to Claude G. Bowers

January 16, 1926
Terre Haute, Indiana

My dear Claude Bowers:

The good letter from you under date of the 6th. was read with keen interest and full appreciation. We have been reading all about the phenomenal sale and success of your work on Jefferson and Hamilton and we have been immensely gratified by it. You have been making steady progress as a historian since first that splendid work on the Orators of Ireland came from your gifted pen, but your Jackson book brought you fame over night and this has been made overwhelmingly by your latest historic work.

I am ashamed to have to admit that I have read neither your book on Jackson nor your later work but I shall certainly do so as soon as I can possibly find the time. When your Jackson book appeared I was ill and for more than a year I did not know whether I would last from day to day, and since then I have been so extremely busy travelling about and trying to catch up that my substantial reading has been shamefully neglected. I shall read your books first and then I want to go through Carl Sandburg's Lincoln of which I have read a part. I suppose you know Sandburg. I sat with him in the jungle in his backyard when he was engaged in this work. He comes nearer bringing the real Lincoln to us vividly, his own breathing self, than anyone who has ever written about him. Sinclair Lewis, Carl Sandburg and I had some happy hours together when I was under treatment at the sanitarium at Elmhurst, where Sandburg lives. There are also two or three books of Dreiser's especially the big one just out, that I must have as soon as time will allow. The trouble is I am on the road so much and when I am back there is such an accumulation that it keeps me busy until it is again leaving time.

In your letter you have a line that struck me very forcibly and I have been thinking a good deal about it ever since. You say: "Socialists as a rule appear to look contemptuously on everything political before their party came into active being." You are absolutely right in regard to many socialists, perhaps most of them, and this is one of the reasons why there has never been the kind of a socialist movement in this country there should be and would be if it were rooted in American traditions, American history and American conditions. The fundamental principles are of course everywhere the same but there is a different psychology in every nation, different economic and political conditions, and these have not been wisely reckoned with by socialists or they would be much farther along with the American movement.

We have traditions peculiarly favorable to socialist development and we have history of like nature which unfortunately is almost wholly unknown. History writers in the past have ignored the common herd. They have not deemed the people of sufficient historic importance to write about. McMaster took a new departure in his history of the people of the United States and he has many facts and details of the most vital importance of which there is no trace in Bancroft or any of the other so-called standard histories.

I know you are very busy but I wish it were possible for you and "Jim" Oneal, Editor of the New Leader of New York to have an hour or two together. I have written him at some length about you and your work and I have asked him to send you an article written by him some time ago entitled "An Early American Socialist." I have also asked him to send you a copy of his "Workers in American History." You will find both interesting, especially the latter in which there is history that has not only been ignored but covered up and suppressed by other writers. I know your method of history writing is your own and that it is different from the standardized writer, and the same is true of "Jim" Oneal who would really be a great historian if he had the chance to devote himself to that line of literary work. He used to work in the rolling mill here and possibly you remember him. He had little schooling but has a wonderful mind, especially for history and he has dug up more vital American history from the workers' point of view than anyone else I know. You will see by his history, although a modest volume, and done at night after a hard day's work, that he also understands the philosophy of history and the reason of Hegel's generalization that "We learn from history that we learn nothing from history."

I feel quite sure that you would find Oneal very well worth while and that you and he would be mutually {enlightening and} inspiring. If some time you have leisure enough to see him call him on the phone, the New Leader, 7 E. 15th. st. And by the way, have you ever been at Rand School? The New Leader has its office in the Rand

School and you would find a visit there worth your time. Oneal would be delighted to show you through. There is a special department there containing my books, letter-files, scrap books, pictures etc. which I made a gift to the School. I wish you might let the fine people there know you. Sam A. De Witt, the beautiful and brilliant Jewish poet is associated with Oneal on the Leader. I have just given the title of your history to a woman visiting here from Chicago and recommending that she read it. She will purchase the work immediately upon her return and give it careful reading.

I thought of you while in New York, you may be sure, but as usual there I was whipped through without half time enough to go around. I intended one afternoon to call you but had an engagement to have a picture taken at the lower end of Coney Island. They assured me it would take a couple of hours. It took all afternoon and until so late at night that I could make no calls before having to leave.

By even mail I am sending you copies of the paper we have just started. Let me say in closing {about your last history} that I do not think any book published in recent years, if ever before in this country, drew such overwhelming praise from such a great variety of competent critics. And this is monumental achievement and rare and enviable distinction.

Cordial greetings and warmest wishes to you and Mrs. Bowers from Mrs. Debs and Theodore and his wife and

Yours always
Eugene V. Debs

TLS, InU, Lilly Library, Bowers MSS.

☐ *The appeals of Nicola Sacco and Bartolomeo Vanzetti were still being carried through the courts by William Goodrich Thompson when Vanzetti wrote the following letter to Debs.*

Bartolomeo Vanzetti to EVD

January 30, 1926
Boston, Massachusetts

Dear Comrade E. Debs: —

I am indeed ashame and remorseful of my long silence with you — a silence filled with love and remembrances, for, I think of you every blessing day of my life.

I have been translating, from Italian to English, "Selected Pages of The War and the Peace," by J.P. Proudhon;[1] and I wish to finish it before the C's decition. And this is the reason, or better, the cause of my silence.

The book is magistral; it will be, if such thing is possible, a real blow, not to the war, but to its very causes. You will received a copy as soon as it will be possible to send you one. I am confident that you will like and approve the book, and forgive me. But, please, do not mention this in your answer: the cat shall not know of the cheese, else, they will spoil it worstly than the rats.

Of the case, of the brave, great argument of Mr. Thompson, I will not speak, because you are surely informed—and have read the brief of exemption.

Are you felling well now? This is what I hope and wish with all my heart.

Give my regards to all of your family—to you, my comrade and Maestro, all my love.

Always yours;
Bartolomeo V.

ALS, InTI, Debs Collection.

☐ *The following letter was Debs's response to a letter seeking information on a number of subjects: the major parties' adoption of ideas originally advocated by the Socialist Party of America, the impact of the war on the SPA, the SPA's reasons for supporting Robert M. La Follette in the 1924 presidential election, and the status of Debs's citizenship.*

EVD to Mrs. Edward H. Weber

February 3, 1926
Terre Haute, Indiana

My dear Mrs. Weber:

Your good letter of the 1st. inst. was received this morning. I appreciate fully your interest in social and economic questions and would gladly answer you in detail, giving you such data and information as are available here, but unfortunately I am having to leave and my time is so completely occupied that I can only make inadequate and I fear sadly unsatisfactory answer to your interrogatories.

Allow me to suggest that you write to Marx Lewis, Secretary of Victor L. Berger, House of Representatives, Washington, and ask him "How great a proportion of the social legislation sponsored by the Republican and Democratic parties has originated in socialist party platforms." Mr. Marx is exceedingly well informed upon this subject, has ready access to the sources of information and will be able, I am sure, to give you a good approximation upon the subject. You are of course at liberty to use my name if you wish and say to Mr. Marx that you write at my request, he being a personal friend.

If you will write to Josephine Conger, Woman's Column American Appeal, 2653 Washington Blvd., Chicago, she can and I am sure will be glad to tell you what women have been the greatest leaders in the American movement.

As to the effect the war had upon the socialist movement it all but crushed it by the governmental exercise and encouragement of brute force, including assaults, and mobbings and almost every imaginable form of repression and persecution. Socialist meetings were prohibited, socialist newspaper offices were invaded and sacked, only three or four of several hundred surviving; speakers were assaulted, kidnapped and even murdered, while meetings were broken up and ruffians in uniform rode roughshod through peaceable socialist parades. The Socialist party was reduced to a shadow of its former self but the party lived through it all and is today recuperating. The people are coming to know the truth about the war, who was responsible for it, and what its net results were in the way of slaughter and sacrifice to the common people and of a harvest of gold to the profiteers. The hysteria following the war has now largely subsided with the result that the Socialist party is being revived and reorganized, and within three years more will be larger and more powerful and militant, in my opinion, than ever before.

Let me suggest that there are two books in which you will find invaluable facts for use in your paper. The first is Frederick G. Howe's "Confessions of a Reformer," published by Scribner, a wonderful book presenting truths and facts in connection with the war and its results upon progressive movements of startling significance.

The other is "Shall it be Again" by John Kenneth Turner, the book that tells more naked and terrible truths about the war, supported by documentary evidence, than any other I have yet seen.

By even mail I am sending you a copy of the Survey in which you will find a series of articles upon the subject that may be of a little service to you.

The Socialist party did not nominate candidates of its own for several reasons, the principal of which was that for the first time in the history of American politics the organized workers entered a national campaign as a class, as an organized force, and the Socialist party which from the beginning has been essentially a working class party felt that here was the opportunity to make common cause with the great body of organized workers, and even though the platform was not at all a socialist platform, it embodied so many socialist principles and so much of the socialist program that the Socialist party, enfeebled and decimated by the war, felt justified in casting its lot with the progressive organized workers who had declared their withdrawal from the old capitalist parties, and I feel satisfied that the future will vindicate the wisdom of this policy.

Answering your personal inquiry, my political and civil rights have not been restored. I have been disfranchised and I am not a citizen of the country in which I was born.

I hope the foregoing will be of at least a small measure of service, and with regret that I am unable to give you more detailed information, and with all good wishes in the preparation and reading of your paper I am,

Yours faithfully,
Eugene V. Debs

TLS, IaH.

☐ *From the time of his release in 1921 Debs remained convinced that his imprisonment had resulted in his loss of citizenship, as he argues in the following letter to Morris Hillquit, who had written to him to say (correctly, as it turned out) that "you are still a full-fledged citizen of the United States."*

EVD to Morris Hillquit

March 4, 1926
[Terre Haute, Indiana]

My dear Morris:
    Your communication of the 1st. inst. has been received and carefully read. The discovery that you have made in my case is something of a surprise to me. You inform me that I have not forfeited my citi-

zenship in any respect, that I have not been disfranchised, that I have the right to vote and hold office, and that in fact my citizenship has not been impaired in the slightest by my conviction.

Now of course I cannot presume to question the correctness of your finding for aside from the attention you have given the case from purely kind personal consideration I know you to be a first class lawyer and entitled to full credit in all such matters. But it appears strange to me that I am nertheless without a vote and shorn of my civil rights in respect to the franchise and other matters, and that there has never been a question about it until now, so far as I know, since my release from prison.

Now let me show you what a formidable array of high "authorities" are pitted against you and declare exactly the opposite view to that taken by you.

President Harding stated in my personal interview with him in the White House on my release from prison that I was disfranchised and I now quote his precise words to me: "The restoration of your citizenship is a matter for after-consideration." This after-consideration, so-called, has yet to materialize. Now it seems to me that the President who commuted my sentence ought to know whether or not it affected by citizenship. If you are right he was wrong. President Coolidge has taken exactly the same position as I chance to know from correspondence that has come from the White House. Two Attorneys General, at the head of the Department of Justice at Washington have held me disfranchised and my citizenship forfeited to that extent and beyond, and whether they are right or wrong my status is fixed by their opinion, so far as the matter in question is concerned. Clarence Darrow is of the same opinion and so is Joe Sharts. And so are all the lawyers here in Terre Haute.

Whatever you may have found in the law as to my being a full-fledged citizen the fact is that I am not permitted to register here by the election board and not permitted to vote here by the election officials. My case in the light of your finding is analogous to that of the chap in the old story who was in jail when a friend called upon him and said "Why they can't put you in jail for that," to which the answer was "Whether they can or not I'm in jail just the same."

Now as against your opinion—and I do not say that you are not right—there stand two Presidents of the United States, two Attorneys Generals, Finch, the Pardon Attorney at Washington, Clarence Darrow, Joe Sharts, the lawyers here, the election boards and officials here and various others not necessary to mention.

There is one point in your finding, however, that I know to be wrong. You say that I am entitled to hold office. In this you are mistaken. The legislature of the state of Indiana enacted a law now on the statute books at the time I was in Atlanta, perhaps for my particular benefit, which specifically provides that a person convicted of a felony shall forever be ineligible to hold public office. Under this law I am absolutely barred from holding office and to that extent my citizenship certainly limps on three feet.

If you will write to the Attorney General or to the Pardon Attorney at Washington they will tell you that I am disfranchised and that my civil rights have been forfeited and that if I wish these restored I must personally apply for a pardon to the president of the United States and that the matter of restoring my citizenship and civil rights will then be considered by the president. That is the answer that has been sent out repeatedly from the Department of Justice to inquiring and protesting correspondents, and now perhaps you can tell me whether I am bound by this or not and whether these high officials have or have not the authority to decide the matter and to determine my legal status as a citizen or non citizen.

Please let me thank you sincerely for your very kind and prompt attention to my request and for the service thus rendered me of which I have full and grateful appreciation.

I note particularly your recommendation of Bermuda and am very glad to have this advice and recommendation which decides the matter in favor of Bermuda and my wife and I if nothing else happens to prevent will leave for there next week.

Hoping this finds you well as usual and not too busy I am always,

Yours faithfully,

[Eugene V. Debs]

TLc, InTI, Debs Collection.

□ *By 1926 the "noble experiment" of Prohibition was widely recognized as a disastrous public policy, bringing in its wake many of the social ills Debs had predicted in the years before World War I. In the following letter he explains his position to J. A. C. Meng, who was both an ardent socialist and an ardent Prohibitionist. Meng had written to Debs to attack a recent article on Prohibition in which Debs said that the "liquor traffic" was "more iniquitous and debauching under prohibition than it was in the days of the open saloon."*

EVD to J. A. C. Meng

March 12, 1926
[Terre Haute, Indiana]

My dear Comrade Meng:

Your communication of the 9th. inst. with enclosure from Comrade Victor L. Berger, herewith returned, came last evening. I took it home with me that I might give it careful reading and consideration without interruption, and after having done so I am answering this morning with the regret that I am on the eve of leaving here to be gone several weeks, and in the little time that remains I am so busy that I shall not be able to answer you as fully as I should be glad to do under other circumstances.

First of all, allow me a little personal explanation. My wife has been suffering with the flu, more or less severe and menacing, all winter, and nothing will relieve her but the change to a warmer climate. I myself am tired and worn after many months of continuous and exhausting labor, especially since the new paper was started and my correspondence has so largely increased, as well as other demands upon my time and strength until I have about reached once more the limits of my physical endurance. Under these circumstances my wife and I are now leaving here for the South, to Bermuda, probably, and perhaps to Havana and Mexico. How long we will be gone will depend upon circumstances. I am told that if we go to Bermuda I will be denied entrance to this country on the ground of my having been deprived of my citizenship and civil rights. But my plans will not be changed on that account.

Now please allow me to say in the first place that your letter, although I take issue, positive issue, with many statements in it, does not in the slightest degree affect my love for you or my perfect faith in your personal honor and your moral rectitude. All the years that I have known you have but served to confirm my faith not only in your honesty, in your sincere idealism, but in your extremely kind, delicate, considerate regard for the rights and feelings of your comrades. I know how modest you have been, all too modest, in the fear that you might intrude upon me, and I am not only not insensible to your personal loyalty and devotion, especially in the hours of supreme test, but I am filled with appreciation of the spirit of it and grateful for it beyond expression. This much for my personal feeling and attitude towards you, no matter though we differ as widely as the poles on every phase of the question in controversy.

"Love is not love that alters when it alteration finds."

Shakespeare wrote that immortal line and I am profoundly impressed with the truth of it. I have no fear, whatever our differences, that your love for me will alter for it is of the kind and of the warp and woof of the character of a man not susceptible to alteration unless it be to grow more steadfast and abiding.

Now let me say to you in all frankness that it is hard, very hard indeed for me to understand how you could conclude for a single instant that I had you and honest men of your kind in mind when I wrote my article in denunciation of the rotten and utterly damnable administration of the enforcement laws of prohibition.

I had in mind a certain type of prohibitionists which you cannot fail, it seems to me, to recognize, and to hold in the same contempt and detestation that I do. Now let me call your attention to the fact that the paragraph upon which you have centered your bitterest criticism reads as follows:

"Thousands of SO-CALLED PROHIBITIONISTS ARE SIMPLY BOOTLEGGERS IN DISGUISE AND ENOUGH OF THEM HAVE BEEN CAUGHT RED-HANDED AND PUBLICLY EXPOSED TO PLACE ALL THE REST UNDER RANK SUSPICION."

Now I mean just that, every word of it, and I was never more positively convinced that I dealt with the real truth than when I penned that paragraph. The charge has been made over and over again that "so-called" prohibitionists without number are bootleggers and profiting in the crime. I met one on the street in New York the last time I was there. He had been in penitentiary with me at Atlanta. He was a prohibitionist and a bootlegger. I admonished and warned him but without avail. He assured me that he was playing safe and his personal appearance certainly confirmed him. He was dressed in style and told me he was in close relation with prohibition enforcement officials, and then frankly said: "We are all prohibitionists and all bootleggers and believe me, it's a paying game."

Now how in the world you could infer that I meant you and your friend Goode and your father of sainted memory in writing this paragraph is simply beyond my understanding. You certainly could not imagine me, dear comrade, could you, referring to you and your revered father as "so-called" prohibitionists? Then how could you feel for an instant that I had you in mind when you must have known, unless you totally misread the paragraph, that I had only the miserable hypocrites, frauds, impostors, false-pretenders in mind who thrive in their rottenness in the prohibition that has not prohibited, cannot prohibit, and never will prohibit.

And here let me say to you with equal frankness that I am the uncompromising enemy of prohibition and always have been. Not only to liquor prohibition but to the whole body of abominable doctrine based upon the vicious BLUE LAW FALLACY that men can be made moral and decent by prohibition and repression and by the enforcement of brutal punitive regulations, the surest way of making criminals I know and I think I am in position to prove it.

From the beginning of creation or at least from the beginning of social contact among human beings the narrow, bigoted, hateful, intolerant spirit of prohibition and repression has been the curse of the race. Read for example the shocking expose by Rupert Hughes with unquestioned documentary evidence taken from contemporary sources about the unspeakable, unmentionable immoralities of the so-called Puritans, the hypocritical pietists who treated a smile as a crime, who thrust their insolent noses into all privacies, and who drastically prohibited and suppressed everything except the right to be a hypocrite like themselves. They had prohibition with a vengeance but drunkenness ran riot along side of some other vices and crimes compared with which drunkenness was a virtue.

You enclose a letter to me from Comrade Berger and I thank you for the privilege of reading it. You surely do not imagine that Comrade Berger agrees with you in the position you have taken toward my article. If you are under that delusion please drop him a line and you will find that he entertains the same views I do on prohibition and while he is strong for temperance he is opposed to prohibition under the present vicious enforcement laws, than which there can scarcely be anything more intemperate.

Prohibition in its present form was foisted upon the country during the war and its leaders know it and would not dare to submit the issue to the people. You believe in the right of the people to rule themselves and so do I. Why do the prohibitionists oppose submission of the issue to the people, the only ones who have the right to decide it? Is it because they do not trust the people or because they do not trust themselves?

The Fort Wayne Journal-Gazette, the leading paper of that city in Indiana has just concluded a poll of the question of its readers. The result was 875 for prohibition and 20,950 against prohibition. I enclose the press dispatch making the report. This may not represent the general sentiment but it is at least highly significant.

You say that only the poor are deprived of whisky under prohibition and you are willing that the rich shall have it and perish and rot in their indulgence of it. You are sadly mistaken. White mule is accessible here in Terre Haute and elsewhere to anyone who wants it and the filthy poison is just as cheap as was whiskey in the open saloon. Every morning our papers contain a string of names of poor devils arrested for drunkenness. There is not a rich man in the bunch. They are all poor creatures and the jails everywhere are stuffed with them to overflowing, all beneficiaries of the great blessing of prohibition enforcement. From Washington comes a press dispatch which I hold in my hand, under date of March 5th. I quote the opening paragraph as follows: "Criminal convictions under federal statutes have increased 350% in the last fifty years causing an overcrowding of federal penitentiaries far beyond their normal capacity." And for this condition prohibition is largely responsible.

It is true that the open saloon has gone but there are today more closed saloons, more underground saloons, more saloons in general and particular than ever before in the history of the country. If you will write to Victor Berger he will tell you as he told me that while prohibition closed a score of breweries {in Milwaukee} it opened a hundred thousands by making every home a brewery where they manufacture their own concoctions and where no prohibition enforcement will ever reach or stop them. The difference is that they used to go into the front door of a saloon and get a drink and now they get their drinks like a sneak and a hypocrite and hold themselves in contempt instead of self-respect.

From Philadelphia there comes a dispatch that "A new cheap process of making alcohol which government officers asserted would, unless checked, make prohibition enforcement all but impossible." Vinegar {is used} in this process and who shall prohibit vinegar making.

Whiskey, wine and beer will be made as long as corn and wheat and grapes grow, and instead of foolishly and vainly trying to stamp it out with the iron heel of prohibition and suppression it is infinitely saner to educate and enlighten the people and to give attention to surrounding them with conditions that make for temperance, morality and sane and sweet human living.

We have thousands, multiplied thousands of laws national, state, and municipal, and grinding out more thousands of laws prohibiting everything under the sun, and what good do they do? If they could all be repealed by some magic of power the people would be far better off.

For myself I would rather appear at the bar of judgment drunk a free soul and plead guilty and take the consequences than to appear there in a straitjacket and confess that I was sober because prohibition had given me no chance to do otherwise. I have not one particle of use of that kind of morality, the kind made by prohibition and suppression. That kind of virtue(?) does not appeal to me in the least. True manliness and self-respect are not the product of prohibition and suppression but of freedom and independence. If a man is only sober because he can't get whisky or if he is only honest because he is handcuffed and has no chance to steal he is not my kind of a man.

Here let me make the incidental mention of a fact in connection with the writing of my article. It was written just after two government officials, prohibition agents, came to this city, engaged the service of a prostitute and had her inveigle a man into a hotel room where she surrendered her body to him, when these prohibitionists stepped into the room, arrested the man, charged him with violating the narcotic law, and that man, the victim of the conspiracy of these two prohibition scoundrels, is now serving a year in the penitentiary at Leavenworth, utterly ruined and his future blasted. And this is but one of hundreds of instances of the kind that are taking place all over the country in the name of prohibition, and if there was ever anything lower, viler, more utterly despicable and infamous than this connected with the open saloon I confess never to have heard of it.

There is a great deal more that might be said but time presses and I have already been at too great length in trying to make my position clear.

I have only to say in closing as I said in the beginning that for you as a man, as a comrade, as a clean, white, noble soul I have the same attachment, the same appreciation and devotion that I have always had since first you and I came into each other's lives.

Yours fraternally,
[Eugene V. Debs]

TLc, InTI, Debs Collection.

□ *Emma Goldman's book and articles, based on her experiences in the Soviet Union, were attacked by elements of the left as a sellout and praised by conservatives as proof of the failure of the Russian Revolution. In the following let-*

*ter Goldman seems to agree with Debs's position of support for the revolution
and his grave misgivings about the nature of the Soviet government.*

Emma Goldman to EVD

March 18, 1926
London, England

Dear good Comrade,

Comrade Van Valkenburgh was good enough to send me your
letter to him of Jan. 15. It reached me in France where I had gone
to escape the dreadful London climate. Since then I have been very
busy preparing a course of lectures on Ibsen and which I am now
delivering in this city. That explains the delay in answering your very
kind letter.

I cannot tell you how much your high opinion of me and your
splendid comradeship for both Alexander Berkman and myself mean
to me. So very few people realize the true meaning of comradeship.
With most of them it implies a denial of intellectual independence. I
suppose that is the reason why so many of my so-called friends and
co-workers have repudiated me because of my independent stand on
Russia. But you, dear Comrade, show by your broadmindedness and
your generous spirit that you realise one may differ from you and
yet be honest and beyond reproach. I thank you for it.

There is one thing in your letter which I would like to correct. It
is where you refer to the harsh treatment which Berkman and myself
were made to suffer in Russia. I do not know how you came to think
that the Soviet government subjected us to the same persecution as
other political offenders. In justice to the ruling power in Russia I
wish to say that never once by word or deed were we molested or
interfered with. Quite the contrary. Everything was done to gain our
confidence and cooperation. It is this which made it so difficult for
us to take a definite stand against the persecution of brave men and
women which was carried on during our stay and if anything has
increased since we left. No, we have no personal grievances against
the Bolshevik regime. Our criticism is impelled by our fervent belief
in political freedom and by our knowledge of the integrity and idealism
of the political victims of the present regime.

It seems strange that so many imagine that one may not see evils
except from a subjective personal standpoint. That unless one has

one-self suffered under these evils one may not know their effect or undertake to point them out. I feel that it is because Berkman and I have no personal reasons to oppose the dictatorship and the terror that we can speak with GREATER authority. However, I feel in justice to the Bolsheviki that it is necessary to dissuade you from your impression that we were in any way made to suffer. I often wish we had been able to share the martyrdom of the unfortunates now slowly being done to death in Bolshevik prisons.

Yes, dear Comrade, we have all "heartily favoured Soviet Russia from the hour it was born and have supported it with pen and from the platform to the full extent." But when we came face to face with the conditions in Russia we had to admit to ourselves that what we considered "Soviet Russia" was a delusion and a snare. That in its stead there is a {crushing} machine which has a stranglehold on the Russian masses and which is undermining the true revolutionary elements as represented by the socialist and anarchist ranks in the country. Hence we had to speak out.

Naturally we were and are feeling interested in protecting the revolution against counter-revolutionary attempts, but that is quite another issue than when you say that it is "necessary to protect the government and its institutions against counter-revolution." Even if I admitted that the govt of Russia represented the majority of the Russian people I should still insist that as a govt it is contrary to the interests of the revolution. But in Russia the govt is composed of an infinitesimal minority, a small political group, which by means of terror and the complete monopoly of every avenue of life is maintaining its power over the masses. What particular reason is there to protect such a govt? And is it not itself the most counter-revolutionary force? However, the people who are in Russian prisons, concentration-camps and exile are not those who have ever attempted by means of arms to overthrow the present govt. Even ~~if they had~~ though they dared to disagree with it and to oppose it.

Yes, one would have assumed that the Labour, and Radical elements in England would lend a willing ear to an expose of the actual conditions in Russia. Unfortunately the labour elements here believe as little in free speech for those they do not agree with as the Tories do. Therefore I have not succeeded in reaching the rank and file of labour either from the socialist and labour platforms or their press. And as I never have and never will mix with the Tories I have had a desperate struggle to plead in behalf of the thousands suffering in Russia. After no end of difficulties and correspondence "the New leader" published PART of a letter which I sent to the Daily Herald and which the latter had no courage to publish. That is some gain after eighteen months of effort. Besides that I have been able to speak from my own platform even though the attendance has been painfully small. I know at least that the people who did come are willing to learn and that is more than can be said for the leaders of the labour movement in England.

In this city I am stopping with very dear friends whom it is my fortune to have met during my visits to Bristol. Dr. Beckh is an American who has been abroad since his childhood, studying in Marburg and Oxford. For fifteen years he has been at the head of a free church in this city, but as he is a rebellious spirit and capable of growth the ministry proved too limited for his rapid advance. He has therefore resigned and is going to America. I am very glad of that because I feel that since I myself can no longer disturb the sluggish peace of the "hundred percentors" that a man of the knowledge and ability of doctor Beckh is going back to his native land to {do} my job and more. That does not mean that Dr. Beckh is an anarchist. But his sympathies are all with the masses and his intentions are to reach all people who can be aroused to the pressing questions of our time. I have told him about you, dear good comrade and what a force you are in the United States. I am hoping that you two will meet and that if you can help him at any time to get a good hearing you will do it.

I hope you are keeping well. I am sure you are keeping your youthful spirit.

Fraternally,
Emma Goldman

TLS, InTI, Debs Collection.

☐ *Sinclair Lewis was living in Kansas City, gathering material for and starting to write* Elmer Gantry, *when he wrote the following letter to Debs. The Unitarian preacher he mentions was Leon Milton Birkhead, who served as an adviser to Lewis in the writing of* Elmer Gantry.

Sinclair Lewis to EVD

April 8, 1926
Kansas City, Missouri

Dear Gene:
    After drifting all over the United States for the eleven months since I returned from Germany, I have now settled permanently in

Kansas City — that is to say, for two months or so. I have heard in a vague way that you are editing a magazine in Chicago. Are you living there or are you remaining in Terre Haute? Whatever I do, I must have the privilege and pleasure of seeing you again before I return to Europe, which will probably be next October.

Is there any conceivable chance that you will be coming to Kansas City before June? If there isn't, I shall see to it that I come to wherever you are and pay my respects to you, even though you may be, like that son-of-a-sea cook, Mussolini, surrounded by nine thousand guards.

Gene, I still haven't been able to do *our* novel, "Neighbor." But you know that some day I shall do it. And I am now starting on the nearest novel to Neighbor — the real approach to Neighbor — the other novel of which I told you at such great length — the novel about the preachers. As you know, it will be a sweet and sanctified novel filled with praise for all of the capitalistic preachers. I am here in Kansas City largely because here I have to work with me a Unitarian preacher who admires you less than I do only because he has not had the privilege of meeting you as often as I have.

Do please let me know your plans for the next three or four months. and let me particularly know when it may be convenient for me to come and spend a day or two with you.

God bless you, comrade!
Sinclair Lewis

My *special* love to Theodore.

TLS, InTI, Debs Collection.

☐ *Pauline Rauschenbusch was the widow of Walter Rauschenbusch, a leader in the Social Gospel movement in America until his death in 1918. In the following exchange of letters Rauschenbusch describes her late husband's admiration for Debs and Debs assures her of his own great respect for her husband.*

Pauline Rauschenbusch to EVD

May 3, 1926
Rochester, New York

Dear Mr. Debs,
Whenever I think of you & see your name — I think of what Dr. Levi Powers (of Gloucester Mass) said of Walter Rauschenbusch

"He was one of four or five men I have known in my lifetime who seemed to me to belong to a higher order of the race we hope will some day fill the earth."

July 25 it will be eight years since WR went on—He was a great admirer of yours and a kindred spirit. He was so modest a man— that I think but for that he might have sent you a copy of "Christianity and the Social Crisis—when it came out in 1907. He was often called a Christian Socialist. One time Rose Pastor Stokes was in the city and came to visit us—and she said she had come to induce him to join the Socialist Party. He explained to her that things being as they were—he would lose all his influence or most of it if he would. She said {at the end of the day} she understood and now begged him not to join it. That did not prevent his voting the Soc. ticket of course.

One of the books that have had a real influence—our "Prayers of the Social Awakening" (the original edition had the subtitle "For God & the People" Mazzini's motto)

The Pilgrim Press has brot out a new edition lately (for Easter) and I would like to give myself the pleasure of sending you & Mrs. Debs a copy.

I wish you & WR had known each other. You would have been a great comfort to each other. He was a victim of the war as surely as tho he had been shot. He consistently spoke and worked against war. That the churches—who were supposed to be followers of the "Prince of Peace"—cried for war and crucified all {who} did not also cry— broke his heart. To show you how he felt about going when he did— not yet 57—I'll enclose some lines from his "Instructions if case of my death." Since 1888 he had the handicap of deafness—or rather "hard of hearing." He had grippe in that 1888 when the Great Blizzard struck N.Y. & the Dr not understanding it then let him go out to look after the needy in his church (the only one he ever had)—he had a relapse—and deafness was his lot for the rest of his life—with continual headnoises to the end of his life. He was a brave spirit & never grew bitter—only sad. For him I can always be glad he could go on—for us it is the "irreparable loss."

Our five children are out in the world now—all choosing the difficult underpaid jobs of Social service of various kinds. *Winnifred* — who had helped to make a survey of the Oriental people on the coast—has been editing the May Survey Graphic which deals with that subject. Hilmar Stephen —is with the League for Industrial Democracy—& has been a miner & is secy of the Com. on Coal & Giant Power & has been a miner & has a union card. [in margin] Wrote "The Anthracite Question" Book also: The People's Fight for

Coal & Power. [end marginal note] Paul —who married Justice Louis
Brandeis's daughter —teaches economics at the Univ. of Wisconsin.
Carl also taught economics at Cornell is now in N.Y.—with Labor
Bureau (he worked in the Steel Mills.—(12 hrs.) Elisabeth is in N.Y.
too—trying to find her niche. I stay on in the old home & by sharing
it with a no. of interesting girls in that way manage to keep up the
home & can thus offer shelter & sanctuary to my own children &
others. Pardon this long digression—I do want you to get acquainted
with WR.

I think you will find that the "Prayers" express your own longings
for this world of ours.

The Memorial No of the Rochester Seminary Bulletin gives one a
sort of Birds Eye view of WR—they are getting rare—having been
sent to his pupils—to all corners of the world—but I'd like to lend
you my copy which you can return at your convenience.

Your life I know has been the Inspiration of great numbers of
people—as it has to us.

With gratitude to God that such as you live among us—and with
all good wishes and prayers for your well being.

Gratefully yours
Pauline Rauschenbusch
Mrs. Walter

I send special greetings to Mrs. Debs—I can appreciate what she
has been to you.

P.S. To show you how he felt about going when he did—I enclose
some lines from his

"Instructions in case of my death"

For him I can always be glad—for us it is the irreparable loss—
and "to the world" (I think Jane Addams said that.)

I am glad he could go and that not be here for this aftermath of
the war—he suffered too intensely—and I'm sure wherever he is he
is serving in some way.

I leave my love to those of my friends whose souls have never
grown dark against me. I forgive the others and hate no man. For
my many errors and weaknesses I hope to be forgiven by my fellows.
I have long prayed God not to let me be stranded in a lonesome and
useless old age, and if this is the meaning of my present illness, I shall
take it as a loving mercy of God toward his servant. Since 1914 the
world is full of hate, and I cannot expect to be happy again in my
lifetime. I had hoped to write several books which have been in my
mind, but doubtless others can do the work better. The only pang is

to part from my loved ones and no longer to be able to stand by
them and smooth their way. For the rest I go gladly, for I have carried
a heavy handicap for thirty years, and have worked hard.

Mar 31/18   WR

From "Instructions in case of my death"

ALS, InTI, Debs Collection.

EVD to Pauline Rauschenbusch

May 22, 1926
Terre Haute, Indiana

My dear Mrs. Rauschenbusch:

This belated acknowledgment of your very kind letter of the 3rd.
inst. and the accompanying book and pamphlet is due to severe illness
in our family during the last three weeks, I myself having been unable
during that time to give attention to my personal correspondence and
other affairs. I was unable on that account to attend the Socialist party
convention at Pittsburgh beginning May 1st., and for the same reason
I am not now at Indianapolis where the state convention of Indiana
is being held.

Mrs. Debs and I have carefully read your beautiful and gracious
letter and we beg to return our most sincere thanks for the very kind
and generous consideration you have shown us.

I had long looked forward to the great pleasure of meeting Doctor
Rauschenbusch, your distinguished husband, but the fates somehow
denied me that privilege and I felt keenly disappointed at the time
of his death to think that, with all I felt I owed him for his great life-
work in general and for his high-souled and inspiring example to me
in particular, I had never been permitted to take him by the hand
and to tell him how very deep my love was for him, how I admired
his sublime courage, his utter unselfishness, his noble idealism, and
how I honored him for his whole-hearted consecration to the cause
of humanity.

It is indeed gratifying to me to know that I had a place in the great
heart of Doctor Rauschenbusch, and though we were not permitted
to come into personal contact I am sure we were not separated by
the miles that lay between us, but that on the contrary we were in
spiritual communion and giving to each other aid and comfort in the
trying hours that came to us both, especially during those cruel years

of the terrible war. I can well imagine what agony your noble husband suffered, and how his tender, sensitive nature was shocked and outraged by the horrors of the war, and I do not wonder that his great, loving heart was broken and ceased to beat during that frightful ordeal.

His was the prophetic vision and the martyr spirit and he assuredly did not live and struggle and suffer in vain. He wrought with that divine consecration and self-effacement that made him and his work immortal. He lived and will live through generations yet unborn for he was indeed of "the few, the immortal few, who were not born to die."

Please accept our added thanks for the inscribed copy of "Prayers of the Social Awakening," a most precious little volume, kindly sent by you, in the pages of which we shall find comfort and inspiration.

The pamphlet containing "The Record," issued by the Rochester Theological Seminary, and containing the Memorial of Doctor Rauschenbusch will be carefully gone over and in due time returned as requested. For the privilege of glancing through the pages of this precious document we feel grateful to you beyond expression.

And now thanking you again and again for your loving kindness and with all affectionate esteem and good wishes to you and all of your blessed household from Mrs. Debs and myself I remain,

Yours faithfully,
Eugene V. Debs

TLS, NRAB.

☐ *In their final exchange of letters Debs shared with Sinclair Lewis his views on the kind of preachers who were the targets of Lewis's* Elmer Gantry.

EVD to Sinclair Lewis

May 13, 1926
Terre Haute, Indiana

My dear Sinclair Lewis:

We have been having all kinds of experiences here, save pleasant ones, during the last two or three weeks, or you would have heard from me days ago as promised in the hurried line I sent you in acknowledgment of your extremely kind letter of the 8th. ult. and the precious enclosures, including the newspaper account of your "sermon" which my long experience with reports of that kind enables me to read with understanding, however crudely the reporter caught or the paper printed what you actually said.

Allow me first of all to compliment you as a "preacher." Never before in Kansas City has a pulpit resounded with so much blunt, refreshing frankness and honesty.

And now to answer your questions: I am one of the editors of the American Appeal published at Chicago, copies of which have been sent you. This paper began with the present year and has already achieved a considerable circulation. My editorial work is done here or wherever I may chance to be, and my residence continues here at Terre Haute.

It is not at all possible that I shall be able to get out to Kansas City this month or next.

My long absence on the trip to Bermuda and my illness since my return have disorganized my plans and it will be some time before I shall be able to make my next trip to the Western states. It is possible that I may go to California later in the season as there is a campaign there in progress in which I am much interested, and if I go out to the coast I shall make it a point to stop at Kansas City if possible to have an hour or two in your inspiriting companionship if you are still there.

I am also expecting to have to make a trip to New York some time next month but I shall put that off for a few weeks if I can so arrange it.

As for your coming here I need not say that you {can} make the schedule to suit yourself. You have the right of way and you can come at your convenience and the joy will be great when your flaming dome rounds the curve and comes into sight.

I can understand perfectly why you have not yet been able to do the novel, "Neighbor." That will have to come in its regular order and in its own time. You are a prodigious worker, you grow steadily greater, and with steady steps you are approaching your masterpiece.

I am sure your novel on the preachers will make the gentry of the "cloth" see red and shake their pulpits throughout the country. They are among the mainstays of the existing order. To obtain their license they must share in its corruption. They wear the livery of Christ in the service of his betrayers and crucifiers. They are all followers of the Prince of Peace until Wall street sounds the tocsin of war and then they all wrap the flag about the pulpit with patriotic unction and join in the howl of the pack for blood and slaughter. But after all most of them are to be pitied rather than condemned. Many of them are so weak, so abject from fawning that it seems cruel to scourge them. They are more menial in their mental and moral abasement than are the scavenger-slaves in the wage-pens.

But there are the "higher-ups" who voluntarily sell their souls to Mammon that they may fawn at the feet of the ruling masters and dress in purple and fine linen and riot and rot in "high living," and they deserve no mercy. Newton Dwight Hillis, the ministerial prostitute, is a fair specimen of these intellectual and moral degenerates.

I am enclosing a little acknowledgment to dear Ethel Barrymore, supposing she is still there and that you will be able to hand it to her. You were very kind in enclosing her beautiful and flattering message. Her handwriting may not be Spencerian but her head and heart are in good working order.

The letter from Comrade Birkhead is nearly all poetry. It touches me to the heart. I can see him clearly, I catch his spirit, and I reach out and hail him brother. He is the rare preacher who atones for the entire tribe. The choice spirit, the royal soul of him, glow in all his lines. I know him and I love him. Kindly hand him the enclosed note. You are both lucky to have each other and you will certainly be mutually and creatively inspiring.

Theodore is able to be up again but still weak. This means the flesh only. His spirit is always the same. He joins me as does my wife in love to you and a thousand endearing wishes.

Always yours steadfastly,
Eugene V. Debs

TLS, NSyU, Dorothy Thompson Collection.

Sinclair Lewis to EVD

May 16, 1926
Kansas City, Missouri

Dear Gene:—

God bless you for your fine long letter, and for the letters to Birkhead and Ethel Barrymore. I have delivered Mr. Birkhead's letter to him, and I will try to get the other to Ethel though I don't know exactly where she is—she is out on the road touring.

Curse it, if you do come through Kansas City, and I shall not be here because I am leaving tomorrow for the woods of northern Minnesota where I shall get a cabin and work all summer.

Last night you were formally canonized and whether or not you like to be a saint (which I suppose will necessarily include being a Catholic) you are now stuck for it because the job is done. I was dining with Birkhead, the Rev. William L. Stidger and Edwin Markham, who is here for a couple of days as Stidger's guest, and they all agreed that the one real honest-to-God saint of whom they had ever known was Eugene V. Debs. Of course, I defended you and said that you were a thoroughly bad actor, and a drinker of liquor, but they threw me out and there you are stuck with a halo for keeps. But perhaps a halo will be lighter for summer wear than a straw hat.

I don't know what my address is going to be in northern Minnesota, but I will be sending you a note bye and bye when I get settled, so don't trouble to answer this.

God bless you Gene!

Ever.
Sinclair Lewis

TLS, InTI, Debs Collection.

□ *In a note to Debs on October 18, 1924, Sandburg wrote to say that, "When the book [Sandburg's* Lincoln*]—in which you have collaborated—comes out next year a copy will go to you."*

Carl Sandburg to EVD

May 18, 1926
Chicago, Illinois

Dear Gene—

Thank you for good words of many kinds you send. I am glad you like the Lincoln book. Sometime I hope to do an extended sketch of you that will have some of the breath and feel of the Lincoln. Luck and health be yours.

Carl [Sandburg]

TLS, InTI, Debs Collection.

☐ *Debs's "Appeal to Save Sacco and Vanzetti" first appeared in the* American
Appeal, *May 22, 1926, and was widely reprinted.*

Bartolomeo Vanzetti to EVD

May 31, 1926
Boston, Massachusetts

Dear Comrade and Maestro: —
    I have read in The Daily Worker of May 27, your letter-appeal to
the American Labor in our behalf. For Nick and I and our dear
ones, I thank you with all my heart for that letter in which you putted
all yourself and worth of better time and better men.
    I learnt to-day that the Massachusetts S. Court have repelled the
quest of the defence for a re-hearing; and that the District Attorney
of the Norfolk County minds again to fix a near date for our sen-
tensing.
    The plutocratic press-editorial on the Court decision was as bestial
as the decision itself.
    Hating us mortally, believing to free himself by killing us, the enemy
is going to execute us as soon as possible. Once, we ded, the enemy
thinks, the agitation will stop and the dangers of retaliation and revenge, dissappear. And it seems to happen very soon. But I am innocent, my faith is firmer than ever, the infamous death will not stain
our names; people are positive of our innocence, and we will pass
sure that our blood and our name will be rivendicated.
    Dear Comrade Debs, I am sorry that your health is not quit well
now, and I wish you a good health. Have care of yourself and do not
whorry about us. Mankind need you; others will take our place.
    And, please, do not bother to answer this. I can receive and benefit
your sentiments and thoughts even if you do not answer by mail.
                                    With figlial love I am yours,
                                        Bartolomeo Vanzetti

ALS, InTI, Debs Collection.

□ *Among socialists and others a "Restore Debs's Citizenship" movement gained considerable momentum in late 1925 and early 1926, including a resolution introduced in Congress by Victor Berger calling for the "restoration" of Debs's citizenship. In the following exchange of letters Debs raises the question with the judge who presided at his 1918 trial in Cleveland.*

EVD to D. C. Westenhaver

June 3, 1926
Terre Haute, Indiana

Dear Judge Westenhaver:

You are quite likely aware of the fact that there has been considerable discussion and difference of opinion as to the status of my citizenship since my conviction in your Court several years ago. Upon my release from prison I was given to understand from various sources that seemed authoritative that my citizenship had been forfeited, or at least impaired to an extent by reason of said conviction that I was deprived of the right to vote, and consequently I have not since attempted the exercise of the elective franchise. Quite recently, however, a lawyer of high standing, after a thorough investigation as to the legal aspects of the case, expressed the opinion in writing that I never had been disfranchised by reason of my conviction in your Court, that you had made no pronouncement to that effect, and that so far as said conviction was concerned my citizenship remained intact and my right to vote unimpaired and unquestioned.

Meanwhile, however, the question of the restoration of my citizenship was raised in Congress and made an issue by a resolution in the House and a petition in the Senate demanding full restoration of my constitutional and civil rights as an American citizen. When the matter was thus brought to the attention of Congress the administration leaders in both branches declared that my citizenship had never been forfeited nor my right to the franchise revoked by reason of my conviction in your Court or by any act of the federal government.

As I am still in doubt in the matter I venture to ask your opinion as to whether my conviction in your Court resulted in the forfeiture of my citizenship and the revocation of my elective franchise and my civil rights, and if so if such forfeiture and revocation are still operative and binding.

An answer at your convenience will much oblige

Yours very truly,
[Eugene V. Debs]

TLc, InTI, Debs Collection.

D. C. Westenhaver to EVD

June 5, 1926
Cleveland, Ohio

Dear Sir:

Replying to your letter of the 3rd inst., respecting the effect of your conviction and sentence upon your qualifications as citizen and elector I trust you understand that my position prevents me from giving legal opinions, and that you should regard my reply entirely as furnishing information in response to a request. Upon this basis, and in order that you may not feel that a failure to reply was for any other reason or might be a discourtesy, I am venturing to make some suggestions on this subject which you may submit to your legal adviser for his consideration. Suggest to him whether or not a person who is once a citizen of the United States does not always remain a citizen unless he abandons his country and goes to live in another country and voluntarily acquires there a new citizenship, or in those limited situations in which a naturalized citizen may have his naturalization cancelled. Now I assume that you are and have always been a citizen of the United States. My information is that you were born in the United States, or if not so born therein, that your parents were naturalized before you arrived at the age of 21 years, in which event, my understanding of the law is that you are a full citizen of the United States despite the conviction and sentence.

Consider also this further fact. The Constitution of the United States does not confer the right to vote at elections, either State or national. It establishes certain qualifications for elective federal officials. The XVth Amendment merely provides that the rights of citizens of the United States to vote shall not be denied or abridged by the United States or by any State on account of race, color, or previous condition of servitude. The XIXth amendment provides that the rights of citizens of the United States to vote shall not be denied or abridged by the United States or by any State on account of sex. These provisions, as I recall, have been held by the United States Supreme Court not to confer the right to vote or the privileges of an elector, but merely to prevent the United States or any State from denying the right to vote because of race, color, sex, or previous condition of servitude. In this way, laws of the States which limited the right to vote to white persons or to male persons, have been overridden and the right to vote has been obtained despite qualifications.

If your counsel reaches the conclusion that the foregoing suggestions are in fact sound, then the answer to the inquiries propounded in your letter must be found in the Constitution and the laws of the State of Indiana of which you are a citizen and resident. I am not familiar with those laws and they are not now accessible to me. For purposes of illustration, however, I take the State of Ohio. Its Constitution provides certain qualifications for voters or electors. Generally speaking, every citizen of the United States, male or female, over the age of twenty-one, shall be entitled to vote. Certain residential qualifications are also required. The particular disqualification in which you are interested is as follows: "The General Assembly shall have power to exclude from the privilege of voting or of being eligible to office, any person convicted of perjury, bribery, or other infamous crime."

You will perceive, therefore, one must turn to the statutes of Ohio to answer the question whether your conviction would prevent you from voting in Ohio. It is unnecessary to review these statutes except to say that they have disqualified persons convicted of certain crimes until pardoned. An inquiry along these lines as to the constitutional statutes of Indiana should answer the question of whether or not you are disqualified from voting in that State.

The qualifications, however, to hold office are different in many respects from the qualifications which entitle a citizen of the United States to vote. The Constitution of the United States has provided certain disqualifications. For instance, age limits for senators and representatives, and birth within the United States for the presidential office. What other disqualifications are or have been provided either by constitutional or federal statute is a matter your counsel probably has already investigated. In the State of Ohio, unless otherwise provided by the Constitution or by statute, any one who is by law a voter or elector, may hold office. An inquiry in Indiana along the same lines will be necessary to determine whether any disqualification exists to hold office in that State as a result of your conviction.

The suggestions will indicate to you and your counsel that the questions propounded in your letter are much complicated and depend upon a great variety of constitutions, statutes, and conditions. It might even be true that neither the United States Constitution or its statutes impose any disqualification either to vote or to hold federal office as a result of the conviction, and yet, disqualification to vote may be imposed by a State Constitution or statute, or to hold a State office. It might also be true that Congress has no power to remove these disqualifications imposed by the State Constitution and statute in so far as voting at any election is concerned, for the reason already stated, that the XVth and XIX Amendments merely prevent discrimination because of race, color, sex, or previous condition of servitude.

These suggestions are for the information and consideration of you and your counsel. They are not intended to express any opinion, legal or official. I shall be pleased if you find them of any service.

Very truly yours,
D. C. Westenhaver
United States District
Judge

TLS, InTI, Debs Collection.

□ *Throughout the summer of 1926 Debs declined speaking engagements and requests for articles, citing poor health as the reason. In September he returned to the Lindlahr Sanitarium.*

John Haynes Holmes to EVD

August 18, 1926
New York City

Dear Mr. Debs—

Word has just come to me that you are still sick —and I cannot refrain from sending you just a word to tell you of my concern, and to convey to you my sympathy. It seems impossible to think of you as ill—you {who} have lived so energetically and momentously all these years; and it seems as though the world grew somehow dark— darker than it is—with you not well and strong. But, alas—even such a soul as yours must defer now and then to the flesh, and make the payment it exacts!

But I count upon you soon being yourself again. There are great days ahead—we cannot meet them without you!—A million hearts are loving you, as they have done these many years, and such love must bring you strength.—No man has been more denounced and persecuted in his time than you—but no man also so truly *loved*. In both cases, it is because you also have truly loved, as did Jesus.

With best wishes to you for a speedy recovery—and affectionate regards to your brother—I remain—

Very sincerely
John Haynes Holmes

ALS, InTI, Debs Collection.

□ *Nicola Sacco's letter was written on the day of Debs's death at Lindlahr.*

Nicola Sacco to EVD

October 20, 1926
Boston, Massachusetts

My Dear Debs:—

The day of yesterday were so sad and gloomy, but this morning it seems more bright that ever; yes, it's so, because this morning just sooner I get up my eyes were turn toward the daylight, and upon the tops at the oak tree between the gold leaves, smillen, the old vegliant image of Eugene Debs in my eyes appear, and the affable smile of his noble face were telling me that he feel all better. Therefore, the appear of your dear image at my vision it was that, the guarder were telling me last night that their have read in the Boston newspaper that you were at the hospital badly sick. So this morning my first thought was to sent you these few lines, for I know that it will relief you noble soul. just as much as your unforgettable dearest letter they have and [one word illegible] to relieve my soul.

I am so really ashame to say to you, dear comrade, courage! But however, you will be good to let me tell you that, more the once in the struggle lifetime and even when a man were lying in bet saying the good old courage, win victoriously the depressed state body. Therefore, I am merely thout it—by remind your old intrepid good spirit, would revive the life in you; and I hope from the bottom of my heart So see you sooner image your old and the young brother comrades {again}, because they need the thought and the sincere radiant words from the sweet Voice of Euge Debs.

So — dear comrade, courage! because before were pass at the eternity world — I want see you, kiss you and so tight you in meni embrace warmly.

Best wishes to you dear wife — Theodore and all his family — from all my dear household kiss from my little one join with most warmly and brotherly embrace

Won and forever your faithful comrade
Ferdinando N. Sacco

ALS, InTI, Debs Collection.

□ *The following are a few of the thousands of letters and telegrams sent to Theodore Debs and Katherine Metzel Debs at the time of Gene's death. Ruth Crawford was a young reporter for the* Terre Haute Saturday Spectator *who conducted one of the last interviews with Debs. J. H. Hollingsworth was a long-time Terre Haute friend who had compiled the 1912 campaign booklet "What Debs' Neighbors Say about Him."*

Claude G. Bowers to Theodore Debs

October 22, 1926
New York City

THEODORE DEBS

WE HAVE ALL LOST A FRIEND   YOUR BROTHER HAD THE MOST LOV-ABLE WINSOME AND BRILLIANT PERSONALITY I HAVE KNOWN AND HIS GREAT HEART BEAT IN TENDER SYMPATHY WITH THE POOR AND UN-FORTUNATE   THE WORLD IS POORER IN HIS PASSING

CLAUDE G BOWERS

Telegram, InTI, Debs Collection.

Nicola Sacco to Theodore Debs

October 22, 1926
Dedham, Massachusetts

Dear Theodore:—

You can so well imagine how badly I felt when I heard the death news of your and the brother and comrade of all the workers class, the father and the friendship of the children, it was worse and a thunder stormy that pass above my heart. I know that it is our fate and the struggle of lifetime that one after another we all got to die, but the death of this taught master, the statuor of this grand American socialist, the giant oak of this faithful idealiste it is a great lost for all the humanity. I would if I could describe you all the pain I feel for the lost of this martyr of idea, but it seems that all my ideas, all mine homble expression words they dying in my brain; But—Whatever, I want that these few lines reach at yours in these sadness day, so I could write with you and join together with the painful that the lost companionship of the poor old dear mother of Mrs. Debs have brought for he, with surely short it would comfort her and all yours dear household.

Meanwhile—best Wishes to all of your warm kisses to Mrs Debs from my little ones from all my dear household join with the bet fraternal and brotherly embrace.

Your sincerely
Nicola Sacco

ALS, InTI, Debs Collection.

Herman Rahm to Theodore Debs and Katherine Metzel Debs

October 23, 1926
Staunton, Illinois

Dear Comrade,

At the meeting of the Socialist Party Local of Staunton held on Oct 23, I was delegated to send you the simpity of the Local. You have our simpity in the loss of your kind and loving Brother and fathfull husband. What a pitie this noble heart should be called to the great silence. It is impossible for me to find words to express our heart felt sorrow, for Comrade Debs was so well known here and liked that we thought him on of us. Dear Comrade our hearts are with you and we share your bereavement, as his soul goes marching and radiates with the passing years.

> With simpithy and Love I Remain First Yours
> Herman Rahm Secty S. P.
> Staunton, Ill

ALS, InTI, Debs Collection.

Ruth Crawford to Theodore Debs

October 25, 1926
[Terre Haute, Indiana]

My dear Mr. Debs,

It is hard to know that one no longer can have one's faith restored by talking to 'Gene. Yet it must be good to know that your brother left behind such a memory that those who ever knew him will be ashamed, because of the life he led, to ever doubt but that somehow good will be our destined end or way.

Will you please offer my sympathy to Mrs. Debs? You have been a splendid brother to Gene, and played your part well in helping him carry on his great work.

> Sincerely,
> Ruth Crawford

ALS, InTI, Debs Collection.

J. H. Hollingsworth to Theodore Debs

October 25, 1926
Bradenton, Florida

My dear Theodore:

The world seems terribly empty. Where is there another just like 'Gene? They cannot be found. Who is there to stand up and fearlessly rebuke the wrongs of this country and of the world as did he? Such sublime courage as his is mighty scarce. Truly, a great, generous, noble, and courageous soul has left us. The sordid world that traduced him when he was with us, will now do him homage when [he] is gone. Like Lincoln, his fame will increase with the passing years. His marvellous life of activity and self-sacrifice shames and rebukes my own comparatively inactive and self-coddling life. If good works count for anything in the other life, he will certainly stand in the highest ranks. I cant help but believe that SOMEWHERE and sometime he will be fully rewarded for all the good he has done and for all he so nobly and heroically endured.

To you, dear Theodore, my whole heart goes out in loving sympathy. I know that upon you the stroke has fallen with tremendous weight. How I long to help you carry your burden! Your pain, is my pain; your tears my tears, your sufferings my sufferings. Not an hour of these days passes that you are out of my mind and heart. Tho absent from you in body, I am with you in spirit. To you, a silent and unseen worker, may be attributed much of 'Gene's usefulness. He could not have accomplished the great work he did without your faithful and highly efficient labor. You have fought many battles and have suffered and endured much, and thro it all you have ever shown a true and brave spirit. You will be just as brave now to face this great bereavement that has befallen you. My heart's desire is that you may retain health and strength to continue your important work.

Please convey my best wishes to your estimable wife and daughter. With all my heart I wish you and your's well in all things and at all times.

Affectionally.
J. H. Hollingsworth

TLS, InTI, Debs Collection.

Index